WITHDRAWN

The Longman Companion to

Nazi Germany

Longman Companions to History

General Editors: Chris Cook and John Stevenson

Now available

THE LONGMAN COMPANION TO THE TUDOR AGE
Rosemary O'Day

THE LONGMAN COMPANION TO NAPOLEONIC EUROPE
Clive Emsley

THE LONGMAN COMPANION TO EUROPEAN NATIONALISM, 1789–1920
Raymond Pearson

THE LONGMAN COMPANION TO THE MIDDLE EAST SINCE 1914
Ritchie Ovendale

THE LONGMAN COMPANION TO BRITAIN IN THE ERA OF THE TWO
WORLD WARS, 1914–45
Andrew Thorpe

THE LONGMAN COMPANION TO COLD WAR AND DETENTE, 1914–91
John W. Young

THE LONGMAN COMPANION TO NAZI GERMANY
Tim Kirk

The Longman Companion to

Nazi Germany

Tim Kirk

Longman
London and New York

Longman Group Limited
Longman House, Burnt Mill,
Harlow, Essex CM20 2JE, England
and Associated Companies throughout the world

Published in the United States of America
by Longman Publishing, New York

© Longman Group Limited 1995

First published 1995

ISBN 0 582 06376 0 CSD
ISBN 0 582 06375 2 PPR

British Library Cataloguing-in-Publication data

A catalogue record for this book is
available from the British Library

Library of Congress Cataloging-in-Publication Data

Kirk, Tim.
   The Longman companion to Nazi Germany / Tim Kirk.
     p.   cm. – (Longman companions to history)
   Includes bibliographical references and index.
   ISBN 0-582-06376-0 (CSD). – ISBN 0-582-06375-2 (PPR)
   1. Germany–Politics and government–1933–1945. 2. Germany–
History–1918–1933. 3. National socialism–Germany–History.
4. Jews–Germany–Persecutions–20th Century. I. Title.
II Series.
DD256.5.K475 1995
943.086–dc20
                                               94-1131
                                                 CIP

Set by 7 in 10/11 New Baskerville
Produced by Longman Singapore Publishers (Pte) Ltd.
Printed in Singapore

Contents

List of Maps   vii
Acknowledgements   viii

**Section I: Politics and the State: the Weimar Republic and
the Rise of Nazism**   1

1. Weimar Republic: Introduction   3
2. Chronology   9
3. Major Political Parties, 1918–33   16
4. Elections   21
5. Weimar Republic: Cabinets   24
6. The Rise of Nazism   40

Section II: Politics, State and Party: the Third Reich   45

1. The Consolidation of Power   47
2. Chronology   49
3. The Political System of the Third Reich   56
4. The Nazi Party   61
5. The Police State   65

Section III: Economy, Society and Culture, 1918–1945   71

1. Area, Population and Territorial Divisions of the
   Reich, 1871/1918–45   73
2. Social and Economic Structure of the Reich   79
3. Agriculture   83
4. Industry   85
5. Trade   88
6. Transport and Communications   89
7. Labour   91
8. Consumption   98
9. Religion   101
10. Health   102
11. Education   104
12. Press   111

13. German Cultural and Intellectual Life, 1918–45: A
    Chronology   114

Section IV: Diplomacy, Rearmament and War, 1918–1945   121

1. Chronology   123
2. Diplomacy and International Relations   137
3. Rearmament   144
4. The Consolidation of a Greater Germany   146
5. Defeat and the Division of Germany   151
6. War Losses   152
7. Maps   153

**Section V: Anti-semitism, Racial Politics and the Holocaust,
1933–1945**   157

1. Chronology   159
2. Jewish Population of Germany, 1933   167
3. Nationality of Jews Resident in Germany, 1933   168
4. Jewish Population of Germany by Economic Sector,
   1933   169
5. Jewish Emigration from Germany, 1937–39   170
6. Destination of Jewish Emigrants from the Reich,
   1937–39   171
7. Mass Murder   172

Section VI: Glossary of Terms and Abbreviations   173

Section VII: Biographies   191

Section VIII: Bibliography   243

Section IX: Sources   261

Index   268

List of Maps

Nazi Party *Gaue*, 1944   64

The Versailles Settlement: Territory lost by Germany   153

Nazi Germany and Europe   154

Poland during World War II   155

Post-war Germany   156

Acknowledgements

I should like to thank Elizabeth Harvey, Ian Kershaw and Tony McElligott for reading and commenting on various drafts at various stages, Stephen Salter for his advice, and Roger Newbrook for help with preparation of the manuscript. I should also like to thank the staff of the library at the University of Northumbria at Newcastle, in particular Jane Shaw, Department Librarian with responsibility for History (surely the world's most helpful librarian), and Kath Holmes and the staff of the Inter-Library Loans Section. Thanks too to Chris Cook and John Stevenson, for their advice and encouragement, and to all the staff at Longman for their help.

The publishers would like to thank the following for granting permission to reproduce textual material: Cambridge University Press and Professor V Berghahn for tables 3.1 (Section IV), 7.3 (Section III) and 7.4 (Section III); University of Exeter Press and Professor Jeremy Noakes for tables 6.2 (Section V), 6.4 (Section I), 7 (Section V) and 11.5 (Section III) and map 7.3 (Section IV); R Piper GmbH & Co KG, Munich, for table 5.2 (second table) (Section II); Dr Michael Freeman for tables 8.5 (Section III) and maps 4.4 (Section II), 7.1, 7.2 and 7.4 (Section IV); Klett-Cotta for table 2.2 (Section IV).

Whilst every effort has been made to trace the owners of copyright material, in a few cases this has proved to be problematic and so we take this opportunity to offer our apologies to any copyright holders whose rights we may have unwittingly infringed.

Politics and the State: the Weimar Republic and the Rise of Nazism

1. Weimar Republic: Introduction

In 1918 Germany was in a state of considerable upheaval. The war had been lost, and although the country was not occupied, as in 1945, peace terms were to be imposed by the Entente: territory would be lost, and reparations demanded. In addition, the strains of war had led to industrial unrest and, eventually, to a political revolution which would bring about the internal collapse of the German Empire.

The informal domestic peace (*Burgfrieden*) agreed in 1914 between the labour movement and Germany's ruling class had been eroded by the cumulative effects of material deprivation on the morale of the German population during the war. The divergent expectations of the parties involved in the 'truce' were exposed: the left had agreed to the truce in the expectation of internal political reform; the nationalist and conservative right hoped for a victorious peace which would obviate the need to reform the domestic political system. In July 1917 the increasing political polarisation within Germany was formalised when the left of centre parties (who supported transformation of the empire into a parliamentary constitutional monarchy) tabled a resolution in the Reichstag demanding peace without annexations. These parties were to form the political nucleus of 'Weimar' or 'republican' parties after the end of the war. On the other hand, the Fatherland Party, supported by Hindenburg, Ludendorff, army and industry had over a million members by 1918. This political grouping would form the nucleus of the nationalist and conservative opponents of the republic.

The dismissal of the Chancellor, Bethmann-Hollweg, and his replacement by a civil servant, Georg Michaelis, also in July 1917 strengthened the quasi-dictatorial power of Hindenburg and Ludendorff. At the same time, however, industrial unrest and political disaffection were intensifying. In April 1917 there were mass strikes across Germany, and the labour movement split when Hugo Haase left the SPD to form the Independent Social Democratic Party of Germany (USPD). Further mass strikes broke out in January 1918, within weeks of the October revolution in Petrograd. It was the Bolshevik revolution, however, and the Treaty of Brest Litovsk, which helped to contain the situation, albeit temporarily. Troops were transferred from the eastern front to France, but the Allies too had reinforcements (from the United States) and the new German offensive was repulsed and the tide of the war turned decisively against Germany by September.

The war was effectively lost. If the German government went to war in 1914 primarily to forestall a gathering domestic political crisis, it now found itself confronted with a crisis much more intense. It was recognised that if a Bolshevik revolution from below were to be avoided, concessions would have to be made to the parliamentary left. The Chancellor duly resigned, and was replaced by Prince Max von Baden. That the opinion of the Reichstag should be a criterion in the selection and appointment of a new chancellor was a major constitutional development in itself. The German political system had ceased to be a quasi-autocracy dominated by the Prussian army, and had become (on paper) a constitutional monarchy with a representative parliament. There were, of course, ulterior motives for this move: firstly, the liberal and democratic parties would be identified with Germany's defeat and would have to confront the disbelief and anger of the German public, who were thoroughly unprepared for anything other than a victory; secondly, it was hoped that the Allies would respond more positively to a 'democratic' government, and deal with it less harshly. In the event the German public proved more predictable than the Allied negotiators proved lenient.

The smooth implementation of these plans was disrupted by the intransigence of the imperial navy, which determined to undertake a last sea battle to save its 'honour'. The result was a naval mutiny in Wilhelmshaven and Kiel which sparked the very 'revolution from below' the army had tried to prevent. These events also generated the 'stab-in-the-back myth' which fuelled the paranoid demonology of the right throughout the Weimar Republic and the Third Reich. Neither the army nor the SPD could control the pace of events. On 7 November Kurt Eisner declared Bavaria a Socialist Republic, and on 9 November Max von Baden announced the Kaiser's abdication and resigned. It was not without constitutional significance at this point that the outgoing chancellor formally handed over power to his successor, Friedrich Ebert, the SPD leader. This invested Ebert's provisional government with a constitutional legitimacy based on a perceived continuity of authority. The political complexion of Ebert's provisional administration (an SPD-USPD coalition) might otherwise have provoked disloyalty on the part of the army and the bureaucracy.

+ As in Russia a year earlier the political situation was complicated by the effective emergence of 'dual power'. +

Constitutional legitimacy existed alongside the real political power of the Workers' and Soldiers' Councils, which had no formal position in the constitution. By seeking the approval of the Berlin Councils on 10 November, the Ebert government had taken steps to found its authority on both the existing state and the organs of the revolution.

Yet although the government called itself the Council of People's Deputies, its members were committed to a parliamentary constitution, rather than one based on councils. The position of the government was strengthened by moves to stabilise the situation on the part of the army and business. Ludendorff's successor, General Groener, provided the Chancellor with an assurance of support from the army in maintaining order, and a comprehensive agreement between employers' and workers' representatives (the Stinnes-Legien Pact) provided a similar guarantee of stability in industry. Elections were held to a National Assembly in January 1919.

Political upheavals in Berlin compelled the National Assembly to withdraw to Weimar to draw up the constitution. This provided Germany with a parliamentary system of government based on a seven-year presidency and a bicameral legislature in Berlin elected by proportional representation. Federal rights were also guaranteed, however, and the federal states (*Länder*) had extensive autonomy in internal matters.

The architects of this constitution were the so-called 'republican parties': SPD, DDP and Centre. However, the creation of the republic constituted something of a compromise between the interests of the old ruling groups of imperial Germany and the more moderate of the forces for change. Despite the extensive achievements of the left in the fields of social policy, industrial relations and welfare, neither the 'November revolution' nor the Weimar constitution brought any fundamental change in economic relations in Germany, either in industry or on the land. The old ruling groups of Wilhelmine Germany, who were for the most part hostile to the republic and its liberal institutions, continued to dominate the bureaucracy, the diplomatic service, the army, the churches and the universities, ensuring fundamental continuities with the empire beneath the surface of parliamentary government.

The new republic immediately found itself in economic difficulties. Germany had lost 13 per cent of her territory under the Versailles Treaty, along with all her colonies (which became League of Nations mandates). Industrial production suffered severe dislocation, the German merchant fleet was decimated and export markets had disappeared. In addition, the imperial government had expected to win the war and finance it through the imposition of reparations payments. Its successor now found the tables turned, was unable either to pay off war debts inherited from the monarchy or to pay the reparations demanded by the Allies. Unable for political reasons to raise taxation to the levels required by the economic situation, the government inflated the currency.

This new inflation came on top of inflationary pressures brought about by the economic policies of the imperial government during the war. It had a disastrous impact on holders of war bonds and liquid financial assets, and these often belonged to middle class groups already impoverished by the new circumstances: civil servants and other public employees whose salaries had fallen in real terms; career officers who had become redundant with the enforced contraction of the armed forces. The grievances of such groups and of others alienated by the policies of early Weimar governments – such as the large landowners east of the Elbe – helped create a constituency of hostility and opposition to the republic from the outset. This anti-republican, counter-revolutionary opposition was successfully held in check during the post-war crisis which culminated in the hyper-inflation of 1923. Counter-revolutionary coups, such as those of Wolfgang Kapp in 1920 and Adolf Hitler in 1923, were unsuccessful. Nevertheless, fundamental opposition to the republic was firmly established. In the political arena it was articulated by the Conservative German Nationalist People's Party (DNVP), to a lesser extent by the German People's Party (DVP) and by a number of political organisations and semi-political associations on the extreme radical right. Together, the groups across this spectrum of political opinion constituted a 'national opposition', not only to the government and its policies, but to the republic itself, whose constitution, political system and institutions they sought to change as quickly as possible.

The republic was able to withstand the post-war crisis because a sufficient number of such opponents – whether politicians, industrialists, officers or civil servants – were prepared to work with it rather than against it. They did so for pragmatic reasons rather than out of conviction, although their hostility to the republic was perhaps tempered by a significant swing to the right in the first elections to the Reichstag in 1920. The republic might well be a 'Bolshevik' creation which had come into existence because patriots had been 'stabbed in the back' by Jews and Communists in 1918, but the damage might still be contained and even, eventually, reversed by participation in the system. Individually and collectively Conservatives and German Nationalists might leave Weimar governments on points of principle (such as the decision to follow a policy of 'fulfilment' of the Versailles Treaty), but on the whole their willingness to administer the system they sought to undermine kept the left out of office for most of the 1920s.

The period of illusory stability after 1923, when the German economy benefited from the Dawes Plan and the recovery of the world economy, and German governments built a fragile and limited prosperity on short term foreign loans, is associated with the name of just such an opponent of the republic who was nevertheless prepared to hold its highest offices: Gustav Stresemann. An ardent German Nationalist during the war, Stresemann emerged as the leader of the 'fulfilment' wing of the German right during the post-war crisis and was Chancellor from August to November 1923, when the hyper-inflation reached its peak. As the economic and political situation began to stabilise he recognised that the interests of his own party (the DVP) and of those it represented in the German business community would be better served from within the government than outside it. As Foreign Minister from 1923 to 1929 he made the DVP the indispensable lynch-pin of Weimar coalition governments, ensuring that the party's views were always taken into consideration. His achievements, however, reflected the ambiguities of his political position. Relations with the West improved, and Germany's western borders were confirmed by the Locarno Pact of 1925. He also succeeded in negotiating a reduction in reparations payments and the Allied evacuation of the Rhineland. Such policies, presented as 'flexible revisionism' for domestic consumption, nevertheless attracted vehement opposition from the nationalist right at home. Such opposition was arguably mistaken: Stresemann continued to believe that Germany should dominate Europe, and there was indeed a shift in the continental balance of power, from France to Germany, as the latter's industrial economy and military potential began to recover. Furthermore, the question of Germany's eastern frontiers remained largely unresolved. 'Fulfilment' was always reluctant and partial.

The domestic policies of Weimar Germany turned on the issue of another revisionism. The government of Germany during the 1920s was constructed around a 'bourgeois bloc' whose twin pillars were the DVP and the Roman Catholic Centre Party. Even with the support of the Liberal DDP, these parties could not form a majority government, which was only possible either with the support of the DNVP – whose hostility to the entire republican system was profound – or of the SPD. In the event the DNVP did join the government, but left again in 1925 over the issues of the Locarno Pact, forcing the government to rely on SPD support for the necessary legislation. Once the treaties were successfully ratified the focus of politics switched to the domestic sphere, where it was now considered essential to minimise the role of organised labour and its representatives in the drafting of social and economic policy. Consequently, the SPD was excluded from decision-making and the government once again relied on the support of the DNVP which rejoined the government in 1927. The SPD finally returned to power shortly before the depression, following gains in the elections of May 1928. Even an SPD Chancellor was unable to overcome the hostility of the right on questions of social welfare, and it was on the issue of proposed increases in unemployment benefit that the SPD left the government again in 1930, triggering the final demise of Weimar parliamentarism.

2. Chronology

1918

30 Sep.	Chancellor von Hertling resigns.
3 Oct.	Prince Max von Baden becomes Chancellor.
23 Oct.	USA refuses to conclude peace with an authoritarian government of Germany.
24–8 Oct.	Constitutional reform to make government responsible to Reichstag.
26 Oct.	Dismissal of Ludendorff. Groener is appointed his successor.
28 Oct.	Mutiny of the German Fleet begins.
29 Oct.	Kaiser leaves Berlin.
3 Nov.	Sailors mutiny in Kiel. Workers' and sailors' councils established.
6 Nov.	Revolution spreads to Hanseatic ports of Hamburg, Bremen and Lubeck.
7 Nov.	Revolution in Munich. Bavaria declared a republic.
8 Nov.	Government of Workers', Peasants' and Soldiers' Councils set up in Bavaria under Kurt Eisner (USPD).
9 Nov.	General strike in Berlin. German republic proclaimed by Philipp Scheidemann. Friedrich Ebert becomes Chancellor.
10 Nov.	Emperor Wilhelm II flees to the Netherlands. Establishment of Council of People's Deputies.
11 Nov.	Armistice signed.
15 Nov.	Stinnes-Legien agreement: establishment of *Zentralarbeitsgemeinschaft* (ZAG) as a co-operative forum for workers and employers.
16–20 Dec.	Reich Congress of German Councils meets in Berlin.
30 Dec.– 1 Jan. 1919	Founding conference of Revolutionary Communist Workers' Party (later KPD).

1919

Jan.	German Workers' Party (DAP) founded in Munich.

5–11 Jan.	General strike and Communist ('Spartacist') uprising in Berlin.
9 Jan.	Founding of the *Deutsche Arbeiterpartei* (DAP, German Workers' Party) which subsequently (April 1920) became the Nazi Party (NSDAP).
15 Jan.	Murder of Rosa Luxemburg and Karl Liebknecht by *Freikorps* officers.
19 Jan.	National Assembly elected.
11 Feb.	National Assembly is convened in Weimar. Ebert becomes provisional Reich President.
13 Feb.	Formation of SPD-led Scheidemann administration.
21 Feb.	Assassination of Kurt Eisner by right-wingers.
6 Apr.	'Soviet' Republic (*Räterepublik*) established in Bavaria.
2 May	Bavarian republic suppressed.
21 Jun.	Gustav Bauer replaces Scheidemann as Chancellor and head of new SPD-Centre coalition.
28 Jun.	Treaty of Versailles signed.
21 Aug.	Ebert takes the oath as Reich President without further confirmation by election.
Sep.	Beginning of financial reforms of Matthias Erzberger.
8 Oct.	Assassination attempt on Haase, leader of the USPD. He died on 17 November.

1920

13 Jan.	42 killed when a USPD-KPD demonstration in front of the Reichstag is dispersed by machine-gun fire.
4 Feb.	Ratification of Works Councils' Bill.
10 Feb.	75 per cent vote for Denmark in the plebiscite in the northern zone of North Schleswig.
24 Feb.	Programme of the German Workers' Party adopted. Party changes name to National Socialist German Workers' Party (NSDAP).
12–17 Mar.	Kapp-Lüttwitz putsch. →
14 Mar.	80 per cent majority for Germany in the plebiscite in the southern zone of North Schleswig.
15 Mar.–20 May	Communist insurrection in the Ruhr valley.
27 Mar.	Formation of new government (SPD-DDP-Centre) by Hermann Müller (SPD, 1876–1931).
31 Mar.	Adolf Hitler leaves army.

6 Apr.	French occupation of Frankfurt, Darmstadt and other towns as a response to the disturbances in the Ruhr.
6 Jun.	'Weimar Coalition' parties lose heavily in Reichstag elections.
25 Jun.	Formation of new centre-right government under Konstantin Fehrenbach (Centre).
11 Jul.	Plebiscites in the districts of Allenstein (East Prussia) and Marienwerder (West Prussia): 98 per cent and 92 per cent in favour of Germany.
20 Sep.	Transfer of Eupen and Malmédy to Belgium resolved by League of Nations.
16 Oct.	USPD splits. Left wing (majority) subsequently joins KPD (December).

1921

24–9 Jan.	Paris Conference on Reparations.
21 Feb.–14 Mar.	London Conference on Reparations.
8 Mar.	Allied occupation of Düsseldorf and Duisburg as sanction for German rejection of reparations terms.
20 Mar.	60 per cent majority for Germany in Upper Silesia plebiscite.
Mar.	Communist disturbances in Hamburg and central Germany.
Apr.	First branch of NSDAP established outside Munich (Rosenheim, Bavaria).
27 Apr.	Allied Reparations Commission sets payment at 132 million gold marks.
4 May	Resignation of Fehrenbach government to avoid responsibility for fulfilment of Allied reparations demands.
5 May	'London Ultimatum': Allies threaten to occupy Ruhr if their demands are not met.
10 May	Formation of new Weimar Coalition government (SPD-DDP-Centre) under Chancellor Josef Wirth (Centre).
29 Jul.	Hitler becomes the first chairman of the NSDAP.
26 Aug.	Assassination of Matthias Erzberger by radical right group.
4 Nov.	Foundation of the Nazi *Sturmabteilung* (SA, stormtroopers).

1922

16 Apr.	Treaty of Rapallo between Germany and the USSR.
24 Jun.	Murder of Foreign Minister Walter Rathenau by

	radical right-wingers.
14 Nov.	Resignation of Wirth administration on reparations issue.
22 Nov.	Centre-right minority government formed by Wilhelm Cuno, a businessman.

1923

11 Jan.	Occupation of the Ruhr by French and Belgian troops.
12 Aug.	Resignation of Cuno administration.
13 Aug.	Formation of a Grand Coalition cabinet by Gustav Stresemann (DVP).
Aug.	Beginning of hyper-inflation.
26 Sep.	Conflict between Bavaria and the Reich: Bavarian government responds to the end of the 'passive resistance' in the Ruhr with declaration of a state of emergency. Gustav von Kahr (1862–1934) becomes General State Commissar in Bavaria.
27 Sep.	Reich government declares a national state of emergency as a counter-measure.
Oct.	SPD and KPD form a 'government of republican and proletarian defence' in Saxony, deposed by *Reichswehr*, 28 October.
Oct./Nov.	Disturbances spread to Thuringia and Hamburg.
21 Oct.	Declaration of the French-sponsored Rhenish Republic.
29 Oct.	Reich Commissar installed in Saxony.
3 Nov.	Social Democratic ministers leave the government in protest at government policy in Saxony and Bavaria.
8 Nov.	Abortive Hitler-Ludendorff 'beer hall' putsch following a meeting at the Munich *Bürgerbräukeller* to protest at 'growth of Bolshevism' in Germany. The coup attempt fails, its leaders are arrested, and the NSDAP is banned.
15 Nov.	New currency (*Rentenmark*) introduced.
23 Nov.	Prohibition of KPD and NSDAP. Stresemann government resigns.
30 Nov.	Formation of new centre-right government under Chancellor Wilhelm Marx (Centre).

1924

| 26 Feb. | Munich putsch leaders tried for high treason. |
| 1 Apr. | Hitler sentenced to five years. In prison he begins work on *Mein Kampf*. |

9 Apr.	Dawes Plan on reparations issued.
4 May	Reichstag elections with gains for KPD and far right.
29 Aug.	Reichstag approves Dawes Plan.
11 Oct.	Introduction of *Reichsmark.*
7 Dec.	Reichstag elections. Gains for SPD and moderate right at the expense of the Communists and nationalists.
15 Dec.	Resignation of Marx government.
20 Dec.	Hitler released from Landsberg prison.

1925

15 Jan.	Formation of new centre-right government under non-party Chancellor Hans Luther.
27 Feb.	Nazi Party refounded.
28 Feb.	Death of President Friedrich Ebert.
25 Apr.	Hindenburg elected President.
14 Jul.–1 Aug.	Allied evacuation of Ruhr.
16 Oct.	Locarno Pact agreeing Germany's western frontier.
25 Oct.	German Nationalist ministers leave coalition over terms of Locarno Pact.
1 Dec.	Locarno Pact signed.
5 Dec.	Resignation of Luther administration.
8 Dec.	Official publication of *Mein Kampf.*

1926

20 Jan.	Luther forms minority centre-right government.
12 May	Luther resigns as Chancellor.
16 May	Marx becomes Chancellor; other ministers remain in place.
8 Sep.	Germany joins the League of Nations.
1 Dec.	Goebbels becomes *Gauleiter* of Berlin.
17 Dec.	Government defeated in vote of no confidence.

1927

29 Jan.	Marx forms new centre-right government (without the DDP).

1928

6 Jan.	Himmler appointed *Reichsführer* SS.
20 May	Shift to left in Reichstag elections.
28 Jun.	Formation of broad coalition government by Hermann Muller (SPD-DDP-Centre-DVP-BVP).

1929

7 Jun.	Publication of Young Plan, revising German

	reparations payments.
9 Jul.	Nazis and DNVP join forces in opposition to Young Plan.
6 Aug.	Young Plan agreed.
3 Oct.	Death of Gustav Stresemann.
24–9 Oct.	US stock market crash.

1930

23 Jan.	Wilhelm Frick (NSDAP) becomes Interior Minister in Thuringia.
27 Mar.	Fall of Müller government.
30 Mar.	Heinrich Brüning (Centre, 1885–1970) becomes Reich Chancellor at the head of a minority right of centre government.
30 Jun.	French troops withdraw from the Rhineland.
16 Jul.	Government by presidential decree begins with measures on economy.
18 Jul.	Dissolution of Reichstag following SPD protests.
14 Sep.	Large Nazi gains in Reichstag elections.

1931

9 Feb.	Withdrawal of 'national opposition' (DNVP, NSDAP) from Reichstag.
20 Mar.	Announcement of proposed Austro-German customs union.
11 May	Collapse of Austrian Credit-Anstalt with repercussions for the German banking system following French pressure in protest at the proposed customs union.
20 Jun.	Hoover moratorium on reparations.
11 Oct.	Anti-Republicans hold meeting at Bad Harzburg and form an alliance, the 'Harzburg Front'.

1932

27 Jan.	Speech by Hitler to Rhineland industrialists in Düsseldorf.
10 Apr.	Hindenburg re-elected.
13 Apr.	Prohibition of SA and SS.
30 May	Resignation of Brüning cabinet.
1 Jun.	Franz von Papen becomes Chancellor.
14 Jun.	Lifting of ban on SA and SS.
20 Jul.	*Preussenstreich*: coup d'état against Prussian state government by von Papen.
31 Jul.	NSDAP becomes the largest party in Reichstag after elections.
12 Sep.	Dissolution of Reichstag.

6 Nov.	Last genuinely free Reichstag election; German Nationalist and Communist gains – NSDAP loses 34 seats.
3 Dec.	Resignation of Papen.
4 Dec.	Kurt von Schleicher becomes Chancellor.

1933

| 4 Jan. | Secret meeting of Hitler and von Papen. |
| 30 Jan. | Hitler appointed Chancellor. |

3. Major Political Parties, 1918–33

NSDAP 'Nationalsozialistische Arbeiterpartei' (Nazis)
One of a number of fringe parties within the radical nationalist and racist *Völkisch* movement, the NSDAP grew out of the DAP (*Deutsche Arbeiterpartei*), founded by Anton Drexler in Munich in 1919. The party was renamed in 1920 and Hitler became chairman in 1921. Between early 1922 and the failed coup attempt of November 1923 party membership rose from about 6,000 to approximately 55,000. The party was banned after the coup and relaunched in 1925; it abandoned putschist politics in favour of a parliamentary route to power, and extended its organisation substantially beyond Bavaria for the first time. Its electoral breakthrough came with the depression and the final collapse and fragmentation of the German right between 1929 and 1932. Its ideology, policies and electoral base coincided to a great extent with those of other nationalist and conservative groups on the far right; it was distinguished from them by its adept use of propaganda techniques, readier resort to political violence and, ultimately, by its ability to mobilise a mass electoral base.

DNVP 'Deutschnationale Volkspartei' (German National People's Party)
Founded in November 1918, the DNVP was a German nationalist party which was heir to the conservative and radical right tradition of Wilhelmine Germany. The DNVP fundamentally rejected the Republic, the Versailles settlement and parliamentary government. Its uncompromising defence of landed agrarian interests limited its appeal both socially and geographically, and its best electoral performances tended to be in the Junker dominated East Elbian provinces. It also attracted support among the urban lower middle class. During the last years of the Republic its leaders co-operated with the Nazis, and it dissolved itself in June 1933. Its associations with the ruling class of Wilhelmine Germany and with the Third Reich ensured the eclipse of German nationalism in both East and West Germany after World War II.

DVP 'Deutsche Volkspartei' (German People's Party)
A right-wing Liberal party, founded in December 1918 and led by

Gustav Stresemann, the DVP absorbed those National Liberals who felt excluded from the DDP (q.v.). The DVP was essentially an anti-republican party, and one committed to the revision of the Treaty of Versailles. It was consistently represented in Weimar coalition governments, where it defended the interests of the upper middle class and the employers. Its electoral support was eroded during the depression as voters deserted to splinter parties representing sectional economic interests, and to the Nazis.

'Zentrum' (Centre Party)
The name Centre was first used in 1859 by Prussian Catholics. The party was formed in 1870 to defend Catholic interests in the new Reich, which was dominated by Protestants. Although it advocated political reform it was generally to the right of the Liberals under William II, and despite a shift to the left during World War I, it was also often to the right of the DDP (q.v.) during the Weimar Republic. Its electoral support was remarkably stable between 1918 and 1933, and it was consistently represented in Weimar governments. The votes of the Catholic lower middle class and large numbers of Catholic workers were crucial to this consistent performance. The Centre was a committed pro-republican party until the depression when it shifted back to the right. It was dissolved in July 1933, but re-emerged as the technically non-denominational Christian Democratic Union after World War II.

BVP 'Bayerische Volkspartei' (Bavarian People's Party)
A Roman Catholic party, and essentially a Bavarian wing of the Centre. The BVP was a particularist rather than a separatist party, and placed great emphasis on Bavaria's independence within a national federal framework. Its resolute opposition to co-operation with the SPD in Bavaria prompted it to form alliances at the regional level (carrying ministerial posts) with anti-democratic parties and politicians of the right. It voted for the Enabling Act and dissolved itself in 1933. Its post-war successor is the Christian Social Union (CSU).

DDP 'Deutsche Demokratische Partei' (German Democratic Party)
A left-wing Liberal party of limited electoral appeal formed by a group of intellectuals and businessmen in November 1918. It inherited much of the membership of the Wilhelmine Progressive Party and some of the National Liberals'. Its members played an important part in the drafting of the Weimar constitution, but its electoral support declined rapidly after the formation of the DVP. It was renamed the German State Party in 1930, and dissolved itself in 1933.

SPD 'Sozialdemokratische Partei Deutschlands' (Social Democratic Party of Germany)

Formed in 1875 by the union of Ferdinand Lassalle's Workers' Associations and the Socialist Workers' Party of August Bebel and Wilhelm Liebknecht, the SPD was persecuted under Bismarck from 1878 to 1890, but re-emerged to become the largest single party in the Reichstag by the outbreak of the First World War. In 1917 the majority expelled its leftist opposition, which formed the *Unabhängige* (independent) *Sozialdemokratische Partei Deutschlands* (USPD). This party competed with the majority 'MSPD' until the USPD itself split, with some members re-joining the majority, and others the Communists. The party drew its support from the industrial working class and sections of the lower middle class, but lost support to the Communists during the depression. It was resolute in its support of the Republic, and was banned by the Nazis in 1933. Some 6,000 Social Democrats went into exile during the Nazi dictatorship. An Exile Committee (*Vorstand*) was constitued in Prague (1933) under Otto Wels and Hans Vogel (SOPADE). It moved to Paris in 1938 and London in 1941. After the Second World War the SPD became the major left-of-centre political party in West Germany.

KPD 'Kommunistische Partei Deutschlands' (Communists)

The KPD was founded in December 1918 by members of the Spartacist League. It was led by Karl Liebknecht and Rosa Luxemburg, both of whom were murdered by members of the right-wing paramilitary *Freikorps* movement in the wake of the Berlin uprising of January 1919. The party became affiliated to the Comintern in 1919. Support for the KPD was negligible during the post-war crisis, and its attempts to seize power by insurrection all failed. It attracted members and voters first from the USPD in 1920, and further support came from disillusioned SPD supporters during the depression. Many of these new members were unemployed, and often young, and party members were frequently involved in street fights with the Nazis. Directed by the Comintern, the KPD refused to form a common front against fascism with the 'social fascist' SPD. It was dissolved in 1933, and some 8,000 KPD members fled abroad. From 1935 a Central Committee and Politburo were established in Moscow. The KPD underground resistance movement was numerically by far the most important in Germany. The party resumed legal activity after the war, but was subsumed in the Socialist Unity Party in the Soviet Occupation Zone and was prohibited in West Germany in 1956.

Minor Parties

The following are some of the more significant minor parties and political groupings active during the Weimar Republic.

BBB *'Bayerischer Bauernbund' (Bavarian Farmers' League)*

Founded in 1895 it became the *Bayerischer Bauern- und Mittelstandsbund* in 1922. Anton Fehr, a League member and Bavarian minister was Minister for Food in the Second Wirth administration from 31 March 1922. The BBB was anti-clerical and republican, favoured land reform and drew support from small farmers. Its value as a potential coalition party in Bavaria influenced the formation of BVP policy. Outside Bavaria it ran in elections as the *Deutsche Bauernpartei* from 1928. The League was dissolved in 1933.

CVP *'Christliche Volkspartei' (Christian People's Party)*

Rhineland particularist splinter from the Centre Party which polled over 65,000 votes in the 1920 Reichstag election. Some members defected to the *Wirtschaftspartei* the following year.

KVP *'Konservative Volkspartei' (Conservative People's Party)*

Founded in 1930 by the union of the *Volkskonservative Vereinigung* (VKV) and German Nationalist Reichstag delegates for the purposes of fielding candidates in the 1930 Reichstag election. It was dissolved in 1931.

'Landbund' (Agricultural League)

Founded in 1921 as a union of the *Bund der Landwirte* (Farmers' League) and *Deutscher Landbund* (German Agricultural League), it was formally dissolved in 1933 but its organisation was subsumed into the Reich Food Estate. Its organisational strength lay disproportionately east of the Elbe, although the local agricultural organisations there never joined its election lists.

'Bund der Polen' (Polish League)

A union, for electoral purposes, of Polish interest groups, which co-operated with other national minorities to campaign for the promotion and defence of national minority rights.

VNB *'Völkisch-Nationaler Block' (People's Nationalist Party)*

Founded in 1922 by a DNVP splinter group, it was officially the *Deutsch-Völkische Freiheitsbewegung* (German People's Freedom Movement). Although ostensibly a nationwide party it was effectively the northern counterpart of the NSDAP in the 1924 elections. It was both anti-semitic and anti-clerical, and drew support from officers and wealthier sections of the rural population.

'*Wirtschaftspartei (des deutschen Mittelstandes)*' (*Business Party*)

Founded in 1920 by lower middle class (*Mittelstand*) groups, it received steadily increasing numbers of votes (over a million between 1928 and 1932), largely from the urban middle classes. In the 1932 Reichstag elections it ran on a common list with the BVP.

4. Elections

The Weimar constitution provided for a directly elected president, elected every seven years, and two houses of parliament. The lower house (the *Reichstag*) was directly elected at least every four years on the basis of proportional representation by all citizens over twenty. The suffrage was universal, equal and secret. The upper house (*Reichsrat*) was indirectly elected: members were appointed by the parliaments of the federal states (*Landtage*), which were directly elected. In addition the constitution provided for the holding of plebiscites, in response to a petition with support from a tenth of the electorate. The most controversial aspect of the Weimar electoral system has been proportional representation. This was used in elections to the National Assembly and subsequently built into the constitution, and was not considered revolutionary at the time. Its adoption had long been advocated by German (and European) Social Democrats, and it was adopted by many other European states. The system was subjected to some criticism towards the end of the republic, but more thoroughly after 1945, and the insistence on the relationship between Weimar's political weakness and the proportional voting system should be understood within the contemporary context. It was felt by some that a similar (albeit qualified) system might pose a similar threat of destabilisation to the Federal Republic. The persistent political stability of West Germany has done much to undermine the thesis. The demise of the Weimar Republic cannot in any case be explained entirely in constitutional terms, and constitutional explanations must also take account of the difficulties experienced by the larger parties in forming coalitions; the hostility of the bourgeois parties to the left; the compromise between federalism and centralisation; and the provision of exceptional emergency powers for the president.

4.1. Elections for the Reichstag during the Weimar Republic (% of vote)

Party	1919*	1920	1924 (1)	1924 (2)	1928	1930	1932 (1)	1932 (2)	1933
NSDAP	–	–	6.6**	3.0	2.6	18.3	37.3	33.1	43.9
DNVP	10.3	14.9	19.5	20.5	14.2	7.0	5.9	8.8	8.0
DVP	4.4	13.9	9.2	10.1	8.7	4.5	1.2	1.9	1.1
Z/BVP	19.7	17.9	16.6	17.3	15.1	14.8	15.9	15.0	14.1
DDP†	18.6	8.3	5.7	6.3	4.9	3.8	1.0	1.0	0.9
SPD	37.9	21.6	20.5	26.0	29.8	24.5	21.6	20.4	18.2
USPD	7.6	17.9	0.8	0.3	0.1	–	–	–	–
KPD	–	2.1	12.6	9.0	10.6	13.1	14.3	16.9	12.2
Turnout	*82.7*	*79.1*	*77.4*	*78.8*	*75.6*	*81.9*	*84.0*	*80.6*	*88.5*

4.2. Elections for the Reichstag during the Weimar Republic (Seats)

Party	1919*	1920	1924 (1)	1924 (2)	1928	1930	1932 (1)	1932 (2)	1933
NSDAP	–	–	32	14	12	107	230	196	288
DNVP	44	71	95	103	73	41	37	52	52
DVP	19	65	45	51	45	30	7	11	2
BVP	20	16	19	16	19	22	20	18	
Z	91	64	65	69	62	68	75	70	74
DDP†	75	39	28	32	25	20	4	2	5
SPD	163	102	100	131	153	143	133	121	120
USPD	22	84							
KPD		4	62	45	54	77	89	100	81
Other	7	10	29	29	51††	72††	11	12	7
Total	*421*	*459*	*472*	*493*	*491*	*577*	*608*	*584*	*647*

* Elections to the National Assembly
** Together with *Völkisch-Nationaler Block*
† *Deutsche Staatspartei* after July 1930
†† Includes Business Party (*Wirtschaftspartei*).

4.3. Presidential Election, 1925 (Votes in Millions)

	First Round (29 March)	Second Round (26 April)
Ernst Thälmann	1.87	1.93
Paul von Hindenburg		14.66
Wilhelm Marx	3.89	13.75
Karl Jarres	10.41	
Erich Ludendorff	0.29	
Heinrich Held	1.01	
Hellpach	1.57	
Otto Braun	7.80	
Splinter votes	0.03	0.13

4.4. Presidential Election, 1932 (Votes in Millions)

	First Round (13 March)	Second Round (10 April)
Adolf Hitler	11.340	13.420
Paul von Hindenburg	18.650	19.360
Ernst Thälmann	4.980	3.710
Winter	0.110	
Theodor Duesterberg	2.560	
Splinter votes	0.005	0.005

5. Weimar Republic: Cabinets

Council of People's Deputies, 9 November 1918
(Revolutionary Government)

The government which was formed in the wake of the revolution of November 1918 contained only Socialists. In theory all were equal, but in practice the senior members were Friedrich Ebert and Hugo Haase. Ebert's position derived a certain legitimacy from the handover of power by Prince Max von Baden and Haase's authority derived from the relationship of the more radical USPD with the revolutionary movement.

Friedrich Ebert	(MSPD)
Hugo Haase	(USPD)
Otto Landsberg	(MSPD)
Philip Scheidemann	(MSPD)
Wilhelm Dittmann	(USPD)
Emil Barth	(USPD; Revolutionary Shop Stewards)

The legitimacy of the new government was confirmed by a meeting of the Workers' and Soldiers' Councils in Berlin, which also elected an Executive Committee in which all executive and legislative rights were invested. A form of 'dual power' emerged not entirely dissimilar to that in Petrograd during the spring of 1917. In Germany, however, this 'dualism' was immediately contained by the councils' agreement (22 November) not to interfere unduly with the work of the government. Moreover, when the National Congress of Workers' and Soldiers' Councils met on 16 December the majority were mainstream Social Democrats and agreed to hold elections for a constituent National Assembly on 19 January 1919.

Scheidemann Administration: 13 February–20 June 1919

The first 'Weimar coalition', Scheidemann's government was formed on the basis of the elections to the constituent National Assembly. It consisted of the genuinely pro-republican parties: the 'Majority Social Democrats' (MSPD), the Roman Catholic Centre Party (Centre) and the left-liberal German Democratic Party (DDP).

Chancellor	Philip Scheidemann (MSPD)
Vice Chancellor	Eugen Schiffer (DDP)
Foreign Minister	Ulrich Graf von Brockdorff-Rantzau (non-party)
Interior Minister	Hugo Preuss (DDP)
Finance Minister	Eugen Schiffer (DDP) replaced by Bernhard Dernburg (DDP) from 11 April 1919
Economics	Rudolf Wissell (MSPD)
Treasury	Georg Gothein (DDP) from 21 March 1919
Justice	Otto Landsberg (MSPD)
Defence	Gustav Noske (MSPD)
Food	Robert Schmidt (MSPD)
Posts	Johann Giesberts (Centre)
Labour	Gustav Bauer (MSPD)
Without portfolio	Georg Gothein (DDP) to 21 March 1919
	Matthias Erzberger (Centre)
	Eduard David (MSPD)

The Allied peace terms, published on 1 May, were unacceptable to some members of the government, particularly members of the Liberal DDP, and the government resigned in June. A new administration was formed, without further elections, under the leadership of Gustav Bauer. The Bauer government was made up of ministers from the Majority SPD and Centre parties. Although the Versailles Treaty was accepted by the Reichstag in a vote of 23 June, the DDP voted against the government. DDP ministers rejoined the government in October.

Bauer Administration: 21 June 1919–27 March 1920 ('Weimar Coalition': MSPD – Centre – DDP from October)

Chancellor	Gustav Bauer (MSPD)
Vice Chancellor	Matthias Erzberger (Centre)
	Eugen Schiffer (DDP) from 2 October 1919
Foreign Minister	Hermann Müller (MSPD)
Interior Minister	Eduard David (MSPD)
Finance Minister	Matthias Erzberger (Centre)
	Unoccupied from 11 March 1920
Economics	Rudolf Wissell (MSPD)
	Robert Schmidt (MSPD) from 15 July 1919
Treasury	Wilhelm Mayer (BVP*)
	Unoccupied from 19 January 1920
Justice	Eugen Schiffer (DDP) from 2 October
Defence	Gustav Noske (MSPD)
Food	Robert Schmidt (MSPD) combined with economics portfolio from 15 September

Posts	Johann Giesberts (Centre)
Labour	Alexander Schlicke (MSPD)
Transport	Johannes Bell (Centre)
Reconstruction	Otto Gessler (DDP) from 25 October 1919
Without portfolio	Eduard David (MSPD) from 5 October 1919

* *Bayerische Volkspartei* (Bavarian People's Party). Mayer resigned and became ambassador in Paris when the BVP broke with the Centre, partly as a result of Erzberger's tax policies, in January 1920.

The Bauer administration fled to Stuttgart during the ultimately abortive Kapp putsch of March 1919, which was thwarted by a general strike. The trades unions then tried unsuccessfully to have a purely Socialist government appointed. Bauer, in any case, was forced to resign. Differences between the army and Defence Minister Noske during the crisis had already prompted the resignation of the latter on 22 March.

First Müller Administration: 27 March–25 June 1920 (Weimar Coalition: MSPD – DDP – Centre)

Bauer's administration was replaced by that of Hermann Müller in March 1920, again without further elections and against the background of continued agitation by the Communists.

Chancellor:	Hermann Müller (MSPD)
Vice Chancellor	Erich Koch (DDP)
Foreign Minister	Hermann Müller (MSPD)
	Adolf Köster (MSPD) from 10 April 1920
Interior Minister	Erich Koch (DDP)
Finance Minister	(Dr) Josef Wirth (Centre)
Economics	Robert Schmidt (MSPD)
Treasury	Gustav Bauer (MSPD)
Justice	Andreas Blunck (DDP)
Defence	Otto Gessler (DDP)
Food	Andreas Hermes (Centre)
Posts	Johann Giesberts (Centre)
Labour	Alexander Schlicke (MSPD)
Transport	Johannes Bell (Centre)
	Gustav Bauer (MSPD) from 1 May 1920
Without portfolio	Eduard David (MSPD)

The Müller administration failed to survive the first Reichstag elections, which were held on 6 June. The results reflected a polarisation in political attitudes which constituted a rejection of the 'Weimar coalition' or 'republican' parties. The Independent Social Democrats won a proportion of the vote almost as large as that of the Majority SPD, while the German Nationalist Party and

Stresemann's conservative German People's Party on the right of the political spectrum also increased their share of the vote.

Fehrenbach Administration: 25 June 1920–4 May 1921 (Centre-right Coalition: DDP – Centre – DVP)

The composition of the new government, led by Konstantin Fehrenbach of the Centre Party, reflected the electorate's shift to the right. The SPD was excluded from power, and the German People's Party (DVP) included instead.

Chancellor	Konstantin Fehrenbach (Centre)
Vice Chancellor	Rudolf Heinze (DVP)
Foreign Minister	Walter Simons (non-party)
Interior Minister	Erich Koch (DDP)
Finance Minister	(Dr) Josef Wirth (Centre)
Economics	Ernst Scholz (DVP)
Treasury	Hans von Raumer (DVP)
Justice	Rudolf Heinze (DVP)
Defence	Otto Gessler (DDP)
Food	Andreas Hermes (Centre)
Posts	Johann Giesberts (Centre)
Labour	Heinrich Brauns (Centre)
Transport	Wilhelm Groener (non-party)

The Fehrenbach government fell on the issue of reparations. The Allied Reparations Commission set the figure for repayment (132 million gold marks) higher than any amount agreeable to the Germans, and the government resigned rather than accept responsibility for agreeing to the figure. The following day the Allies threatened to occupy the Ruhr on 12 May if their conditions were not met. A new administration was formed on 10 May to deal with the new crisis.

First Wirth Administration: 10 May–26 October 1921 (Weimar Coalition: MSPD – DDP – Centre)

Fehrenbach was replaced by Josef Wirth, another Centre Party politician. Wirth was from Baden and his administration and policies reflected his background in the liberal democratic tradition of south-west Germany. He moved the government to the left by bringing back the Social Democrats and dispensing with the services of the DVP, and adopted a policy of 'fulfilment' and accepted the Allied ultimatum on 11 May.

Chancellor	(Dr) Josef Wirth (Centre)
Vice Chancellor	Gustav Bauer (MSPD)

Foreign Minister	(Dr) Josef Wirth (Centre)
	Friedrich Rosen (non-party) from 23 May 1921
Interior Minister	Georg Grandauer (MSPD)
Finance Minister	(Dr) Josef Wirth (Centre)
Economics	Robert Schmidt (MSPD)
Treasury	Gustav Bauer (MSPD)
Justice	Eugen Schiffer (DDP)
Defence	Otto Gessler (DDP)
Food	Andreas Hermes (Centre)
Posts	Johann Giesberts (Centre)
Labour	Heinrich Brauns (Centre)
Transport	Wilhelm Groener (non-party)
Reconstruction	Walther Rathenau (non-party) from 29 May 1921

Wirth reshuffled his cabinet on 26 October.

Second Wirth Administration: 26 October 1921–22 November 1922 (Weimar Coalition: SPD – DDP – Centre)

Chancellor	(Dr) Josef Wirth (Centre)
Vice Chancellor	Gustav Bauer (MSPD)
Foreign Minister	(Dr) Josef Wirth (Centre)
	Walther Rathenau (non-party) from 1 February 1922
	(Dr) Josef Wirth (from 25 June 1922)
Interior Minister	Adolf Köster (MSPD)
Finance Minister	Andreas Hermes (Centre) from 3 March 1922
Economics	Robert Schmidt (MSPD)
Treasury	Gustav Bauer (MSPD)
Justice	Gustav Radbruch (MSPD)
Defence	Otto Gessler (DDP)
Food	Andreas Hermes (Centre)
	Anton Fehr (BBB*) from 31 March 1922
Posts	Johann Giesberts (Centre)
Labour	Heinrich Brauns (Centre)
Transport	Wilhelm Groener (non-party)

* BBB = *Bayerischer Bauernbund* (Bavarian Farmers' League)

Walther Rathenau was assassinated on 24 June and Wirth himself took over the Foreign Ministry portfolio the next day. In September the MSPD and USPD were re-united, precipitating a government crisis. The united Social Democrats were now perceived as a more radically left-wing party, and their liberal coalition partners wanted to compensate for this shift by drawing the DVP back into the government. The SPD chose instead to leave the government, and a new (minority) administration was formed by Wilhelm Cuno.

Cuno Administration: 22 November 1922–12 August 1923 (Centre-right Coalition: DDP – Centre – DVP)
Cuno was not officially affiliated to any party but his sympathies as a businessman were with the DVP, so that the government now shifted significantly to the right. In addition *Fachminister* or non-party experts were appointed to a number of departments.

Chancellor	Wilhelm Cuno (non-party)
Foreign Minister	Frederic von Rosenberg (non-party)
Interior Minister	Rudolf Oeser (DDP)
Finance Minister	Andreas Hermes (Centre)
Economics	Johannes Becker (DVP)
Treasury	Heinrich Albert (non-party) to 31 March (post abolished 31 March 1923)
Justice	Rudolf Heinze (DVP)
Defence	Otto Gessler (DDP)
Food	Karl Müller (Centre)
	Hans Luther (non-party) from 25 November
Posts	Joseph Stingl (BVP)
Labour	Heinrich Brauns (Centre)
Transport	Wilhelm Groener (non-party)
Reconstruction	Gustav Müller (deputising)
	Heinrich Albert (non-party) from 31 March 1923

In January the French and Belgians occupied the Ruhr. The government ordered passive resistance and simultaneously tried to come to terms with the French. By August it was clear that this policy, conducted against a background of accelerating hyper-inflation, could not be continued, and Cuno's administration resigned to make way for a grand coalition under Gustav Stresemann.

First Stresemann Administration: 13 August–6 October 1923 (Grand Coalition: SPD – DDP – Centre – DVP)

Chancellor	Gustav Stresemann (DVP)
Vice Chancellor	Robert Schmidt (SPD)
Foreign Minister	Gustav Stresemann (DVP)
Interior Minister	Wilhelm Sollmann (SPD)
Finance Minister	Rudolf Hilferding (SPD)
Economics	Hans von Raumer (DVP)
Justice	Gustav Radbruch (SPD)
Defence	Otto Gessler (DDP)
Food	Hans Luther (non-party)
Posts	Anton Höfle (Centre)
Labour	Heinrich Brauns (Centre)
Transport	Rudolf Oeser (Centre)

| Reconstruction | Robert Schmidt (SPD) |
| Occupied Areas | Johannes Fuchs (non-party) from 24 August 1923 |

Stresemann's coalition cabinet was reshuffled on 6 October, following the declaration of a national state of emergency. This effectively transferred executive authority to Otto Gessler, the Defence Minister, and to General Hans von Seeckt, the head of Army Command (*Chef der Heeresleitung*). This power was reinforced by the use of presidential decree based on Article 48 of the constitution.

Second Stresemann Administration: 6 October–30 November 1923
(Grand Coalition: SPD to 3 November – DDP – Centre – DVP)

Chancellor	Gustav Stresemann (DVP)
Foreign Minister	Gustav Stresemann (DVP)
Interior Minister	Wilhelm Sollmann (SPD)
	Karl Jarres (DVP) from 11 November 1923
Finance Minister	Hans Luther (non-party)
Economics	Josef Koeth (non-party)
Justice	Gustav Radbruch (SPD) to 3 November 1923
Defence	Otto Gessler (DDP)
Food	Gerhard Graf von Kanitz (non-party, formerly DNVP)
Posts	Anton Höfle (Centre)
Labour	Heinrich Brauns (Centre)
Transport	Rudolf Oeser (DDP)
Reconstruction	Robert Schmidt (SPD) to 3 November 1923
Occupied Areas	Johannes Fuchs (non-party) to 3 November 1923

Following the successful suppression of putschist threats from the right and Communist agitation (leading to a ban on both the NSDAP and KPD), and the stabilisation of the currency, the cabinet resigned on November and the SPD withdrew from the coalition.

First Marx Administration: 30 November 1923–3 June 1924
(Centre-right Coalition: DDP – Centre – BVP – DVP)

Chancellor	Wilhelm Marx (Centre)
Vice Chancellor	Karl Jarres (DVP)
Foreign Minister	Gustav Stresemann (DVP)
Interior Minister	Karl Jarres (DVP)
Finance Minister	Hans Luther (non-party)
Economics	Eduard Hamm (DDP)
Justice	Erich Hemminger (BVP)
	Curt Joël from 15 April 1924
Defence	Otto Gessler (DDP)

Food	Gerhard Graf von Kanitz (non-party)
Posts	Anton Höfle (Centre)
Labour	Heinrich Brauns (Centre)
Transport	Rudolf Oeser (DDP)
Reconstruction	Gustav Müller to 11 May 1924 (post abolished)
Occupied Areas	Anton Höfle (Centre)

The Marx administration was a minority government operating under a state of national emergency. When the state of emergency came to an end with the relinquishing of executive authority by von Seeckt in February and the refusal of the Reichstag to vote an extension of special powers, new elections were held on 4 May.

Second Marx Administration: 3 June 1924–15 January 1925 (Centre-right Coalition: DDP – Centre – DVP)

The election resulted in gains for the nationalists (DNVP and a nationalist bloc representing former Nazis and the DVFP) and Communists at the expense of the government parties. A new administration was formed with minor changes and new elections held on 7 December. In the meantime the government relied on informal SPD and some DNVP members' support to steer the ratification of the Dawes Plan through parliament, initiating a period of government from the centre-right where the SPD opposition was called on to support contentious foreign policies rejected by the right.

Chancellor	Wilhelm Marx (Centre)
Vice Chancellor	Karl Jarres (DVP)
Foreign Minister	Gustav Stresemann (DVP)
Interior Minister	Karl Jarres (DVP)
Finance Minister	Hans Luther (non-party)
Economics	Eduard Hamm (DDP)
Justice	Curt Joël (non-party)
Defence	Otto Gessler (DDP)
Food	Gerhard Graf von Kanitz (non-party)
Posts	Anton Höfle (Centre)
Labour	Heinrich Brauns (Centre)
Transport	Rudolf Oeser (DDP)
	Rudolf Krohne (DVP) from 11 October 1924
Occupied Areas	Anton Höfle (Centre)
	Wilhelm Marx (Centre) from 10 January 1925

First Luther Administration: 15 January–5 December 1925 (Centre-right Coalition: Centre – DVP – DNVP – BVP)

Both Communists and Nationalists lost heavily in the December elections. The SPD gained substantially but the possibility of a 'Grand Coalition' was excluded by the DVP which was prepared only to join a bourgeois bloc government. For the first time, therefore, the DNVP entered government. Although Gessler remained Defence Minister, the DDP was not formally part of the coalition.

Chancellor	Hans Luther (non-party)
Foreign Minister	Gustav Stresemann (DVP)
Interior Minister	Martin Schiele (DNVP)
	Otto Gessler (DDP) from 26 October 1925
Finance Minister	Otto von Schlieben (DNVP)
	Hans Luther (non-party) from 26 October 1925
Economics	Albert Neuhaus (DNVP)
	Rudolf Krohne (DVP) from 26 October 1925
Justice	Josef Frenken (Centre)
	Hans Luther (non-party) from 21 November 1925
Defence	Otto Gessler (DDP)
Food	Gerhard Graf von Kanitz (non-party)
Posts	Karl Stingl (BVP)
Labour	Heinrich Brauns (Centre)
Transport	Rudolf Krohne (DVP)
Occupied Areas	Joseph Frenken (Centre)
	Heinrich Brauns (Centre) from 21 November 1925

Continued DNVP participation in government depended on an uncontroversial foreign policy, and the opportunity for the party's inclusion had arisen only with the successful resolution of the reparations problem in August 1925. However, DNVP ministers came under internal party pressure to resist Stresemann's foreign policy, based as it ostensibly was on republican *Erfüllungspolitik*, and in particular to vote against the Locarno Treaties. The Nationalists resigned (25 October) before the Reichstag vote on the issue (27 November). The remaining rump of the cabinet resigned after the vote (5 December).

Second Luther Administration: 20 January–12 May 1926 (Centre-right Coalition: Centre – DDP – DVP – BVP)

The government crisis lasted for several weeks. Its outcome was determined by the intervention of Hindenburg, the new Reich President, who made it clear that if a 'bourgeois bloc' could not be formed, a minority government was preferable to one which included the SPD. Accordingly, Luther constructed a new minority government on 20 January 1926.

Chancellor	Hans Luther (non-party)
Foreign Minister	Gustav Stresemann (DVP)
Interior Minister	Wilhelm Külz (DDP)
Finance Minister	Peter Reinhold (DDP)
Economics	Julius Curtius (DVP)
Justice	Wilhelm Marx (Centre)
Defence	Otto Gessler (DDP)
Food	Heinrich Haslinde (Centre)
Posts	Karl Stingl (BVP)
Labour	Heinrich Brauns (Centre)
Transport	Rudolf Krohne (DVP)
Occupied Areas	Wilhelm Marx (Centre)

The government was brought down by a further intervention of the Reich President in politics. Hindenburg's 'flag decree' (5 May) prompted a vote of no confidence in which DDP members voted against the government. Luther resigned.

Third Marx Administration: 17 May–17 December 1926 (Centre-right Coalition: DDP – Centre – DVP – BVP)

Apart from the new Chancellor, the cabinet remained virtually unchanged.

Chancellor	Wilhelm Marx (Centre)
Foreign Minister	Gustav Stresemann (DVP)
Interior Minister	Wilhelm Külz (DDP)
Finance Minister	Peter Reinhold (DDP)
Economics	Julius Curtius (DVP)
Justice	Johannes Bell (Centre) from 16 July 1926
Defence	Otto Gessler (DDP)
Food	Heinrich Haslinde (Centre)
Posts	Karl Stingl (BVP)
Labour	Heinrich Brauns (Centre)
Transport	Rudolf Krohne (DVP)
Occupied Areas	Johannes Bell (Centre)

Another minority government could only be seen as a provisional measure and the DNVP and DVP maintained contacts with a view to forming a broad conservative coalition at some point. This would mean the termination of SPD 'tolerance', and the working agreement between the SPD and the government did indeed break down in December. The DNVP supported a successful SPD no confidence motion, bringing down the government on 17 December 1927.

Fourth Marx Administration: 29 January 1927–12 June 1928 (Centre-right Coalition: Centre – DVP – DNVP – BVP)

The new administration was very much one of the right. The DDP were excluded, and the DNVP brought in.

Chancellor	Wilhelm Marx (Centre)
Vice Chancellor	Oskar Hergt (DNVP)
Foreign Minister	Gustav Stresemann (DVP)
Interior Minister	Walter von Keudell (DNVP)
Finance Minister	Heinrich Köhler (Centre)
Economics	Julius Curtius (DVP)
Justice	Oskar Hergt (DNVP)
Defence	Otto Gessler (non-party)
	Wilhelm Groener (non-party) from 19 January 1928
Food	Martin Schiele (DNVP)
Posts	Georg Schätzel (BVP)
Labour	Heinrich Brauns (Centre)
Transport	Wilhelm Koch (DNVP)
Occupied Areas	Wilhelm Marx (Centre)

The government coalition was now a very broad alliance stretched across a range of profoundly divergent interests. However, it was not brought down by the anticipated foreign policy intransigence of its new German Nationalist members, but by a disagreement over education between the Roman Catholic Centre Party and the secular DVP, heir to the nineteenth-century National Liberal Party. The crisis arose in February and resulted in the defeat of the Centre Party, which promptly served notice on the coalition and dissolved the Reichstag. The subsequent elections (20 May 1928) were such a clear victory for the left over the government parties that a new coalition without the SPD was unthinkable.

Second Müller Administration: 28 June 1928–27 March 1930 (Grand Coalition: SPD – DDP – Centre – BVP – DVP)

Chancellor	Hermann Müller (SPD)
Foreign Minister	Gustav Stresemann (DVP)
	Julius Curtius (DVP) from 4 October 1929
Interior Minister	Carl Severing (SPD)
Finance Minister	Rudolf Hilferding (SPD)
	Paul Moldenhauer (DVP) from 23 December 1929
Economics	Julius Curtius (DVP)
	Paul Moldenhauer (DVP) from 11 November 1929
	Robert Schmidt (SPD) from 23 December 1929
Justice	Erich Koch (DDP)
	Theodor von Guérard (Centre) from 13 April 1929

Defence	Wilhelm Groener (non-party)
Food	Hermann Dietrich (DDP)
Posts	Georg Schätzel (BVP)
Labour	Rudolf Wissell (SPD)
Transport	Theodor von Guérard (Centre)
	Georg Schätzel (BVP) from 6 February 1929
	Adam Stegerwald (Centre) from 13 April 1929
Occupied Areas	Theodor von Guérard (Centre) to 6 February 1929
	Dr Josef Wirth (Centre) from 13 April 1929

The most significant of the many ministerial changes during the life of the administration was that caused by the death of Stresemann, whose intervention in negotiations had helped bring the cabinet together in the face of DVP and Centre Party hostility to the Social Democrats. It was an administration marked by conflicts not only between ministers of different parties, but between ministers and their own backbenchers. It fell against the background of the slump and a full frontal attack by industrialists on the basic welfare provisions which were fundamental to the Weimar system. The alteration to the insurance system which was the ostensible reason for the conflict between the SPD and DVP had merely provided the focus for a larger conflict of sectional economic interests.

First Brüning Administration: 30 March 1930–7 October 1931 (Presidential Cabinet)

The crisis led to the effective exclusion of the SPD from government and the formation of a new minority cabinet under Heinrich Brüning. The negotiations and preparations for the installation of an anti-Marxist government which would rule without parliament began long before the crisis of March 1930. The government was defeated on 16 July and used Article 48 to pass its legislation by presidential decree. When an SPD motion to lift the emergency decree was passed two days later the government carried out its threat to dissolve the Reichstag.

Chancellor	(Dr) Heinrich Brüning (Centre)
Vice Chancellor	Hermann Dietrich (DDP to 26 June 1930, then DStP)
Foreign Minister	Julius Curtius (DVP)
Interior Minister	(Dr) Josef Wirth (Centre)
Finance Minister	Paul Moldenhauer (DVP)
	Hermann Dietrich (DStP) from 26 June 1930
Economics	Hermann Dietrich (DDP) to 26 June 1930
	Ernst Trendelenburg (non-party)

Justice	Viktor Bredt (Business Party)
	Curt Joël (non-party) from 5 December 1930
Defence	Wilhelm Groener (non-party)
Food	Martin Schiele (DNVP; from 22 July 1930 CL)
Posts	Georg Schätzel (BVP)
Labour	Adam Stegerwald (Centre)
Transport	Theodor von Guérard (Centre)
Occupied Areas	Gottfried R Treviranus (KVP) to 30 September 1930
Without portfolio	Gottfried R Treviranus (KVP) from 1 October 1930

KVP = *Konservative Volkspartei*;   CL = *Christliches Landvolk*
DStP = *Deutsche Staatspartei.*

Nazi and Communist gains in the elections (14 September 1930) prevented the formation of any majority. The Bruning cabinet survived through SPD 'toleration' by which the Social Democrats hoped to prevent the further marginalisation of parliamentary government through the use of emergency decrees.

Second Brüning Administration: 9 October 1931–30 May 1932 (Presidential Cabinet)

Brüning reshuffled his cabinet in October 1932 to counter criticism from the right, and the last committed republican minister, Josef Wirth, was dropped. Nevertheless, the government only survived thanks to the continued support of the SPD.

Chancellor	Heinrich Brüning (Centre)
Vice Chancellor	Hermann Dietrich (DSP)
Foreign Minister	Heinrich Brüning (Centre)
Interior Minister	Wilhelm Groener (non-party)
Finance Minister	Hermann Dietrich (DSP)
Economics	Hermann Warmbold (non-party)
	Ernst Trendelenburg (non-party) from 6 May 1932
Justice	Curt Joël (non-party)
Defence	Wilhelm Groener (non-party)
Food	Martin Schiele (CL)
Posts	Georg Schätzel (BVP)
Labour	Adam Stegerwald (Centre)
Transport	Gottfried R Treviranus (KVP)
Osthilfe	Hans Schlange-Schöningen (CL) from 5 November 1931

DStP = *Deutsche Staatspartei*;   KVP = *Konservative Volkspartei*
CL = *Christliches Landvolk*

Brüning's government, appropriately enough, fell not by defeat in the Reichstag but by the refusal of Hindenburg's assent to a presidential decree (to break up the large and uneconomic East Elbian estates for resettlement as small farms). Brüning was effectively dismissed and replaced by Franz von Papen's 'cabinet of barons'.

Papen Administration: 1 June–3 December 1932 (Presidential Cabinet)
Papen immediately dissolved the Reichstag and elections were held on 31 July. The Nazis emerged as by far the largest party and Hitler refused not only to 'tolerate' the Papen government but even to join it, except as Chancellor.

Chancellor	Franz von Papen (non-party from 3 June 1932)
Foreign Minister	Konstantin Freiherr von Neurath (non-party)
Interior Minister	Wilhelm Freiherr von Gayl (DNVP)
Finance Minister	Johann Ludwig Graf Schwerin von Krosigk (non-party)
Economics	Hermann Warmbold (non-party)
Justice	Franz Gürtner (DNVP)
Defence	Kurt von Schleicher (non-party)
Food	Magnus Freiherr von Braun (DNVP)
Posts	Paul Freiherr Eltz von Rübenach (non-party)
Labour	Hugo Schäffer (non-party)
Transport	Paul Freiherr Eltz von Rübenach (non-party)
Osthilfe	Magnus Freiherr von Braun (DNVP)
Without portfolio	Franz Bracht (non-party)
	Johannes Popitz (non-party) from 29 October 1932

Papen's cabinet was massively defeated in a no confidence vote on 12 September and the Reichstag was dissolved. The Nazis joined forces with the Centre Party to force new elections against the wishes of the President and his associates who had not intended to set a date for them. Despite Nazi losses the election results failed to provide a way out of the impasse: the work of Papen's government could be blocked at any time if any of the other major opposition parties joined forces. Plans for a revision of the constitution along authoritarian lines, to be implemented by force if necessary, were blocked by Schleicher. As a result Papen was dismissed on 17 November and Schleicher himself formed a government.

Schleicher Cabinet: 3 December 1932–30 January 1933 (Presidential Cabinet)
Schleicher's attempts to bring the NSDAP into his government by appointing Gregor Strasser Vice-Chancellor were blocked by Hitler and other leading Nazis. Schleicher therefore attempted to

venture into populist politics himself, which only served to arouse the suspicion and hostility of the right.

Chancellor	Kurt von Schleicher (non-party)
Foreign Minister	Konstantin Freiherr von Neurath (non-party)
Interior Minister	Franz Bracht (non-party)
Finance Minister	Johann Ludwig Graf Schwerin von Krosigk (non-party)
Economics	Hermann Warmbold (non-party)
Justice	Franz Gürtner (DNVP)
Defence	Kurt von Schleicher (non-party)
Food	Magnus Freiherr von Braun (DNVP)
Posts	Paul Freiherr Eltz von Rubenach (non-party)
Labour	Friedrich Syrup (non-party)
Transport	Paul Freiherr Eltz von Rübenach (non-party)
Osthilfe	Günther Gereke (*Christliches Landvolk*)
Without portfolio	Johannes Popitz (non-party)

The government was short-lived and fell victim to a German Nationalist censure motion in January. Schleicher requested the dissolution of the Reichstag followed by a limited period of unconstitutional government supported by the President; but Hindenburg refused, and instead appointed Hitler Chancellor.

Hitler Cabinet: 30 January 1933
Since the beginning of January Hitler had worked with von Papen to bring about the fall of the Schleicher administration. He had also insisted on his own claim to the Chancellorship, which von Papen had conceded. Otherwise there were few changes in the political complexion or even the composition of the cabinet. Von Papen himself became Vice Chancellor and Reich Commissioner of Prussia, the latter post arising as a consequence of his own unconstitutional suppression of the elected Prussian government in November 1932.

Chancellor	Adolf Hitler (NSDAP)
Vice Chancellor and Reich Commissioner for Prussia	Franz von Papen
Foreign Minister	Konstantin Freiherr von Neurath (non-party)
Interior Minister	Wilhelm Frick (NSDAP)
Finance Minister	Johann Ludwig Graf Schwerin von Krosigk (non-party)
Economics, Food and Agriculture	Alfred Hugenberg (DNVP)
Justice	Franz Gürtner (DNVP)
Defence	Werner von Blomberg (non-party)

Posts and Transport	Paul Freiherr Eltz von Rübenach (non-party)
Labour	Franz Seldte (non-party)
Employment	Günther Gereke (*Christliches Landvolk*)
Without Portfolio	Hermann Goering (NSDAP)

The government was a presidential cabinet as Hitler had insisted. New elections on 5 March 1933 under conditions of extreme intimidation failed to provide the NSDAP with an absolute majority.

Rise of Nazism

6.1. The Origins of the Nazi Party (NSDAP)

The precursors of the Nazi Party are to be found in the *völkisch* and Pan-German movements of both Germany and Austria at the end of the nineteenth century. The radical right of German-speaking Europe was organisationally fragmented, but shared an ideology characterised to a greater or lesser extent by a number of common features. Among these was a militant exclusive nationalism related to a 'scientific' racism which claimed to be founded on the principles of 'social Darwinism'. This racism was most virulent when directed against the Jews, but others, particularly Slavs, were not exempt. There was also a shared general antipathy among such circles to modern industrial society and all its manifestations, whether political (liberalism, parliamentarism, democracy, Marxism and the labour movement), economic (capitalism – and in particular the concentration of capital in the hands of big business, workers' co-operatives), social (urbanisation, the perceived disintegration of traditional family life, women's emancipation) or cultural (modernist or abstract art, cultural decadence). The response of the radical right to such phenomena was to call for the purging and rejuvenation of the nation, the restoration of 'traditional' values, and ultimately the 'restoration' of a stable and organic rural society from a mythical golden age in the Germanic past. Elements of this arguably 'proto-fascist' ideology were reflected on many levels, from the work of a radical right university-educated intelligentsia to the anti-semitic pornography of street pedlars, and late imperial Vienna in particular was a centre for the production of such material.

The *völkisch* precursors of the Nazi Party remained relatively marginal to the mainstream of central European politics before World War I. The earliest party of a recognisably Nazi type (also called the German Workers' Party) was formed in Bohemia in 1904 in response to the creation of a separate Czech labour party and the influx of cheap Czech labour from the Bohemian countryside which undermined the wage levels of urban, ethnically German industrial workers. The social composition and ideology of this first DAP was strikingly similar to its Munich namesake of

1919. Its members were manual or clerical workers (especially railway workers) and its ideology was nationalist and at the same time anti-capitalist, anti-Marxist and anti-semitic. The party's strength remained largely in Bohemia (the Sudetenland) and although it was refounded as the German National Socialist Workers' Party (DNSAP) in 1918, with branches in both Austria and the new Czechoslovakia, it failed to attract members. The party was finally absorbed into the German NSDAP in 1926.

The origins of the Munich DAP were in a militantly nationalist anti-semitic group called the Thule Society, which served as a focus for the extreme right in the city. The party itself was very much a local group of relatively minor significance when Hitler joined it in 1919. It was refounded as the National Socialist German Workers' Party the following year (1 April 1920) and Hitler was chairman with dictatorial powers by July 1921. The formation of the 'sports' section (later the *Sturmabteilung* or SA) was announced in the following month.

On 8–9 November 1923 Hitler attempted an unsuccessful coup in Munich and was subsequently arrested along with other putsch leaders, including General Ludendorff. The ringleaders were tried for high treason and Hitler was sentenced to five years (the minimum term possible) in Landsberg prison. Ludendorff was acquitted. The Nazi Party was banned and Hitler withdrew from active politics during the term of his imprisonment. Other former party members co-operated with the German People's Freedom Party in a *völkisch*-social bloc which presented a joint list in the May 1924 Reichstag elections and won 9% of the vote. Hitler was released from prison in December 1924 and the party was refounded on 27 February 1925. During the period of in-fighting which followed, Gregor Strasser founded a 'working-group' of *Gauleiters* in northern and western Germany, a development which quickly came to be perceived in Munich as a threat to Hitler's leadership. The conflict came to a head in Bamberg, Bavaria, in February 1926; a turning point where Hitler's authority as party leader was re-asserted.

The party had little electoral success until the onset of the depression. It made gains in local elections in 1929, winning power at regional level for the first time (as coalition partner in the government of Thuringia). Despite pressure for a 'Socialist' commitment from the Strasser wing of the party, whose own 'Socialism' amounted to little more than a nationalistic populist appeal to the working class, the propaganda effort of the party was increasingly (and successfully) directed at the middle classes and peasants. While the details of electoral support for the Nazis in the elections of 1930 and 1932 are still the subject of controversy, three features are strikingly clear: support was much stronger in predominantly middle-class constituencies than in industrial working-class districts; it was also much stronger in the countryside and in small towns than in large cities; and it was stronger in Protestant regions than in predominantly Roman Catholic ones.

Despite the electoral breakthrough of the depression years the Nazis were no more successful than any other party in their attempt to win an absolute majority in the Reichstag. (This was true even of the election of March 1933, which was conducted under conditions of intimidation and repression.) However, the government had already ceased to rely on parliamentary majorities long before Hitler's appointment as Chancellor. The cabinets of Heinrich Brüning, Franz von Papen and Kurt von Schleicher dispensed with the necessity of Reichstag majorities by ruling through presidential decree. These governments failed, in three consecutive general elections, to win sufficient support to form a parliamentary majority, and many conservatives, both within and outside parliament, were considering a permanent authoritarian solution to replace the Weimar constitution. In the meantime, after the fall of von Schleicher, the parliamentary base of the governing coalition was broadened by bringing the Nazi Party into the cabinet, something which Hitler was only prepared to accept if he himself were appointed Chancellor.

6.2. Social Structure of the Nazi Party Membership

NSDAP Party Members as of 1 January 1935

	To 1930	1930-33*	1 January 1935	
			Party	*Society*
I. Employed	93.5%	93.1%	94.5%	
1. Workers	26.3%	32.5%	29.7%	46.3%
2. White-collar	24.0%	20.6%	18.6%	12.4%
3. Self-employed	18.9%	17.3%	19.0%	9.6%
4. Civil servants	7.7%	6.5%	12.4%	4.8%
5. Peasants	13.2%	12.5%	10.2%	20.7%
6. Others	3.4%	3.7%	3.2%	6.2%

* 14 September 1930 to 30 January 1933.

6.3. Occupational Background of Leading Nazi Functionaries, 1934

Occupation	% of Total
Industry and Commerce	23.2
Academics	17.2
Party employees	15.9
Military	14.6
Public service	13.2
Peasants	7.3
Communications	2.6
Artisans	2.0
Other/unknown	4.0

6.4. Nazi Vote by Region in National Elections, 1924–33

	4 May 1924*	7 Dec. 1924*	20 May 1928	14 Sep. 1930	31 Jul. 1932	6 Nov. 1932	5 Mar. 1933
1 East Prussia	8.6	6.2	0.8	22.5	47.1	39.7	56.5
2 Berlin	3.6	1.6	1.4	12.8	24.6	22.5	31.3
3 Potsdam II	6.5	2.9	1.8	16.7	33.0	29.1	38.2
4 Potsdam I	5.8	2.8	1.6	18.8	38.2	34.1	44.4
5 Frankfurt/Oder	5.0	3.2	1.0	22.7	48.1	42.6	55.2
6 Pomerania	7.3	4.2	1.5	24.3	48.0	43.1	56.3
7 Breslau	4.0	1.4	1.0	24.2	43.5	40.4	50.2
8 Liegnitz	1.5	1.5	1.2	20.9	48.0	42.1	54.0
9 Oppeln	2.6	1.5	1.0	9.5	29.2	26.8	43.2
10 Magdeburg	4.9	3.0	1.7	19.5	43.8	39.0	47.3
11 Merseburg	8.7	4.3	2.7	20.5	42.6	34.5	46.4
12 Thuringia	9.9	5.4	3.7	19.3	43.4	37.1	47.2
13 Schleswig-Holstein	7.4	2.7	4.0	27.0	51.0	45.7	53.2
14 Weser/Ems	7.4	4.8	5.2	20.5	38.4	31.9	41.4
15 East Hanover	8.6	4.4	2.6	20.6	49.5	42.9	54.3
16 S. Hanover-Brunswick	7.6	3.4	4.4	24.3	46.1	40.6	48.7
17 Westphalia North	3.5	1.3	1.0	12.2	25.7	22.3	34.9
18 Westphalia South	1.5	1.1	1.6	13.9	27.2	24.8	33.8
19 Hesse-Nassau	5.6	2.5	3.6	20.8	43.6	41.2	49.4
20 Cologne-Aachen	1.5	0.6	1.1	14.5	20.2	17.4	30.1
21 Koblenz-Trier	1.3	—	2.1	14.9	28.8	26.1	38.4
22 Düsseldorf East	3.9	1.6	1.8	17.0	31.6	27.0	37.4
23 Düsseldorf West	2.6	0.9	1.2	16.8	27.0	24.2	35.2
24 Upper Bavaria-Swabia	17.0	4.8	6.2	16.3	27.1	24.6	40.9
25 Lower Bavaria	10.2	3.0	3.5	12.0	20.4	18.5	39.2
26 Franconia	20.7	7.5	8.1	20.5	39.9	36.4	45.7
27 Palatinate	5.7	1.9	5.6	22.8	43.7	42.6	46.5
28 Dresden-Bautzen	4.5	1.5	1.8	16.1	39.3	34.0	43.6
29 Leipzig	7.9	1.8	1.9	14.0	36.1	31.0	40.0
30 Chemnitz-Zwickau	7.7	4.2	4.3	23.8	47.0	43.4	50.0
31 Württemberg	4.1	2.1	1.9	9.4	30.3	26.2	42.0
32 Baden	4.8	1.9	2.9	19.2	33.7	27.2	38.9
33 Hesse-Darmstadt	2.9	1.3	1.9	18.5	43.1	40.2	47.4
34 Hamburg	6.0	2.3	2.6	19.2	33.7	27.2	38.9
35 Mecklenburg	20.8	11.9	2.0	20.1	44.8	37.0	48.0
Reich	6.5	3.0	2.6	18.3	37.3	33.1	43.9
Seats in Reichstag	32†	14†	12	107	230	196	288

* 4 May 1924: Combined list of the *Deutsch-Völkische Freiheitspartei* (German Nationalist Freedom Party, DVFP) or *Völkisch-Nationaler Block* and NSDAP. The Nationalists campaigned in the north and attracted much upper class support, the Nazis in Bavaria and the south, where they attracted predominantly petty bourgeois support. The northern Nationalists were more successful.
7 December 1924: The two parties again combined as the *Nationalsozialistische Freiheitsbewegung* (National Socialist Freedom Movement).

† 4 May 1924: 9 NSDAP seats: 7 December 1924: 4 NSDAP seats.

Politics, State and Party: the Third Reich

1. The Consolidation of Power

The Nazi dictatorship was not established by a revolutionary seizure of power. Hitler was appointed Chancellor by the President in the usual way, and could be dismissed by him at any time. Although parliamentary government had effectively been suspended since 1930 the Weimar constitution technically remained in force. Hitler led a coalition government of Nazis and conservatives and the situation was not altered significantly by the election of March 1933, although this election was by no means free. The Reichstag fire of 27 February had provided the government with a pretext for the promulgation of a 'Decree of the Reich President for the Protection of People and State' (28 February 1933). This suspended civil rights and provided for imprisonment without trial. It formed the basis of the suppression of the Communist Party and the intimidation of other political opponents which characterised the last days of the election campaign.

Despite the 'terror' the Nazis themselves failed to win an absolute majority, and even with the support of other parties had only a meagre overall majority. In order to place the new regime on a firmer footing, and dispense with the need either for parliamentary majorities (and, inevitably, new elections) or for presidential decrees, the government needed to pass an Enabling Law granting it emergency powers for a substantial period of time. This required a two-thirds quorum and majority in the Reichstag. Even with such powers the government would only have control at Reich level. Furthermore, except in Prussia, where the state government had been deposed by the von Papen government (20 July 1932) and other states where the Nazis were already in government (Oldenburg, Mecklenburg, Mecklenburg-Strelitz, Brunswick, Anhalt and Thuringia) the federal states would continue to enjoy a relative degree of autonomy. In addition, institutions such as the civil service, the army, the judiciary and the education system continued to be dominated by non-Nazis (although many joined the party for career reasons), and many Social Democrats and other opponents of the party remained in public office.

The consolidation of power at Reich level was effected by the promulgation of the Enabling Law. This was initially conceived as a measure allowing the government to pass *decrees* without referring to the president. In the event, however, it allowed for the promulgation of further *laws*. The Centre Party was persuaded to lend its support, and the law was passed against 94 SPD votes. The process of 'co-ordination' (*Gleichschaltung*), by which both federal states and institutions were brought into line, occurred in the wake of a series of crises of public order across Germany, provoked by SA violence. The administration of the Reich was purged of oppositional civil servants and Jews by means of the Law for the Restoration of a Professional Civil Service. (A similar procedure had been undertaken in Prussia in the wake of the 'Papen coup'.) Nevertheless, the purge was not sufficient to satisfy the aspirations of radical rank and file Nazis.

The first year of Nazi rule was a period of effectively unrestrained street violence by the SA and repressive measures on the part of the authorities. The regime's opponents were beaten up, arrested and imprisoned in hastily erected concentration camps. This period of 'national revolution' saw Hitler and the Nazi leadership caught between the violence and increasing disaffection of the rank and file (and particularly the storm-troopers) and the disapproval of leading conservatives and army officers. Hitler officially called an end to the 'revolution' in July 1933, but the SA in particular continued to act in a way which alienated not only the party's conservative allies, but the Gestapo and party institutions themselves. It became clear that Hitler had to act not only against the opposition, but against his own rank and file as well. This he did with a purge of the SA which began on 30 June 1934 (Night of the Long Knives), and ensured the co-operation of the army; when after Hindenburg's death a few weeks later he combined the offices of President and Chancellor, he also took a personal oath of allegiance from the army.

2. Chronology

1933

30 Jan.	First cabinet meeting of the Hitler administration.
1 Feb.	Dissolution of the Reichstag.
4 Feb.	Presidential 'Decree for the Protection of the German People' qualifies freedom of the press and freedom of assembly.
17 Feb.	Prussian Interior Ministry (under Goering) permits shooting of 'enemies of the state' with impunity.
22 Feb.	Formation of auxiliary police forces in Prussia composed of SA, SS and Stahlhelm members.
23 Feb.	Homosexual rights groups proscribed.
27 Feb.	Reichstag fire.
28 Feb.	Hitler given emergency powers by presidential decree. The Decree of the Reich President for the Protection of People and State
3 Mar.	Arrest of Ernst Thälmann and other KPD members.
5 Mar.	Reichstag elections. NSDAP wins 288 seats, but fails to gain an overall majority. 'Co-ordination' of Hamburg state government.
6 Mar.	'Co-ordination' of Hesse, Lübeck and Bremen.
7 Mar.	'Co-ordination' of Baden, Saxony, Württemberg. Government of Schaumburg-Lippe resigns.
8 Mar.	Interior Minister Wilhelm Frick announces the establishment of 'concentration camps'.
9 Mar.	Himmler becomes Police President of Munich. Ritter von Epp is appointed Governor of Bavaria.
13 Mar.	Goebbels becomes Reich Minister of Public Enlightenment and Propaganda.
16 Mar.	Hjalmar Schacht succeeds Hans Luther as President of the *Reichsbank*.
17 Mar.	Hitler's 'bodyguard' (*Leibstandarte Adolf Hitler*) of 120 established under the leadership of Sepp Dietrich.

21 Mar.	Reichstag convened in a garrison church in Potsdam: Communist deputies forbidden to take their seats. 'Malicious Practices Law' (*Heimtückegesetz*) prohibits outspoken criticism of the regime. 'Special Courts' established.
22 Mar.	Establishment of a racial hygiene department in the Interior Ministry.
23 Mar.	Enabling Act ratified; 444 to 94 (SPD). All Communists and 26 SPD deputies absent. Centre Party support is nevertheless crucial in winning the necessary two-thirds majority.
30 Mar.	German bishops withdraw their opposition to the Nazis.
31 Mar.	First Law for the Co-ordination of the Federal States.
1 Apr.	Himmler becomes 'Political Police Commander of Bavaria'. Nationwide boycott of Jewish businesses. Literature by Jehovah's Witnesses banned.
7 Apr.	Law for the Restoration of a Professional Civil Service. Second Law for the Co-ordination of the Federal States: Office of Reich Governor (*Reichsstatthalter*) created. Resignation of Papen as Reich Commissioner for Prussia.
1 May	Nazi Party membership frozen.
2 May	Dissolution of the Free Trades Unions.
6 May	Ley announces establishment of German Labour Front (DAF). Hirschfeld's Institute of Sexual Research ransacked and its library burned.
10 May	Further burning of books in university towns. SPD property confiscated.
19 May	Law providing for the regulation of employment contracts by 'Reich Trustees of Labour'.
1 Jun.	Law for the Reduction of Unemployment. German firms begin to contribute 0.5 per cent of wages costs to NSDAP.
5 Jul.	Centre Party disbands.
6 Jul.	Hitler announces the end of the 'national revolution'.
8 Jul.	Concordat between Germany and the Vatican.
14 Jul.	NSDAP formally declared the only political party in Germany, which thereby becomes a one-party state.
20 Jul.	Concordat ratified.
13 Sep.	Law concerning the Provisional Establishment of the Reich Food Estate

22 Sep.	Reich Chamber of Culture established.
29 Sep.	Reich Entailed Farm Law.
12 Nov.	Reichstag Elections and Referendum.
27 Nov.	Establishment of 'Beauty of Labour' (*Schönheit der Arbeit*) and 'Strength through Joy' (*Kraft durch Freude*).
30 Nov.	Gestapo created.
1 Dec.	Law to ensure the Unity of Party and State. Hess and Röhm appointed Ministers without Portfolio.

1934

30 Jan.	Law for the Reconstruction of the Reich.
21 Mar.	'Battle for Work' begins.
20 Apr.	Himmler appointed 'Inspector of the Gestapo'.
20 Jun.	Hindenburg demands the dissolution of the SA.
30 Jun.	'Night of the Long Knives'. Purge of stormtroopers initiates the liquidation of opposition both within and outside the party: 170 leading Nazis are killed, including SA leader Ernst Röhm.
20 Jul.	SS established as an organisation independent from SA (under Himmler).
1 Aug.	'Law concerning the Head of State of the German Reich' provides for the combination of the offices of Chancellor and President.
2 Aug.	Death of President Hindenburg. Hitler becomes President and army swears oath of allegiance to him. Hjalmar Schacht appointed Minister of Economics.
19 Aug.	Hitler proclaims himself Führer and Reich Chancellor.
Sep.	Schacht introduces his 'New Plan'.
24 Oct.	Establishment of German Labour Front (DAF).
26 Oct.	A special department on abortion and homosexuality is set up in Berlin under Joseph Meisinger.
Oct.–Nov.	Nationwide arrests of homosexuals.

1935

13 Jan.	Saar plebiscite returns majority in favour of re-unification with Germany.
17 Mar.	Re-introduction of military service.
27 Mar.	Arrest of underground leadership of KPD.
Apr.	Prohibition of employment of Jehovah's Witnesses in civil service followed by nationwide wave of arrests.

24 Apr.	A decree orders the closure of certain newspapers.
May	Destruction of SPD resistance group *Germania*.
16 Jul.	Ministry of Churches created under Hanns Kerrl, formerly Minister without Portfolio.
24 Jul.	Dissolution of *Freikorps* organisations.
Aug.	Arrest of members of SPD resistance group (*Neu Beginnen*).
17 Aug.	Dissolution of all remaining masonic lodges.
15 Sep.	Nuremberg Laws.
13 Dec.	*Lebensborn* ('Spring of Life') organisation founded.

1936

10 Feb.	Gestapo actions placed above the law.
7 Mar.–28 Mar.	Military reoccupation of Rhineland followed by plebiscite affirming Hitler's policy.
4 Apr.	Goering appointed Commissioner of Raw Materials.
24 Apr.	*Ordensburgen* (Nazi elite schools) founded.
Jun.	Women effectively banned from the legal profession.
17 Jun.	Himmler appointed Head of the German Police.
26 Jun.	Himmler merges the Gestapo and the Criminal Police (*Kripo*) in the Security Police (*Sipo*), under the command of Heydrich. All uniformed police similarly combined as *Ordnungspolizei* (*Orpo*) under Kurt Daluege.
Jul.	First group of Gypsies (Sinti and Roma) sent to Dachau
1 Aug.	Olympic Games open in Berlin.
28 Aug.	Mass arrests of Jehovah's Witnesses.
19 Oct.	Announcement of Four Year Plan under leadership of Hermann Goering.

1937

30 Jan.	Reichstag extends Enabling Law for a further four years.
10 Feb.	*Reichsbank* and *Reichsbahn* subordinated to the government.
9 Mar.	Mass arrests of persons designated 'habitual criminals'.
14 Mar.	Publication of the Papal Encyclical *Mit brennender Sorge* denouncing Nazi persecution of the Church and clergymen.
19 Apr.	First Adolf Hitler School opens.

1 May	NSDAP membership re-opened temporarily (permanently from 1 May 1939).
18 Jun.	Dual membership of Hitler Youth and Roman Catholic youth organisations is prohibited.
1 Jul.	Pastor Niemöller arrested.
26 Nov.	Schacht resigns as Economics Minister.
Dec.	Leading Protestant opponents of the regime arrested.

1938

19 Jan.	Establishment of 'Faith and Beauty' organisation for young women aged between 17 and 21.
25 Jan.	General Werner von Blomberg resigns.
4 Feb.	Political shift within the leadership of the regime is marked by the appointment of Ribbentrop as Foreign Minister; the dismissal of Fritsch as Commander-in-Chief of the Army. War Ministry abolished and replaced by OKW. Hitler assumes personal command of armed forces.
5 Feb.	Last meeting of Reich cabinet.
11 Mar.	Annexation of Austria followed by plebiscite on 10 April.
13 Mar.	Law for the 'Re-unification of Austria with the German Reich'. Resignation of Austrian President Miklas.
1 Oct.	Occupation of Sudetenland.
7-8 Nov.	*Reichskristallnacht,* anti-semitic pogroms.
8 Dec.	All Gypsies (Sinti and Roma) required to register with the police.

1939

21 Jan.	Purge of leading conservatives continues with Schacht's dismissal from the presidency of the *Reichsbank.*
15 Mar.	Occupation of Czechoslovakia.
25 Mar.	All Germans aged between ten and eighteen to be conscripted into the Hitler Youth.
27 Aug.	Food rationing introduced.
1 Sep.	Invasion of Poland.
4–5 Sep.	War Economy Decrees.
21 Sep.	Heydrich draws up guidelines for *Einsatzgruppen* in Poland.
27 Sep.	Unification of security police (including Gestapo) and the office of the Reichsfuhrer SS to form *Reichssicherheitshauptamt* (RSHA).

Oct.	Direct incorporation of western Poland into Reich as *Reichsgaue* Danzig-Westpreussen, Posen (later Wartheland). Other Polish administrative districts incorporated into East Prussia and Silesia.
7 Oct.	Himmler becomes Reich Commissioner for the Consolidation of Germandom.
14 Oct.	Clothing coupons introduced.
8 Nov.	Failure of the attempt of Johann Georg Elser to assassinate Hitler in Munich.

1940

17 Mar.	Fritz Todt appointed Minister for Armaments and Munitions.
9 Apr.	Invasion of Denmark and Norway.
14 Apr.	Division of Austria into seven *Reichsgaue.*
10 May	Offensive against the West begins.
18 May	Re-incorporation of Eupen, Malmédy and Moresnet into Reich from Belgium.

1941

29 Jan.	State Secretary Franz Schlegelberger is commissioned to replace Franz Gürtner at the Justice Ministry.
19 Mar.	Union of German Socialist Organisations in Great Britain established.
6 Apr.	Invasion of Yugoslavia and Greece.
21 Apr.	*Reichsvereinigung Kohle* founded to manage raw materials shortages.
10 May	Flight of Hess to Scotland; Bormann takes over party apparatus.
29 May	Martin Bormann, head of the Party Chancellery is appointed a minister.
May	Reich Press Chamber closes down 550 newspapers.
22 Jun.	Invasion of the Soviet Union.
17 Jul.	Rosenberg becomes Reich Minister for the Occupied Eastern Territories.
15 Aug.	Bialystok incorporated into East Prussia.
11 Dec.	Hitler declares war on USA.

1942

20 Jan.	Wannsee Conference.
8 Feb.	Albert Speer becomes Armaments Minister following death of Todt.
Feb.	Communist resistance movement of Robert Uhrig and Beppo Römer smashed.

Spring	Revolutionary Socialist resistance movement in Bavaria and Austria suppressed.
22 Apr.	Establishment of 'Central Planning' to co-ordinate allocation of raw materials and energy.
Jun.	Beginning of mass murder of Jews in gas chambers at Auschwitz.
20 Aug.	Otto Georg Thierack becomes Justice Minister. Roland Freisler replaces him as President of *Volksgerichtshof.*
Autumn	'*Rote Kappelle*' resistance movement smashed.
Nov.	Communist resistance in Hamburg smashed.

1943

18 Feb.	Goebbels' 'Total War' speech in Berlin sports stadium.
20 Aug.	Himmler replaces Frick as Interior Minister.

1944

Jan.	Gestapo breaks up the Kreisau circle, a focus of conservative resistance.
Jul.	Destruction of Communist resistance centres.
20 Jul.	Assassination attempt on Hitler by Stauffenberg and fellow conspirators.
21 Oct.	Allies occupy Aachen.

1945

30 Jan.	Hitler's last radio speech.
19 Mar.	Hitler orders destruction of all industry useful to the enemy.
25 Apr.	American and Soviet troops meet on the Elbe.
30 Apr.	Hitler's suicide. Admiral Doenitz becomes Head of State.
1 May	Goebbels' suicide.
2 May	Soviet troops reach Berlin.
7 May	Surrender of Germany.
23 May	Dissolution by the Allies of the last Reich government.

3. The Political System of the Third Reich

3.1. The Cabinet under Hitler

Cabinet government was not immediately abandoned by the Nazis, but was circumvented by a process whereby drafts of legislation were circulated among ministers for approval (*Umlaufverfahren*), obviating the necessity for a formal meeting. Hitler was required not so much to achieve a consensus among the cabinet, as to approve or reject the final drafts of legislation. The cabinet appointed in January 1933 remained in office after the March elections, but a number of changes were made during the following two years. On 13 March 1933 a Ministry of Popular Enlightenment and Propaganda was created under Joseph Goebbels and an Air Ministry was created on 5 May 1933 under Hermann Goering. Goering was also appointed to the newly created Forestry Ministry on 3 July 1934. A Ministry of Science and Education was created on 1 May 1934 and Bernhard Rust appointed Minister, and finally a Ministry for the Churches was created on 16 July 1935 and Hanns Kerrl appointed to it.

The following were appointed Ministers without Portfolio: Rudolf Hess (1 December 1933), Ernst Röhm (1 December 1933 to 30 June 1934); Hanns Kerrl (16 June 1934 to 16 July 1935); Hans Frank (19 December, 1934).

Alfred Hugenberg was replaced as Economics Minister by Kurt Schmitt on 29 June 1933, and he in turn was replaced by Hjalmar Schacht, effectively from 30 July 1934. Hugenberg also relinquished the Food Ministry to Walter Darré on 29 June 1933.

There were 72 cabinet meetings in 1933, 19 in 1934 and 12 in 1935.

Reich Government: 1 January 1936

Chancellor	Adolf Hitler (NSDAP)
Foreign Minister	Konstantin Freiherr von Neurath
Interior Minister	Wilhelm Frick (NSDAP)
Finance Minister	Johann Ludwig Graf Schwerin von Krosigk
Economics	Hjalmar Schacht
Justice	Franz Gürtner
Defence	Werner von Blomberg
Food and Agriculture	Walter Darré (NSDAP)

Posts and Transport   Paul Freiherr Eltz von Rübenach
Labour   Franz Seldte (NSDAP from 27 April 1933)
Popular Enlightenment
and Propaganda   ↘ (Dr) Joseph Goebbels (NSDAP)
Air   Hermann Goering (NSDAP)
Science and Education   Bernhard Rust (NSDAP)
Forestry   ↗ Hermann Goering (NSDAP)
Churches   Hanns Kerrl (NSDAP)
Without Portfolio   ⁓ Rudolf Hess (NSDAP)
⁓ Hans Frank (NSDAP)
Hjalmar Schacht from 26 November 1937
Konstantin Freiherr von Neurath
(from 5 February 1938)

Further changes in 1937 and 1938 effectively amounted to a purge of conservative members of the government. On 2 February 1937 Paul Freiherr Eltz von Rübenach was replaced as Minister for Posts and Minister of Transport by two Nazis, Wilhelm Ohnesorge and Julius Dorpmüller. Goering replaced Schacht at the Economics Ministry from 26 November 1937 to 15 January 1938 when he was replaced by Walter Funk. Schacht remained in the government as Minister without Portfolio. Ribbentrop replaced von Neurath on 4 February 1938, and also became Minister without Portfolio. On the same day the post of Defence Minister was abolished and von Blomberg effectively dismissed. The cabinet met four times in 1936 and seven times in 1937. It met for the last time on 5 February 1938.

Reich Government: 1 September 1939

Chancellor   Adolf Hitler (NSDAP)
Foreign Minister   Joachim von Ribbentrop (NSDAP)
Interior Minister   Wilhelm Frick (NSDAP)
Finance Minister   Johann Ludwig Graf Schwerin von Krosigk
Economics   Walter Funk (NSDAP)
Justice   Franz Gürtner
Food and Agriculture   Walter Darré (NSDAP)
Posts   Wilhelm Ohnesorge (NSDAP)
Labour   Franz Seldte (NSDAP)
Transport   Julius Dorpmüller (NSDAP)
Popular Enlightenment
and Propaganda   (Dr) Joseph Goebbels (NSDAP)
Air   Hermann Goering (NSDAP)
Science and Education   Bernhard Rust (NSDAP)
Forestry   Hermann Goering (NSDAP)
Churches   Hanns Kerrl (NSDAP)
Head of Reich Chancellery   Hans-Heinrich Lammers
(minister from 26 November 1937)
Without Portfolio   Rudolf Hess (NSDAP)
Hans Frank (NSDAP)

Without Portfolio	Hjalmar Schacht
	Konstantin Freiherr von Neurath
	Otto Meissner (NSDAP) from 1 December 1937
	Arthur Seyss-Inquart (NSDAP) from 1 May 1939

Otto Meissner was appointed Minister of State and Head of the Reich Chancellery on 1 December 1937, and the leading Austrian Nazi Arthur Seyss Inquart was admitted to the government on 1 May 1939. The designation Minister without Portfolio was abolished on 5 February 1938, but such ministers remained members of the government. Further ministerial changes were made during the war. The Nazi government was replaced by an interim administration under Admiral von Doenitz on 30 April 1945.

Reich Government: 1 September 1939–30 April 1945

Chancellor	Adolf Hitler (NSDAP)
Foreign Minister	Joachim von Ribbentrop (NSDAP)
Interior Minister	Wilhelm Frick
	Heinrich Himmler (NSDAP) from 20 August 1943
Finance Minister	Johann Ludwig Graf Schwerin von Krosigk
Economics	Walter Funk (NSDAP)
Justice	Franz Gürtner to 29 January 1941
	Franz Schlegelberger (non-party) to 20 August 1942 (state secretary)
	Otto Georg Thierack (NSDAP) from 20 August 1942
Food and Agriculture	Walter Darré
	Herbert Backe (NSDAP) from 20 May 1942
Posts	Wilhelm Ohnesorge (NSDAP)
Labour	Franz Seldte (NSDAP)
Transport	Julius Dorpmüller (NSDAP)
Popular Enlightenment and Propaganda	(Dr) Joseph Goebbels (NSDAP)
Air	Hermann Goering (NSDAP)
Science and Education	Bernhard Rust (NSDAP)
Forestry	Hermann Goering (NSDAP)
Churches	Hermann Muhs (state secretary) from 16 January 1941
Head of Reich Chancellery	Hans-Heinrich Lammers
Occupied Eastern Territories	Alfred Rosenberg (NSDAP) from 17 July 1941
Armaments	Fritz Todt (NSDAP) 17 March 1940 – 8 February 1942.
	Albert Speer (NSDAP) from 8 February 1942
	Rudolf Hess (NSDAP) to 10 May 1941

Armaments   Hans Frank (NSDAP)
Hjalmar Schacht to 21 January 1943
Konstantin Freiherr von Neurath
Otto Meissner (NSDAP)
Arthur Seyss-Inquart
Martin Bormann (from 29 May 1941)

The power vacuum brought about by the decline of the cabinet was filled by the Reich Chancellery (under Hans-Heinrich Lammers), which attempted to act in the interests of rational policy formulation. It was checked by conflicting interests located in the Nazi movement itself. The attempt to define the relationship between party and state by integrating the former into the latter proved unsuccessful, not least because Hitler ensured that neither could gain supremacy over the other. In the first months of Nazi rule he was concerned – for various reasons – to limit the power of the party, and bring it to heel; on the other hand he did not want the party reduced to an organisation solely used for propaganda and mobilisation. A further problem was the threat of the party disintegrating into a number of separate semi-governmental organisations: the Labour Front, the Hitler Youth etc.

Hitler's solution was to give considerable personal power to Rudolf Hess as the 'Führer's Deputy for Party affairs'. Hess' authority was gradually extended to give him a supervisory role over new legislation (1934), and the power to vet senior appointments and promotions in the administration (1935); moves which strengthened the power of the party over the state. The 'Staff of the Führer's Deputy' was run by Martin Bormann, who built up an organisation in Munich based on two departments. Department II handled the internal relations of the party, where its chief problem was the continuing autonomy of the *Gauleiter* (something which waned as the *alte Kämpfer* died out and were replaced). Department III dealt with party-state relations. It recruited its own administration from the civil service and developed an administration which soon overshadowed the Reich Chancellery, and became a powerful base for Bormann's own political ambitions, particularly during the war.

The nature of the Nazi state has been hotly debated. Some historians have placed great emphasis on the personal role of Hitler, others have emphasised the incoherent nature of Nazi aims and the chaotic nature of government and administration. Historians identified with the former, 'intentionalist' position assume that Hitler personally had consistent plans for the future of Germany, above all in matters of foreign and 'racial' policy. This approach has also been labelled 'programmatist'. Historians identified with the latter school of 'structuralist' or 'functionalist' interpretations of the Third Reich have accepted that Hitler may well have had consistent policy intentions, but have drawn attention to the external constraints on his ability to act freely, and have cast some doubt on the programmatic nature of his actions.

4. The Nazi Party

4.1. National Leaders and Functionaries, 1936

Führer and Reich Chancellor	Adolf Hitler
Deputy Führer	Rudolf Hess
Staff of Führer's Deputy	Martin Bormann
Party Chancellery	Martin Bormann
Treasurer	Franz Schwarz
Supreme Party Court	W Buch; W Grimm
Leader of Reichstag Delegation	Wilhelm Frick
Political Organisations (Cadres)	Robert Ley
Director of Propaganda	Joseph Goebbels
Press Chief	Otto Dietrich
Reichsleiter, Press	Max Amann
Nazi Literature	Philipp Bouhler
Ideology	Alfred Rosenberg

Reichsamt for Agrarian Policy — Walther Darré
Darré was also Reich Agriculture Minister and Reich Peasant Leader.

Reich Law Office	Hans Frank
NS *Rechtswahrerbund*	Hans Frank
Foreign Policy Office	Alfred Rosenberg
Chief of Colonial Office	Franz von Epp
Youth Leader	Baldur von Schirach
Sturmabteilung (SA)	Viktor Lutze

4.2. Party Organisations

German Labour Front	Robert Ley
Factory Cell Organisation	
Reich Labour Service	Konstantin Hierl
National Socialist Motor Corps	A Hühnlein
Schutzstaffel (SS)	Heinrich Himmler
	Reich Leader SS and Head of
	the German Police

Party Offices and Associations

Local government	K Fiehler	*Deutscher Gemeindetag*
		President: K Fiehler
Civil Servants	H Neef	Reich Association of German
		Civil Servants
		Director: H Neef
Education	F Waechtler	NS Teachers' Association
		F Waechtler
War Victims	H Oberlinder	NS Association for the Care of
		War Victims
		Reich War Victims' Leader:
		H Oberlinder.
Health	G Wagner	NS German Doctors' Association
		Reich Doctors' Leader: G Wagner
Welfare	E Hilgenfeldt	NS Association for National
		Welfare
		E Hilgenfeldt
Technology	Fritz Todt	NS Association of German
		Technology
		Inspector General: Fritz Todt
NS *Frauenschaft*	E Hilgenfeldt	Reich Women's Leader
		G Scholtz-Klink
		NS German Students' Asociation
		Reich Student Leader: G A Scheel
		NS German Lecturers'
		Association W Schultze

4.3. Nazi Party *Gaue*, 1941

		Area (km^2)	Inhabitants (1939)
1	Baden	15,090	2,502,023
2	Bayerische Ostmark (Bayreuth)	29,600	2,370,658
3	Berlin	884	4,338,756
4	Danzig-West Prussia	26,057	2,288,604
5	Düsseldorf	2,672	2,261,909
6	Essen	2,825	1,921,326
7	Franconia	7,618	1,077,216
8	Halle-Merseburg	10,209	1,578,292
9	Hamburg	747	1,711,877
10	Hessen-Nassau	15,030	3,117,266
11	Carinthia	11,554	449,713
12	Cologne-Aachen	8,324	2,447,454
13	Kurhessen	9,200	971,887
14	Magdeburg-Anhalt	13,903	1,820,416
15	Main-Franconia	8,432	840,663
16	Mark Brandenburg	38,378	3,007,933
17	Mecklenburg	15,722	900,417
18	Moselland	11,876	1,367,354
19	Munich-Upper Bavaria	16,411	1,938,447
20	Lower Danube	23,502	1,697,676
21	Lower Silesia	26,985	3,286,539
22	Upper Danube	14,216	1,034,871
23	Upper Silesia	20,636	4,341,561
24	East Hanover	18,006	1,060,509
25	East Prussia	52,731	3,338,978
26	Pomerania	38,409	2,393,844
27	Saxony	14,995	5,231,739
28	Salzburg	7,153	257,226
29	Schleswig-Holstein	15,687	1,589,267
30	Swabia	10,231	946,212
31	Styria	17,384	1,116,407
32	Sudetenland	22,608	2,943,187
33	South Hanover-Brunswick	14,553	2,136,961
34	Thuringia	15,763	2,446,182
35	Tyrol-Vorarlberg	13,126	486,400
36	Wartheland	43,905	4,583,895
37	Weser-Ems	15,044	1,839,302
38	North Westphalia	14,559	2,822,603
39	South Westphalia	7,657	2,678,026
40	Westmark	7,417	1,892,240
41	Vienna	1,216	1,929,976
42	Württemberg-Hohenzollern	20,657	2,974,373
43	Auslandsorganisation		
	Total: Greater German Reich	**680,872**	**89,940,185**

4.4. Nazi Party *Gaue*, 1944

1. Baden	16. Mark Brandenburg	30. Swabia
2. Bayreuth	17. Mecklenburg	31. Styria
3. Berlin	18. Moselland	32. Sudetenland
4. Danzig-West Prussia	19. Munich-	33. South Hanover-
5. Düsseldorf	Upper Bavaria	Brunswick
6. Essen	20. Lower Danube	34. Thuringia
7. Franconia	21. Lower Silesia	35. Tyrol Vorarlberg
8. Halle-Merseburg	22. Upper Danube	36. Wartheland
9. Hamburg	23. Upper Silesia	37. Weser-Ems
10. Hesse-Nassau	24. East Hanover	38. North Westphalia
11. Carinthia	25. East Prussia	39. South Westphalia
12. Cologne-Aachen	26. Pomerania	40. Westmark
13. Kurhessen	27. Saxony	41. Vienna
14. Magdeburg-Anhalt	28. Salzburg	42. Württemberg-
15. Main-Franconia	29. Schleswig-Holstein	Hohenzollern

Source: M Freeman *Atlas of Nazi Germany* (Longman), p. 67.

5. The Police State

The origins of the SS were in the *Schutzstaffeln*, internal party protection squadrons, and the prototype for these was the personal bodyguard of the 'Führer', created by Julius Schreck, Hitler's chauffeur, shortly after his release from Landsberg. The problematic relationship with the SA was thereby built into the SS from the outset. Technically subordinate to the former organisation, its internal party policing function would nevertheless bring it into conflict with unruly stormtroopers. Indeed, the first SS units were created in response to the perceived unreliability of the SA in the mid-1920s.

Himmler joined the SS in 1925. He was appointed its deputy leader in 1927, and its leader in 1929. At that time the organisation had around 250 members. Under Himmler's leadership membership expanded rapidly (1931, c.10,000; 1933, c.52,000; 1935, c.200,000). In 1931 Himmler set up an internal security service within the SS, under the leadership of Reinhard Heydrich: this was the SD (*Sicherheitsdienst*). After the seizure of power the SS developed a further new role in supplying guard troops for the first concentration camps.

The Gestapo's origins lay in Department Ia of the Berlin Police Praesidium which oversaw the political police in Prussia during the Weimar Republic. This was subordinated to the Prussian Interior Ministry (although in practice its functions applied to the whole of Germany). In April 1933 the Prussian Interior Minister (Goering) established a new Secret State Police Office (*Gestapa*) which functioned as a state agency (and therefore acquired executive powers), and was accountable to the Interior Ministry.

The effective fusion of the SS with the Gestapo was a product of the development of Himmler's career. On 1 April 1933 he was appointed 'Political Police Commander of Bavaria'. Himmler's position was considerably strengthened by the development of a power struggle for control of the Prussian police between Goering and Reich Interior Minister Frick, who attempted to create a national police force. On 24 April 1934 Goering appointed Himmler 'Inspector of the Gestapo' in order to strengthen his own position against Frick. This gave Himmler and the SS a foothold in the state police. Heydrich took over the secret state police office (*Gestapa*).

Shortly afterwards the SS was made completely independent of the SA as a reward for its loyalty in the Röhm purge and proceeded to extend its control over the Gestapo, despite complaints from Goering's officials and above all from Frick. The situation was resolved to some extent in 1936 by the intervention of Hitler. Himmler was appointed Head of the German Police, and set about reorganising the security forces: the uniformed police were combined as the *Ordnungspolizei* under Police (and SS) General Kurt Daluege. The detective police (i.e. the criminal police, or *Kripo*) and the political police (or Gestapo) were also brought together as the Security Police (*Sipo*) under Heydrich.

In 1939 the *Reichssicherheitshauptamt* (RSHA: 'Reich Security Head Office') was formed, bringing together Gestapo, *Kripo*, and the *Sicherheitsdienst* (SD: 'Security Service'). Combining as it did the head offices of the police and the SS it brought together and centralised the leadership of the *state* security services and the SS.

The Concentration Camps

Arbitrary arrests of the regime's political opponents began immediately in 1933, and was generally described as 'protective custody' (*Schutzhaft*). The Decree for the Protection of the People and State, which followed the Reichstag fire, permitted arrest and imprisonment without reference to the judiciary, and the first concentration camps were erected to deal with the large numbers of political prisoners (26,789 by 31 July 1933, 14,906 of them in Prussia). By the end of 1934 a number of developments – not least the purge of the SA in June – ensured that jurisdiction over the concentration camp system fell to the SS. During the 1930s new types of prisoners were put in the concentration camps. These were on the whole people whom Nazi ideology categorised as harmful to the interests of the *Volk*, but for whom there was no legislative provision for long-term detention: e.g. homosexuals, Jehovah's Witnesses, so-called 'asocials' and habitual criminals. After the anti-semitic pogrom of 1938 (*Reichskristallnacht*), large numbers of Jews were arrested, and although most of these were released almost immediately, the composition of the concentration camps changed considerably during the war.

The outbreak of war was accompanied by organisational changes in the concentration camp system and the first executions of prisoners; other deaths occurred through overcrowding and ill treatment as the population of the camps expanded. A new wave of arrests brought back those Jews who had been released in 1938 and had not so far emigrated, along with gypsies, suspected saboteurs, the 'workshy', active Communists and Social Democrats and others perceived to be a threat to the state in wartime. New camps were set up in the occupied territories, including Auschwitz (1940). The war provided a cover for the political and biological 'cleansing' of Germany. Between 1935 and 1941 the average number of arrests from within the Reich had increased tenfold.

Most of the new prisoners, however, were foreigners from the occupied teritories, particularly Slavs and – in the first years of the war – above all Poles. From 1941 Hitler's *Nacht-und-Nebel* permitted the removal of resistance activists to camps in the Reich under cover of 'Night and Fog'. From 1941 thousands of Soviet prisoners of war were transferred to the camps (where they were kept apart from other prisoners) to provide forced labour. The exploitation of slave labour was an important function of the camps. In 1938 a company had been formed by the SS to exploit the labour of concentration camp prisoners: *Deutsche Erd- und Steinwerke GmbH* (DEST, German Quarrying Company). From 1941 prisoners at Auschwitz were used by IG Farben for the construction of synthetic rubber (Buna). Separate camps were erected in Poland for the exploitation of Jewish labour, and Jews arriving at Auschwitz (although not at other death camps such as Treblinka, Sobibor, Belzec and Chelmno) were spared the gas chambers for as long as they provided useful labour.

By the end of 1941 it was becoming clear that the function of the concentration camps was changing: they were becoming an increasingly important economic asset to the SS and to the Reich war effort. During 1942 a separation emerged between two projects. The *Wirtschafts- und Verwaltungshauptamt* (WVHA: SS Economic and Administrative Head Office), formed on 1 February 1942, assumed control of the concentration camps on 16 March 1942. It contained within it Group D, the Inspectorate-General of Concentration Camps, and Group W, SS Economic Enterprises. Certain camps were selected as 'extermination' camps, where Jews and other 'undesirable' groups were murdered. Others were primarily sites of forced labour under the auspices of the WVHA. At Auschwitz, one of the largest camps, this dual function was present at the same site.

The imprisonment in concentration camps of large numbers of Russians, Poles and Jews meant that the population of the camps more than doubled between the end of 1942 and August 1943 (from 88,000 to 224,000). By April 1944 there were 20 concentration camps with 165 labour camps attached. Not all concentration camps were 'death camps' used for the mass murder of Jews, but death rates were also high among those Jewish prisoners selected for work, and among the foreign civilians and prisoners of war whose labour was exploited by German industry.

5.1. SS Ranks

SS	Police	Army
Reichsführer		*Generalfeldmarschall*
Oberstgruppenführer	*Generaloberst der Polizei*	*Generaloberst*
Obergruppenführer	*General der Polizei*	*General*
Gruppenführer	*Generalleutnant*	*Generalleutnant*
Brigadeführer	*Generalmajor der Polizei*	*Generalmajor*
Oberführer	*Oberst der Schutzpolizei Reichskriminaldirektor*	*Oberst*
Standartenführer	*Oberst der Schutzpolizei Reichskriminaldirektor*	*Oberst*
Obersturmbannführer	*Oberstleutnant der Schutzpolizei Oberregierungs- und Kriminalrat*	*Oberstleutnant*
Sturmbannführer	*Major der Schutzpolizei Regierungs- und Kriminalrat*	*Major* .
Hauptsturmführer	*Hauptmann der Schutzpolizei Krimimalrat*	*Hauptmann*
Obersturmführer	*Oberleutnant der Schutzpolizei Kriminalkommissar*	*Oberleutnant*
Untersturmführer	*Leutnant der Schutzpolizei Kriminalsekretär*	*Leutnant*

5.2. The SS and the Holocaust: Concentration Camps and Death Camps

Principal Concentration Camps

	Established
Dachau	1933
Sachsenhausen	1936
Buchenwald	1937
Flossenbürg	1938
Mauthausen	1938
Neuengamme	1938
Ravensbrück	1939
Stutthof (Danzig)	1939
Auschwitz I	1940
Gross-Rosen	1940
Natzweiler-Struthof	1941
Lublin Majdanek	1941
Auschwitz II (Birkenau)	1941
Auschwitz III (Monowitz)	1942
Herzogenbusch-Vught	1943
Riga	1943
Bergen-Belsen	1943
Dora-Mittelbau	1943
Warsaw	1943
Kauen	1943
Vaivara	1943
Klooga	1943
Cracow-Plaszow	1944

Death Camps	Operation Span	Murder Victims (estimated minimum figures)
Kulmhof/Chelmno	1941–44	152,000
Auschwitz-Birkenau	1942–44	1,000,000+
Belzec	1942–43	600,000
Sobibor	1942–43	250,000
Treblinka	1942–43	700,000–900,000
Lublin-Majdanek	1942–44	200,000

Economy, Society and Culture, 1918–1945

1. Area, Population and Territorial Divisions of the Reich, 1871/1918–45

1.1. Population and Population Change, 1871–1940

	Population (1,000s)	Marriages	Live Births	Deaths[1]	Excess Births/ Deaths
1871[2]	40,997	392,744	1,619,251	1,175,337	443,914
1881[3]	45,428	354,716	1,704,741	1,185,297	519,444
1891	49,762	399,398	1,840,172	1,164,421	675,751
1901	56,874	468,329	2,032,313	1,174,489	857,824
1911	63,359	512,819	1,870,729	1,130,784	739,945
1913	66,978	513,283	1,838,750	1,004,950	833,800
1914	66,790	460,608	1,818,596	1,291,310	527,286
1915	67,883	278,208	1,382,546	1,450,420	−67,874
1916	67,715	279,076	1,029,484	1,298,054	−268,570
1917[4]	67,378	308,446	912,109	1,345,424	−433,315
1918[4]	66,811	352,543	926,813	1,606,475	−679,662
1919[5]	62,897	844,339	1,260,500	978,380	282,120
1920[6]	61,797	894,978	1,599,287	932,929	666,358
1921	62,469	740,330	1,581,130	869,555	711,575
1922	62,035	690,947	1,424,804	890,181	534,623
1923	62,450	588,069	1,318,489	866,754	451,735
1924	62,486	446,445	1,290,763	766,957	523,806
1925	63,177	489,084	1,311,259	753,017	558,242
1926	63,646	489,685	1,245,471	742,955	502,516
1927	64,023	545,381	1,178,892	765,331	413,561
1928	64,393	594,631	1,199,998	747,444	452,554
1929	64,739	597,014	1,164,062	814,545	349,517
1930	65,084	570,241	1,144,151	718,807	425,344
1931	65,429	422,881	1,047,775	734,165	313,610
1932	65,716	516,793	993,126	707,642	285,484
1933	66,027	638,573	971,174	737,877	233,297
1934	66,409	740,165	1,198,350	724,758	473,592
1935	66,871	651,435	1,263,976	792,018	471,958

	Population (1,000s)	Marriages	Live Births	Deaths[1]	Excess Births/ Deaths
1936	67,349	609,770	1,278,583	795,793	482,790
1937	67,831	620,265	1,277,046	794,367	482,679
1938[7]	75,396	645,062	1,348,534	799,220	549,314
1939	86,910	774,163	1,413,230	854,348	
1940[8]	98,173	612,946	1,402,640	888,736	

1. Excluding still births. From 1939 excluding deaths of members of armed forces.
2. Average 1871–5.
3. Average 1881–5.
4. Excluding Alsace-Lorraine
5. Excluding Alsace-Lorraine and parts of Posen (Poznan) ceded to Poland.
6. Excluding territories in 5, and in addition: Memel, Danzig and territories ceded to Poland, Czechoslovakia, Belgium and Denmark.
7. From 1938 including territorial acquisitions.
8. Provisional figures for 1940.

1.2. Surface Area and Population Density of the German Reich

	Area 1,000s km^2	Population Density km^2
1871	540.6	76
1910	540.9	120
1925	468.7	133
1933	468.8	139
1939(May)	583.4	136

1939 figures include Austria and the Sudetenland.

1.3. Area and Population of the Federal States, 1 August 1941

	Area (km^2)	Population
Prussia	321,788.66	45,328,118
Bavaria	77,785.03	8,222,982
Saxony	14,994.70	5,231,739
Württemberg	19,507.10	2,896,920
Baden	15,069.37	2,502,442
Thuringia	11,760.35	1,743,624
Hamburg	746.62	1,711,877
Hesse	7,690.62	1,469,215
Mecklenburg	5,721.66	900,417
Brunswick	3,570.87	602,873
Oldenburg	5,396.47	577,648
Bremen	324,16	450,084
Anhalt	2,315.53	431,422
Lippe	1,215.18	187,220
Schaumburg-Lippe	340.32	53,195
Saarland	1,924.78	842,454
Reichsgau Vienna	1,215.52	1,929,976
Lower Danube	23,502.01	1,697,676
Upper Danube	14,216.02	1,034,871
Styria	17,383.87	1,116,407
Carinthia	11,553.63	449,713
Salzburg	7,152.96	257,226
Tyrol (inc. Vorarlberg)	13,126.06	486,400
Sudetenland	22,608.23	2,943,187
Danzig-West Prussia	26,057.32	2,288,604
Wartheland*	43,905.19	4,583,895
German Reich	**680,872.23**	**89,940,185**

* The Wartheland incorporated territory which had never previously belonged to Germany, or to Prussia.

1.4. Territories directly under German Rule, 1 August 1941

	Area (km^2)	Population
Government General	142,207.00	16,962,726[†]
Alsace	8,294.03	1,219,381 (1936)
Lorraine	6,227.79	696,246 (1936)
Luxembourg	2,586,36	290,173 (1941)
Lower Styria, South Carinthia and Upper Carniola[*]	9,620.00	775,000[†]

* Formerly part of Yugoslavia.
† Estimated.

The Weimar constitution preserved the federal structure of the German Empire, with extensive autonomy for the federal states (*Länder*), and their legislatures (*Landtage*). This was effectively dismantled by a number of legislative measures in 1933 and 1934: The First Law for the Co-ordination of the Federal States (31 March 1933); the Second Law for the Co-ordination of the Federal States (7 April 1933), which created the post of *Reichsstatthalter* (Reich Governor); and the Law for the Reconstruction of the Reich (30 January 1934), which turned the federal structure of the Reich into a centrally controlled administrative network under Wilhelm Frick at the Interior Ministry.

Austria had a similar federal structure which was modified when it was annexed in 1938. The name Austria, and even the traditional German nationalist designation *Ostmark*, were dispensed with, and the Austrian *Länder* were incorporated directly into the Reich as the *Alpen- und Donaugaue*. The term Austria was also removed from the provincial names of Lower and Upper Austria (which became Lower and Upper Danube respectively). Vienna was enlarged; the Burgenland was absorbed into Lower Danube and Styria, and Vorarlberg reduced to the status of an administrative district within the Tyrol. Upper and Lower Danube gained further territory from the annexed Sudetenland. After the Polish campaign and the division of Poland between Germany and the USSR, territory lost to Germany at Versailles was reincorporated as two new *Reichsgaue*, Danzig-West Prussia and the Wartheland.

The rest of Poland was not incorporated directly into the Greater German Reich, but its administration, under a Governor-General, was directly responsible to Berlin. Other territories bordering the Reich had a similarly ambiguous status during the war, generally under a Head of the Civilian Administration (*Chef der Zivilverwaltung*, CdZ).

1.5. Cities of the Greater German Reich, 1933 (Population, 1,000s)

Berlin	4,243
Hamburg	1,129
Cologne (Köln)	757
Munich (München)	735
Leipzig	714
Essen	654
Dresden	642
Breslau (Wrocław)	625
Frankfurt/Main	556
Dortmund	541
Düsseldorf	499
Hanover	444
Duisburg	440
Stuttgart	415
Nuremberg (Nürnberg)	410
Wuppertal	409
Chemnitz	351
Gelsenkirchen	333
Bremen	323
Königsberg	316
Bochum	315
Magdeburg	307
Mannheim	275
Stettin	271
Altona	242
Kiel	218
Halle	209
Oberhausen	192
Augsburg	177
Kassel	175

1.6. Population Living in Cities with a Population over 100,000 (1871–1939) (Proportion of Total Population of Reich)

1871	5.4
1900	17.2
1910	22.8
1925	26.6
1933	30.2
1939	31.6

1.7. Population Living in Small Rural Communities of less than 2,000 (1871–1939) (Proportion of Total Population of Reich)

1871	62.6
1900	43.9
1910	38.3
1925	35.4
1933	32.7
1939	30.1

1939 figures are for the territory of the Reich in mid–1939.

1.8. Age Structure of the Population of the German Reich

Percentage	1910	1934	1939
Under 10	23.4	15.3	15.5
10–20	20.3	15.8	16.8
20–30	16.3	18.6	14.5
30–40	14.0	16.5	17.4
40–50	10,6	12.7	13.2
50–60	7.6	10.7	10.5
60–65	2.8	4.1	7.8
Over 65	4.9	7.3	7.8

2. Social and Economic Structure of the Reich

2.1. Population by Economic Sector (%), 1882–1939

	1882	1895	1907	1925	1933	1939
Agric. and Forestry	40.0	33.6	27.1	23.0	21.0	18.2
Industry and Crafts	36.9	40.0	41.3	42.0	38.8	40.9
Trade and Commerce	9.6	11.2	14.7	16.7	16.9	15.8
Non-Domestic Services	5.1	5.7	5.9	6.8	7.8	10.1
Domestic Service	3.7	3.4	2.9	2.4	2.0	2.0
Total employed	95.3	93.9	91.9	90.9	86.5	87.0
Independants without occupation	4.7	6.1	8.1	9.1	13.5	13.0

2.2. Employed Population by Economic Sector (%), 1882–1939

	1882	1895	1907	1925	1933	1939
Agric. and Forestry	42.3	36.4	34.0	30.5	28.9	26.1
Industry and Crafts	35.5	38.8	39.7	42.1	40.4	42.1
Trade and Transport	8.4	10.7	13.7	16.2	18.4	17.5
Non-Domestic Services	5.8	6.9	6.8	6.8	8.4	10.4
Domestic Service	8.0	7.2	5.8	4.4	3.9	3.9

2.3. Employed and Unemployed Population by Occupational Status (%), 1925 and 1933

	1925	1933
Independants	5,095,200	5,302,916
(of which unemployed)	565	3,107
Family members	5,437,227	5,312,116
Civil servants/Military and Employees	5,442,295	5,513,137
(of which unemployed)	167,006	875,446
Workers	14,708,991	14,949,786
(of which unemployed)	448,811	4,807,401
Household employees	1,325,587	1,218,119
(of which unemployed)	20,495	169,064
Total	*32,009,300*	*32,296,074*
(of which unemployed)	*636,877*	*5,855,018*

2.4. Structural Changes in Economic Activity (% increase/ decrease in workforce)

	1925–33			1925–39		
	Total	Men	Women	Total	Men	Women
Agric. and Forestry	−4.3	−2.1	−6.4	−8.5	−15.4	−1.8
Industry and Crafts	−3.2	−1.9	−7.7	+7.0	+5.9	+10.8
Trade and Transport	+14.4	+9.3	+26.9	+14.4	+6.5	+33.4
Non–Domestic Services	+23.3	+16.9	+38.6	+67.8	+61.9	+82.9
Domestic Service	−8.9	−45.9	−7.9	−3.6	−66.3	−1.9
Total employed population	*+0.9*	*+1.4*	*0.0*	*+7.4*	*+5.1*	*+10.6*

2.5. Employment of Women

2.5.1. Employment of Women by Economic Sector (1,000s)

	1925	1933	1939
Agric. and Forestry	4,969.3	4,648.8	4,880.6
Industry and Crafts	2,987.4	2,758.8	3,310.3
Trade and Transport	1,514.2	1,920.8	2,083.9
Non-Domestic Services	650.1	901.1	1,093.6
Domestic Service	1,357.1	1,249.6	1,331.8
Total	*11,478.0*	*11,479,041*	*12,700.2*

2.5.2. Employment of Women by Occupational Status, 1925 and 1933 (1,000s)

	1925	1933
Independants	894,617	936,365
Family members	4,132,956	4,149,035
Civil servants/military and employees	1,446,081	1,694,621
Workers	3,693,919	3,488,698
Household employees	1,310,439	1,210,322
Total	*11,478,012*	*11,479,041*
(of which unemployed)	*158,924*	*1,142,586*

2.5.3. Economic Sectors Employing a Majority of Women, 1933

	Total	Women
Agriculture[1]	8,934,971	4,569,868
Confectionery industry	57,321	34,329
Tobacco industry	212,321	143,167
Clothing manufacture	1,477,161	788,443
Catering	762,782	419,694
Churches and religious institutions	165,072	92,027
Accommodation services	67,505	52,408
Nursing	401,448	250,010
Welfare services	104,512	69,895
Domestic service	1,269,582	1,249,636

1. Excluding forestry, fishing and gardening.

2.5.4. Female Workforce by Sector, 1939–44* (1,000s)

	1939	1940	1941	1942	1943	1944	1944 Sept.
Agric./Forestry	6,049	5,689	5,369	5,537	5,665	5,694	5,756
Industry/Crafts	3,836	3,650	3,677	3,537	3,740	3,592	3,636
Finance/Transport/ Commerce	2,227	2,183	2,167	2,225	2,320	2,219	2,193
Domestic Service	1,560	1,511	1,473	1,410	1,362	1,371	1,287
Public Admin./Services	954	1,157	1,284	1,471	1,719	1,746	1,748
Total	**14,626**	**14,386**	**14,167**	**14,437**	**14,806**	**14,808**	**14,897**

* Figures for May, unless otherwise indicated.

3. Agriculture

3.1. Agricultural Population of Regions, 1933

Indented regions are provinces of Prussia and Bavaria.

	Population	% of Total Population
East Prussia	983,717	42.2
Berlin	49,942	1.2
Brandenburg	774,852	28.5
Pomerania	732,632	38.1
Grenzmark Posen West Prussia	149,410	44.3
Lower Silesia	796,566	24.9
Upper Silesia	308,658	25.7
Saxony (Province)	729,219	21.4
Schleswig-Holstein	351,893	22.1
Hanover	998,576	29.7
Westphalia	644,564	12.8
Hessen-Nassau	548,396	21.2
Rhineland Province	924,982	12.1
Hohenzollern lands	35,800	49.1
Prussia	8,101,207	20.3
South Bavaria	1,167,393	34.1
North Bavaria	1,045,636	32.0
Palatinate	208,223	21.1
Bavaria	2,421,252	31.5
Saxony	431,748	8.3
Württemberg	746,510	27.7
Baden	604,461	25.0
Thuringia	296,9997	17.9
Hamburg	25,553	2.1
Hesse	307,291	21.5
Mecklenburg	307,905	38.3
Brunswick	96,228	18.8
Oldenburg	192,952	33.6
Bremen	9,214	2.5
Anhalt	63,160	17.3
Lippe	38,177	21.7
Lübeck	7,287	5.3
Schaumburg-Lippe	10,844	21.7
German Reich	*13,660,786*	*21.0*

3.2. Grain Production, 1935–40

	Rye (1,000t)	Yield (per ha)	Wheat (1,000t)	(Yield per ha)
1935	7,478	16.5	4,667	22.2
1936	7,386	16.4	4,427	21.2
1937	6,917	16.6	4,467	22.6
1938	8,606	20.2	5,578	27.4
	(9,702)	(19.8)	(6,331)	(26.2)
1939	8,342	19.8	4,865	23.6
	(9,301)	(19.2)	(5,518)	(22.7)
1940	6,534	16.4	4,058	21.9
	(9,845)	(15.4)	(4,918)	(20.3)

Figures in brackets include Austria, the Sudetenland and Memel, and for 1940 the incorporated districts of Poland.
Figures for agricultural production reflect the variability of climate and bad harvests.

3.3. Livestock Populations, 1935–40

	Cattle	Pigs	Chickens
1935	18,938	22,827	86,084
1936	20,088	25,892	88,423
1937	20,507	23,847	85,393
1938	19,954	23,567	88,638
	(22,532)	(26,640)	(97,779)
1939	19,948	25,440	89,777
	(23,927)	(29,135)	(103,459)
1940	19,663	21,578	88,277
	(23,662)	(24,662)	(100,585)

Figures in brackets: 1938 includes Austria; 1939 includes Austria, Memel and Danzig; 1940 includes Austria, Memel, Danzig, Eupen-Malmédy and Soldau.

4. Industry

4.1. Index of Industrial Production, 1913–44 (1928=100)

	Capital goods	Consumer goods	Total
1913	99	97	98
1918			56
1919	32		37
1920	56	51	54
1921	65	69	65
1922	70	74	70
1923	43	57	46
1924	65	81	69
1925	80	85	81
1926	77	80	78
1927	97	103	98
1928	100	100	100
1929	102	97	100
1930	84	91	87
1931	62	82	70
1932	47	74	58
1933	56	80	66
1934	81	93	83
1935	99	91	96
1936	114	98	107
1937	130	103	117
1938	144	108	125
1939	148	108	132
1940	144	102	128
1941	149	104	131
1942	157	93	132
1943	180	98	149
1944	178	93	146

4.2. Mineral Extraction, 1918–45 (1913=100)

	Coal	Lignite	Oil	Iron ore
1918	83.2	115.3	31.5	27.7
1919	61.4	107.4	30.9	21.5
1920	69.1	128.3	29.0	22.2
1921	71.7	141.1	31.7	20.6
1922	62.7	157.3	34.7	20.7
1923	32.8	136.2	42.0	17.9
1924	62.5	142.9	49.1	15.6
1925	69.8	160.2	65.4	20.7
1926	76.4	159.5	78.8	16.8
1927	80.8	172.5	80.1	23.2
1928	79.4	189.8	76.1	22.6
1929	86.0	200,1	85.0	22.3
1930	75.1	167.4	144.1	20.1
1931	62.4	152.8	189.2	9.2
1932	55.1	140.6	190.1	4.7
1933	57.7	145.4	196.7	9.1
1934	65.7	157.0	260.4	15.2
1935	75.2	168.5	352.9	21.2
1936	83.3	185.0	367.0	26.5
1937	97.1	211.7	372.8	34.2
1938	98.1	223.5	456.3	43.2
1939	98.9	243.2	612.5	51.4
1940	97.0	257.9	872.8	67.1
1941	98.1	270.7	744.7	63.3
1942	98.8	281.9	614.1	53.6
1943	100.2	290.5	586.9	53.2
1944	87.3	263.0	595.1	
1945	18.7	27.9	452.1	

4.3. Iron, Steel and Chemicals Production, 1918–44 (1913=100)

	Iron	Steel	Chemicals
1918	61.4	68.6	
1919	32.5	39.9	
1920	33.1	48.5	
1921	40.6	57.7	
1922	48.7	64.9	
1923	25.6	36.0	
1924	40.5	56.2	
1925	52.7	69.8	133.0
1926	49.9	70.6	123.3
1927	67.9	93.1	155.1
1928	61.1	84.8	161.1
1929	69.4	92.5	186.1
1930	50.2	65.7	172.2
1931	31.4	47.3	148.0
1932	20.4	32.6	138.4
1933	27.3	43.2	151.9
1934	45.3	67.6	174.6
1935	66.5	93.2	201.9
1936	79.3	108.2	234.8
1937	82.6	110.6	312.3
1938	96.4	129.7	334.8
1939	90.5	129.6	
1940	72.3	110.3	
1941	80.0	120.0	
1942	79.4	118.0	
1943	82.7	119.6	
1944	69.2	105.5	

5. Trade

5.1. Exports and Imports by Volume, 1924–38 (1913=100)

	Exports	Imports
1924	48.7	
1925	66.4	82.3
1926	76.7	72.5
1927	77.4	105.2
1928	87.4	101.7
1929	98.0	96.6
1930	92.2	86.0
1931	82.7	69.9
1932	55.6	62.5
1933	50.7	62.8
1934	47.1	68.4
1935	51.5	60.8
1936	56.9	59.8
1937	64.2	69.0
1938	54.7	74.6

5.2. Food and Raw Materials as a Proportion of Foreign Trade (%)

	Imports		Exports	
	Food	Raw Materials	Food	Raw Materials
1913	38.2	34.9	12.0	13.3
1928	40.9	28.3	6.4	12.2
1932	32.7		3.8	
1937	37.4	6.5	1.5	9.8
1943	40.0	13.5	6.8	13.1

6. Transport and Communications

6.1. Railway Traffic Index (1913 = 100)

	Passenger/km	Goods/km
1913	100	100
1922	182	101
1923	155	63
1924	107	71
1925	121	89
1926	106	97
1927	113	108
1928	118	109
1929	117	114
1930	107	91
1931	91	76
1932	74	66
1933	74	71
1934	86	85
1935	97	95
1936	107	105
1938	138	132
1939	152	
1940	138	
1941	153	

6.2. Radio Listeners by Region: % Households, 1941

Prussia	65.2
Bavaria	57.9
Saxony	72.1
Wurttemberg	64.6
Baden	58.9
Thuringia	67.2
Hamburg	75.0
Hesse	62.6
Mecklenburg	71.2
Brunswick	71.4
Oldenburg	69.1
Bremen	75.0

Anhalt	76.7
Lippe	56.2
Schaumburg-Lippe	55.5
Saarland	44.7
Vienna	60.8
Lower Danube	43.5
Upper Danube	46.4
Styria	43.0
Carinthia	40.8
Salzburg	52.0
Tyrol	54.0
Sudetenland	54.5
Reich	*63.4*
Bohemia	48.7
Moravia	42.4

6.3. Radio Listeners in Cities: % Households, 1941

Berlin	78.7
Hamburg	75.0
Cologne (Köln)	66.6
München (Munich)	77.1
Leipzig	79.5
Essen	61.4
Dresden	77.9
Breslau (Wrocław)	67.6
Frankfurt/Main	76.6
Dortmund	70.6
Dusseldorf	71.6
Hanover	79.1
Duisburg	63.8
Stuttgart	86.3
Nuremberg (Nürnberg)	75.5
Wuppertal	67.3
Chemnitz	78.0
Gelsenkirchen	51.6
Bremen	74.9
Königsberg	80.2
Bochum	61.6
Magdeburg	79.8
Mannheim	73.2
Stettin	71.2
Kiel	84.6
Halle	81.3
Oberhausen	59.2
Augsburg	72.6
Kassel	75.8
Vienna (Wien)	60.8
Danzig	67.5
Linz	76.1

7. Labour

7.1. Working Hours

7.1.1. *Average Annual Working Hours, 1913–50*

1913	3,290
1925	2,910
1929	2,770
1938	2,750
1950	2,640

7.1.2. *Average Weekly Working Hours, 1913/27–1942 (Processing Industries)*

1913/14	c.50–60
1927	46.0
1928	46.0
1932	41.5
1933	42.9
1934	44.6
1935	44.4
1936	45.6
1937	46.1
1938	46.5
1939	47.0
1942	49.2

7.2 Wages

7.2.1. *Average Earnings, 1913/1925–40 (1936=100)*

	Nominal Wages		Real Wages	
	Per hour	per week	per hour	per week
1913/14	64.7	76.0	80.6	94.6
1925	94.6	93.4	83.1	83.2
1926	100.8	97.1	88.3	85.1
1927	110.6	109.6	93.1	92.3
1928	122.9	124.5	100.9	102.2
1929	129.5	128.2	104.7	103.6
1930	125.8	118.1	105.7	99.2
1931	116.3	103.9	106.4	95.1
1932	97.6	85.8	100.7	88.5
1933	94.6	87.7	99.8	92.5
1934	97.0	94.1	99.7	96.7
1935	98.4	96.4	99.6	97.6
1936	100.0	100.0	100.0	100.0
1937	102.1	103.5	101.6	103.0
1938	105.6	108.5	104.7	107.5
1939	108.6	112.6	107.2	111.1
1940	111.2	116.0	106.4	111.0

7.2.2. *Average Earnings (Gross) in Selected Industries, 1937–40 (1935=100)*

	1937		1940	
	per hour	per week	per hour	per week
Mining	102.2	109.6	112.9	132.6
Ironworking	107.4	109.5	111.6	120.4
Non-ferrous metals			107.2	110.0
Metallurgical Industry	106.4	109.6	118.4	125.6
Chemicals	102.3	109.5	110.0	121.0
Rubber	103.5	112.2	115.1	131.0
Quarrying	105.4	107.2	120.9[1]	127.0[1]
Ceramics	102.7	105.2	120.0	123.9
Glass	103.7	104.9	123.4	128.0
Construction	104.4	104.6	113.4	116.0
Textiles	101.1	115.9	112.0	133.5

Figures refer to December of each year, except where otherwise indicated:
1. September

7.2.3. Women's Earnings as a Proportion of Men's (%), 1927–43

	Unskilled	Skilled
1928	66	63
1929	64	63
1933	70	66
1938	70	65
1943	70	65

7.3. Industrial Disputes, 1913/18–1932

	Strikes and lockouts	Employees (1,000s)	Working days lost
1913[1]	2,464	323.4	11,761.0
1918	532	391.6	1,453.0
1919	3,719	2,132.5	33,083.0
1920	3,807	1,508.4	16,755.0
1921	4,485	1,617.2	25,874.0
1922	4,755	1,895.8	27,734.0
1923	2,046	1,626.8	12,344.0
1924	1,973	1,647.1	36,198.0
1925	1,708	771,0	2,936.0
1926	351	97.1	1,222.0
1927	844	494.5	6,144.0
1928	739	775.5	20,339.0
1929	429	189.7	4,251.0
1930	353	223.9	4,029.0
1931	463	172.1	1,890.0
1932	648	129.5	1,130.0

Source: V. Berghahn, *Modern Germany, Society, Economy and Politics in the Twentieth Century* (2nd Edition, 1987, Cambridge University Press), p. 304.

1. Trades union statistics differ from the official Reich statistics. The number of strikes and lockouts is given as 2,600; the number of employees affected 249,000; and the number of working days lost 5,672,000.

7.4. Unemployment

7.4.1. *Official Annual Averages, 1921–40*

	1,000s	%
1921	346	1.8
1922	215	1.1
1923	818	4.1
1924	927	4.9
1925	682	3.4
1926	2,025	10.0
1927	1,312	6.2
1928	1,391	6.3
1929	1,899	8.5
1930	3,076	14.0
1931	4,520	21.9
1932	5,603	29.9
1933	4,804	25.9
1934	2,718	13.5
1935	2,151	10.3
1936	1,593	7.4
1937	912	4.1
1938	429	1.9
1939	119	0.5
1940	52	0.2

Source: Berghahn, *Modern Germany*, p. 284.

7.4.2. *Hidden Unemployment, 1928–33*

	Official Statistics		Total including Hidden Unemployed	
	1,000s	%	1,000s	%
1928*	1,862	9.5	2,977	14.4
	1,012	5.0	1,867	8.8
1929	2,850	14.0	3,710	17.7
	1,251	6.0	1,800	8.4
1930	3,218	15.8	3,920	18.6
	2,765	13.5	3,605	17.1
1931	4,887	24.8	5,982	29.1
	3,990	20.3	5,134	25.0
1932	6,042	32.2	7,619	38.0
	5,392	28.9	7,164	35.4

* Figures for February and August each year.

7.5. Foreign Workers in Germany, 1923–44 (1,000s)

1923	225
1924	174
1925	173
1926	218
1927	227
1928	236
1929	232
1930	219
1931	155
1932	108
1933	148
1934	175
1935	188
1936	229
1936/7	274
1937/8	381
1938/9	435
1939	301
1940	1,154
1941	3,033
1942	4,224
1943	62,460
1944 (May)	7,126
(Sep.)	7,487

The statistics on foreign labour in Germany are incomplete and contradictory. The above table is an attempt to put together an overview of the development of the foreign labour force from different sources: 1923–1936, Herbert, *Fremdarbeiter*, 49; 1936/7–1938/9, ibid. p.56; from 1940 Homze, *Foreign Labor in Nazi Germany*, p.232.

7.6. Trades Unions

Trades unions were not officially recognised in Imperial Germany. Recognition came from the employers and the state in 1918. The right to strike and the employers' right to lock workers out were guaranteed by the Weimar constitution, which also provided for the establishment of works councils (*Betriebsräte*) with elected workers' representatives.

Free Trades Unions
Social Democratic 'Free Trades Unions' centralised their organisation by forming the ADGB (*Allgemeiner Deutscher Gewerkschafts-Bund*) in 1919. Social Democratic clerical unions formed the *Allgemeiner freier Angestellten-Bund* (Afa) the following year.

Christian Trades Unions
Anti-Marxist Catholic trades unions first appeared in the 1890s.

They joined together to form the *Deutscher Gewerkschaftsbund* in 1919.

Hirsch-Duncker Trades Unions
During the Weimar Republic the Hirsch-Duncker Unions were organised in the *Gewerkschaftsring Deutscher Arbeiter-Angestellten und Beamtenverbände* (GdA)

Besides these categories there were several smaller splinter groups and small company unions ('yellow' unions), of little significance.

7.6.1. Trades Union Membership, 1918–31 (1,000s)

	Free	Communist/ Syndicalist	Christian	Hirsch– Duncker	'Yellow'	Total
1890	278					357
1891	277				63	
1895	259		5	67		327
1900	680		77	77		849
1905	1,345		192	116		1,653
1910	2,017		316	122		2,455
1911	2,339		340	122		
1912	2,553		344	107		
1913	2,549		343	107	319	3,024
1914	2,076		283	78		2,437
1915	1,159	·	176	61		1,396
1916	967		174	58		1,199
1917	1,107		244	79		1,430
1918	1,665		405	114	46	2,184
1919	5,479		858	190	150	6,527
1920	7,890	247	1,077	226	190	9,193
1921	7,568	246	986	225	297	8,779
1922	7,895		1,049	231		9,175
1923	7,138		938	216		8,292
1924	4,618		613	147		5,378
1925	4,156	64	588	158	188	4,902
1926	3,977	63	532	163		4,672
1927	4,150	73	606	168		4,924
1928	4,654	55	647	169		5,469
1929	4,906	71	673	169	167	5,740
1930	4,822		659	198		5,679
1931	4,418	35	578	181	123	5,177

Sources: V Berghahn, *Modern Germany*, p.306; H-G Schumann, *Nationalsozialismus und Gewerkschaftsbewegung*, pp.163–5. Most figures and all totals are from Berghahn. Totals include figures not in other columns and are not calculated from the table itself. All figures for Communist and Syndicalist, and 'yellow' trades unions are from Schumann.

7.7. Nazi Labour Organisations

7.7.1. NSBO Regions and Inspectors, 1931

I	North East	(incl. Berlin, Danzig)	W Schuhmann
II	West	(Ruhr, Rhineland, Westphalia)	W Börger
III	North West	(incl. Hamburg, Hanover, Magdeburg)	B Karwahne
IV	Central	(incl. Halle, Hesse, Thuringia)	F Triebel
V	Northern South*	(Franconia, Upper Palatinate)	H Wölkersdorfer
VI	South	(Baden, Württemberg, Swabia, L. Bavaria)	W Dreher

* Nordsüd.

7.7.2. NSBO Regional Leaders (Landesobmänner), 1932

1.	Greater Berlin	J Engel
2.	East	A Kulisch
3.	Central Germany-Brandenburg	H Wolkersdörfer
4.	North	B Stamer
5.	Lower Saxony	B Karwahne
6.	Bavaria	K Frey
7.	South West	F Plattner
8.	Saxony-Thuringia	F Triebel
9.	West	W Börger
10.	Austria	S Kroyer

7.7.3. German Labour Front (DAF) Membership (millions)

1933	(July)	5.32
	(October)	9.13
	(December)	9.36
1934	(April)	c.14
	(June)	c.16
1935	(April)	c.21
1939	(September)	c.22
1942	(September)	c.25

8. Consumption

8.1. Raw Materials Prices, 1913–41 (1913=100)

1913	100
1924	136
1925	139
1926	129
1927	135
1928	136
1929	131
1930	114
1931	98
1932	86
1933	82
1934	87
1935	91
1936	94
1937	96
1938	97
1939	95
1940	99
1941	103

8.2. Retail Prices: Groceries, 1925–38 (Pfennige)

	Beef (kg)	Poultry (kg)	Eggs (each)	Milk (litre)	Fish (kg.)
1925	227	295	15.4	25.6	90
1926	220	294	14.5	23.1	95
1927	233	304	14.3	23.5	95
1928	231	304	14.4	24.2	96
1929	236	317	15.5	24.1	95
1930	232	315	13.1	20.3	95
1931	191	257	11.3	18.1	90
1932	147	197	9.5	15.9	76
1933	143	190	10.2	15.4	74
1934	146	198	10.7	16.9	71
1935	158	219	11.0	16.5	71
1936	165	263	11.0	1.9	71
1937	167	253	11.3	17.1	71
1938	167	250	12.0	17.1	66

8.3. Cost of Living, 1924–40 (1913/14=100)

1924	130.8
1925	141.8
1926	142.1
1927	147.9
1928	151.7
1929	154.0
1930	148.1
1931	146.1
1932	120.6
1933	118.0
1934	121.1
1935	123.0
1936	124.5
1937	125.1
1938	125.6
1939	126.2
1940	130.1

8.4. Proportion of Household Expenditure on Selected Items in Working Class Households, 1940

Food	42.8%
Drinks	2.0%
Tobacco, etc.	1.9%
Rent	12.1%
Heating and lighting	4.4%
Clothing	9.3%
Cleaning and washing	1.4%
Household Goods	2.9%
Travel	1.2%
Insurance	9.1%
Education, entertainment and leisure	3.4%

The table refers to a family with an average yearly income of RM 2,383.88

8.5. Inflation and Hyper-inflation, 1919–23

		Average Dollar Quotations (in Marks)
1919	(Jan.)	8.9
1919	(Jul.)	14.0
1920	(Jan.)	64.8
1920	(Jul.)	39.5
1921	(Jan.)	64.9
1921	(Jul.)	76.7
1922	(Jan.)	191.8
1922	(Jul.)	493.2
1923	(Jan.)	17,972.0
1923	(Jul.)	353,412.0
1923	(Aug.)	4,620,455.0
1923	(Sep.)	98,860,000.0
1923	(Oct.)	25,260,208,000.0
1923	(15 Nov.)	4,200,000,000,000.0

Source: M Freeman, *Atlas of Nazi Germany* (Longman).

9. Religion

Religious Affiliation of the Population of the Greater German Reich, 1933 (%)

	Evangelical	Roman Catholic	Other Christian	Jewish	Other
Prussia	63.57	31.48	.05	.91	3.99
(Berlin)	71.05	10.40	.15	3.78	14.62
Bavaria	28.68	69.92	.05	.55	.80
Saxony	87.03	3.79	.07	.40	8.71
Wurttemberg	67.19	31.14	.02	.37	1.28
Baden	39.10	58.37	.24	.86	1.43
Thuringia	89.52	2.71	.01	.17	7.59
Hesse	65.32	30.72	.06	1.25	2.65
Hamburg	78.16	5.22	.03	1.39	15.20
Mecklenburg	94.98	3.95	.01	.13	.93
Oldenburg	74.66	23.22	.00	.22	1.90
Brunswick	88.55	4.27	.01	.23	6.94
Bremen	85.37	6.49	.01	.39	7.74
Anhalt	88.01	3.57	.00	.25	8.17
Lippe	94.19	4.80	.01	.29	.71
Lubeck	91.53	3.30	.04	.36	4.77
Schaumburg-Lippe	97.91	1.35	.00	.38	.36
Saarland	26.48	72.51	.03	.38	.60
Reich	62.21	32.96	.05	.76	4.02

10. Health

10.1. Life Expectancy at Birth in Years, 1871–1939

	Men	Women
1871/80	36	38
1881/90	37	40
1891/1900	41	44
1901/10	45	48
1924/26	56	59
1932/34	60	63

10.2. Medical Professionals and Hospital Beds per 10,000 Inhabitants

	Doctors	Dentists	Nurses/Carers	Hospital Beds
1909	4.8	1.8	10.8	63.1
1924	6.4	1.2		75.2
1930	7.4	4.2	17.2	90.9
1938	7.3	5.2	19.4	92.9
1954	13.9	5.8	19.7	107.9

10.3. Infant Mortality, 1914–39

	Deaths in First Year per 100 (excluding stillbirths)
1910–14	16.3
1915–19	14.8
1920–24	12.7
1925	10.5
1926	10.2
1927	9.7
1928	8.9
1929	9.7
1930	8.5
1931	8.3
1932	7.9
1933	7.7
1934	6.6
1935	6.9
1936	6.6
1937	6.4
1938	6.0
1939	6.1
1940	6.4

11. Education

11.1. Expenditure on Schools and Universities, 1925–37 (current prices, millions of marks)

1925	1,998
1926	2,143
1927	2,451
1928	2,725
1929	2,865
1930	2,689
1931	2,248
1932	1,919
1933	1,919
1934	2,022
1936	2,100
1937	2,244

11.2. Schools

11.2.1. Elementary Schools (1,000s)

	Schools	Teachers	Pupils
1911	61.6	147.5	1,309.9
1921/2	52.8	195.9	8,894.5
1926/7	52.8	186.9	6,661.8
1931/2	53.0	190.3	7,790.1
1938	51.1	179.3	7,596.4
1941	50.5	180.5	7,724.1

11.2.2. Middle Schools (1000s)

	Schools	Teachers	Pupils
1911	2.0	12.0	354.0
1921/2	1.7	12.9	329.3
1926/7	1.6	12.2	259.3
1930/1	1.5	11.5	229.7
1939	1.2	8.8	259.4

11.2.3. Senior Schools (1,000s)

	Schools	Teachers	Pupils
1911	2.5	35.3	664.2
1921/2	2.4	42.7	799.5
1926/7	2.6	45.1	843.8
1931/2	2.5	44.9	786.7
1938	2.3	43.5	662.4

11.3. Nazi Schools

11.3.1. State Schools

20 April 1933: National Political Educational Institutes (Napolas),
Age 10–18.
23 schools, 5,000 pupils (1940).
Training schools for armed forces.
Run by Education Ministry, SA and SS among
senior personnel from 1936.

Langemarck schools, from mid-teens.
18 months training for university entry for pupils
from poor backgrounds.

Social Background of Pupils in Napola Schools, 1940

Father's occupation	% of Total
Civil servants	26.0
Clerical employees	22.0
Trade and Commerce	16.3
Workers	13.1
Peasants	7.2
Officers	5.6
Other	9.8

11.3.2. Party Schools

20 April 1937:   Adolf Hitler Schools, Age 12-18.
                          Training schools for party leaders.

20 April 1937:   *Ordnungsburgen*
                          For selected graduates of Adolf Hitler Schools.
                          Curriculum of politics, ideology and physical
                          culture.

Social Background of Pupils in Adolf Hitler Schools, 1940

Father's Occupation	% of Total
Trade and Commerce	33.0
Clerical employees	21.0
Civil servants	12.0
Workers	11.0
Peasants	5.0
Officers	3.0
Other	9.0

11.4. Higher Education

The numbers of both students and teachers in German universities declined under the Nazis. In addition, the Nazification of the curriculum, the dismissal of Jewish and other academics unacceptable to the regime, and restrictions placed on academic freedom and the range and nature of scholarship, transformed the universities into much smaller and narrower institutions.

11.4.1. Students in Higher Education

		Total	Women (%)
1912		71,710	c. 3.6
1914	SS	79,511	5.4
1914	WS	36,201	20.4
1918	SS	25,430	29.8
1918	WS	46,180	17.0
1920	SS	115,633	7.5
1922	SS	120,557	7.4
1924	SS	100,751	8.3
1926	SS	95,255	9.0
1928	SS	111,582	11.5
1930	SS	129,708	14.5
1932	SS	127,580	15.7
1934	SS	92,622	13.7
1936	WS	64,482	12.9
1937	WS	58,325	11.5
1939	SS	56,477	11.1
1941	SS	40,968	33.2
1943	SS	61,066	44.5

SS Summer semester
WS Winter semester

11.4.2. Students by Discipline: Winter Semester, 1935-6

	Men	Women
Evangelical Theology	3,975	138
Roman Catholic Theology	4,649	5
Law	7,851	175
Social and Economic	4,077	514
Medicine	16,738	3,818
Dentistry	3,351	749
Veterinary Science	1,522	12
Pharmacy	1,683	510
Education	5,045	1,088
Humanities	4,776	2,633
Chemistry	2,494	271
Mathematics and Natural Sciences	3,015	782
Agriculture and Forestry	1,994	36
Architecture	3,503	62
Engineering	2,699	2
Electrical Engineering	1,920	1
Aircraft Construction	227	2
Mining and Steelworking	461	
Other	482	178

11.4.3. Decline of Theology

Numbers of theology students declined throughout the 1930s. Both Protestant (Evangelical) and Roman Catholic theology were affected. By 1940 the Nazis were able to question the justification for the continued existence of independent theology faculties. Nazi students agitated against the continued existence of theology faculties.

Evangelical Theology: Student Numbers, 1939–40

Faculty	1939	1940
Vienna	40	20
Jena	50	13
Halle	35	17
Kiel	13	5
Münster	20	7
Heidelberg	61	11

Roman Catholic Theology: Staff/Student Ratio, 1940

Faculty	Staff	Students
Bonn	18	5
Heidelberg	17	11
Rostock	7	4
Kiel	11	5
Giessen	4	5
Marburg	12	15
Berlin	37	58

11.4.4. Universities in Greater Germany with a Majority of Women Students, 1943

The conscription of young men to the armed forces altered the gender balance of German universities during World War II.

University	Students		Freshers	
	Men	Women	Men	Women
Vienna	2,335	2,382	169	638
Munich	2,100	2,176	149	375
Heidelberg	1,782	2,352		
Freiburg	1,585	1,973	119	447
Leipzig	1,151	1,204		
Tübingen	1,077	1,169		
Marburg	883	1,189	82	337
Königsberg	647	785	44	236
Jena	637	757	46	242
Posen	198	273		

11.4.5. Men and Women Students by Faculty, 1943

Faculty	Men	Women
Medicine	25,158	15,427
Law	2,495	561
Natural Sciences	1,779	3,868
Humanities	1,751	8,900
Economics	1,860	2,252
Theology	366	40

11.5. Nazi Youth Groups

The Hitler Youth (*Hitlerjugend, HJ*)
Boys of 10–14 were recruited into the *Deutsches Jungvolk* (DJ), and were then organised in the Hitler Youth between the ages of 14 and 18.

The League of German Girls (*Bund Deutscher Mädel*)
Girls of 10–14 were recruited into the *Jungmädelbund*, and were then organised in the League of German Girls between the ages of 14 and 18. The organisation *Glaube und Schönheit* was founded in 1938 for 17–21-year-old girls.

11.5.1. Membership Figures of Youth Groups, 1933–39

	HJ	DJ	BDM	JM	Total (Total 10–18 pop.)
1932	55,365	28,691	19,244	4,656	107,956
1933	568,288	1,130,521	243,750	349,482	2,292,041 (7,529,000)
1934	786,000	1,457,304	471,944	862,317	3,577,565 (7,682,000)
1935	829,361	1,498,209	569,599	1,046,134	3,943,303 (8,172,000)
1936	1,168,734	1,785,424	873,127	1,610,316	5,437,601 (8,656,000)
1937	1,237,078	1,884,883	1,035,804	1,722,190	5,879,955 (9,060,000)
1938	1,663,305	2,604,538	1,448,264	1,855,119	7,031,226 (9,109,000)
1939	1,723,886	2,137,594	1,502,571	1,923,419	7,287,470 (8,870,000)

Figures are for the end of the year, except 1939 figures for the beginning of the year.

12. Press

12.1. German Newspaper Press: Number of Titles, 1914–35

1914	4,200
1918	2,398
1920	3,500
1925	3,152
1928	3,356
1930	3,353
1932	3,426
1934	3,245
1935	2,488

12.2. Major Non-Nazi Newspapers, 1935

	Circulation (1,000s)	
	1932	1935
Berliner Tageblatt	130.0	60.5
Berliner All. Nachtausgabe		223.7
Berliner Lokalanzeiger		190.5
Berliner Morgenpost	454.7	402.3
Berliner Zeitung am Mittag	146.2	110.8
Breslauer Volkszeitung	80.0	165.8
Dresdner Neueste Nachrichten	100.0	94.7
Frankfurter Zeitung		69.2
Mitteldeutschland (Halle)	100.0	55.5
Hamburger Anzeiger	160.0	138.4
Hamburger Fremdenblatt	150.0	110.6
Leipziger Neueste Nachrichten	180.0	146.1
Neue Leipziger Zeitung	100.0	69.8
Münchener Zeitung	105.5	70.2
Münchener Neueste Nachrichten	135.0	94.5

12.3. Circulation Loss of Non-Nazi Press, 1932–35
(By total circulation per region)

	Circulation (1,000s) 1932	1935	% loss, 1932–35
Anhalt	56.8	46.8	− 17.5
Baden	552.0	395.2	− 30.2
Bavaria	1,255.6	886.5	− 39.4
Brunswick	51.0	40.2	− 21.4
Bremen	88.8	84.3	− 5.0
Hamburg	376.2	302.8	− 19.7
Hessen-Darmstadt	265.9	189.4	− 32.5
Lippe	17.2	14.8	− 13.7
Lübeck	53.5	48.3	− 9.6
Mecklenburg	138.7	105.1	− 24.9
Oldenburg	99.5	84.1	− 16.5
Saxony (Free state)	1,153.7	957.4	− 17.0
Thuringia	267.6	211.4	− 20.9
Württemberg	596.1	509.3	− 14.5
Prussia			
Greater Berlin	1,556.8	1,305.5	− 16.1
Brandenburg	402.3	310.7	− 32.3
Hannover	533.8	431.9	− 19.0
Hessen-Nassau	308.4	211.4	− 31.4
Hohenzollern	12.3	13.3	+ 7.3
East Prussia	375.2	274.1	− 26.9
Pomerania	155.3	157.7	+ 1.5
Rhineland (Prov.)	1,266.5	758.9	− 40.0
Saar-Palatinate	401.9	282.0	− 29.8
Saxony (Prov.)	704.7	477.0	− 32.8
Lower Silesia	757.7	634.2	− 16.2
Upper Silesia	229.2	157.7	− 31.1
Schleswig-Holstein	350.8	263.8	− 24.8
Westphalia	641.3	491.4	− 23.3

12.4. Reich Press Chamber

President	Max Amann
Director	Ildephons Reichter (1933–39)
	Anton Willi (1939–45)

Reich Association of German Newspapers

Leader	Edgar Brinkmann
	Max Wiessner
Deputy	Rolf Reinhardt
	Wilhelm Baur

Reich Association of the German Press

Leader	Otto Dietrich
	Wilhelm Weiss

12.5. Circulation of Major Nazi Newspapers, 1935 (1,000s)

	1932	1934	1935
Der Angriff (Berlin)	125.0	67.4	95.0
Westfälische Landeszeitung (Dortmund)	182.0	174.0	171.8
Rheinische Landeszeitung (Düsseldorf)		174.4	166.2
Nationalzeitung (Essen)		158.9	140.6
Westdeutscher Beobachter		185.2	187.3
Der Mitteldeutsche (Magdeburg)		101.4	103.1
Völkischer Beobachter (Munich/Berlin)		358.9	400.7
NSZ Rheinfront (Neustadt)		85.0	122.8

13. German Cultural and Intellectual Life, 1918–45: A Chronology

1918

Revolutionary artists form *Arbeitsrat für Kunst* (Working Council for Art) in Berlin (24 November).

Works

Literature · Heinrich Mann, *Der Untertan* (translated as Man of Straw)

1919

Staatliches Bauhaus established in Weimar by Walther Gropius. Munich police offer 10,000 marks reward for Ernst Toller, who is imprisoned for five years for high treason. Max Reinhardt opens Grosses Schauspielhaus.

Works

Film Robert Biehne, *The Cabinet of Dr Caligari*
Literature Franz Kafka, *In the Penal Colony*
Painting Max Beckmann, *Die Nacht*
Theatre Ernst Toller, *Die Wandlung* (The Transformation)

1920

Death of Max Weber.
Berlin Dada Fair.
Erwin Piscator organises Proletarian Theatre.
Paul Klee begins teaching at Bauhaus.

Works

Architecture 'Einstein Tower' observatory at Potsdam by Erich Mendelsohn
Film Fritz Lang, *Dr Mabuse der Spieler*
Friedrich Murnau, *Nosferatu*
Painting Otto Dix, *War Cripples*
George Grosz, *Republican Automata; Deutschland, ein Wintermärchen*
(Germany. A Winter's Tale)

Theatre   Romain Rolland, *Danton*

1921
                   Einstein awarded Nobel Prize for Physics.
                   Brecht resident dramatic adviser at Munich
                   Kammerspiele.

1922
                   Kandinsky begins teaching at Bauhaus.

Works
Philosophy   Ludwig Wittgenstein, *Tractatus
                   Logico-Philosophicus*
Politics   Oswald Spengler, *Der Untergang des Abendlandes*
                   (Decline of the West)

1923
                   Bauhaus exhibition: 'Art and Technology. A
                   New Unity'. Public broadcasting begins.

Works
Painting   Otto Dix, *Two Victims of Capitalism* (drawing)
Politics   Arthur Moeller van den Bruck, *Das dritte Reich*
                   (The Third Reich)
                   Alfred Rosenberg, *Die Protokolle der Weisen von
                   Zion und die jüdische Weltpolitik* (The Protocols of
                   the Elders of Zion and Jewish World Politics)

1924   Death of Franz Kafka.
                   Erwin Piscator becomes head of *Volksbühne.*
                   First Radio Exhibition in Berlin.

Works
Literature   Thomas Mann, *The Magic Mountain*

1925   Brecht resident dramatic adviser at Deutsches
                   Theater, Berlin. *Neue Sachlichkeit* (New
                   Objectivity) exhibition in Mannheim.

Works
Literature   Posthumous publication of Franz Kafka's *The
                   Trial*
Music   Alban Berg, *Wozzeck* (world premiere at Prussian
                   state opera)
Politics   Hans Grimm, *Volk ohne Raum* (People without
                   Space)
                   Adolf Hitler, *Mein Kampf,* Vol. 1, *Eine Abrechnung*
                   (A Reckoning)

1926

Bauhaus moves to Dessau.

Works

Literature   Franz Kafka, *The Castle*
Painting   Otto Dix, *The Journalist Sylvia von Harden*
Politics   Adolf Hitler, *Mein Kampf*, Vol. 2, *Die Nationalsozialistische Bewegung* (The National Socialist Movement)

1927

Otto Dix appointed to Dresden Academy.
Otto Klemperer takes over Kroll Opera.
Paul Hindemith appointed Professor at Berlin Hochschule für Musik.

Works

Film   Fritz Lang, *Metropolis*
Walter Ruttmann, *Berlin. Symphonie einer Stadt* (Berlin. Symphony of a City).

1928

Edmund Husserl retires from Chair of Philosophy at Freiburg. Martin Heidegger appointed his successor.
First television without cable exhibited in Berlin.

Works

Music   Igor Stravinsky, *Oedipus Rex* (premiere at Kroll Opera)

1929

Thomas Mann awarded Nobel Prize for literature.
Wittgenstein awarded doctorate by Cambridge University.
Eight sound films made in Germany.

Works

Architecture   German Pavilion at International Exhibition in Barcelona, Mies van der Rohe
Literature   Alfred Döblin, *Berlin Alexanderplatz*
Erich Kästner, *Emil and the Detectives*
Erich Maria Remarque, *All Quiet on the Western Front*
Music   Kurt Weill, *Mahagonny, Happy End, Dreigroschenoper* (Threepenny Opera)

1930

Mies van der Rohe succeeds Gropius as director of Bauhaus.
New German sound films outnumber silent films.

Works

Film	Josef von Sternberg, *The Blue Angel*
Literature	Thomas Mann, *Mario and the Magician*
Music	Kurt Weill, *Der Jasager*
Politics	Alfred Rosenberg, *Der Mythus des 20. Jahrhunderts* (The Myth of the 20th Century)

1931

Erwin Piscator leaves Germany for the USSR.
International Photography Exhibition in Essen.

Works

Art History	Walter Benjamin, *Short History of Photography*
Film	Fritz Lang, '*M*'

1932

Nazis close the Bauhaus in Dessau.

Works

Film	Joseph von Sternberg, *Shanghai Express*
Literature	Hans Fallada, *Kleiner Mann, was nun?* (What Now, Little Man?)

1933

Reich Chamber of Culture set up.
First exhibition of 'degenerate art' in Stuttgart Karlsruhe.
Käthe Kollwitz and Heinrich Mann resign from Prussian Academy of Arts.
Ransacking of Max Hirschfeld's Institute of Sexual Research and burning of its library.
Burning of books in German universities (10 May).
Law restricts admission to journalist profession.
A number of artists and intellectuals flee Germany, among them: Hannah Arendt to Paris, 1940 to USA; Max Beckmann to Paris, Amsterdam, 1947 to USA; Bertolt Brecht to Denmark, 1941–47 to USA; Albert Einstein to USA; Wassily Kandinsky to Paris, French citizenship in 1939; Lotte Lenya to France; Heinrich Mann to France; Klaus Mann to Paris,

1936 to USA; Thomas Mann to Switzerland, 1939 to USA; Max Reinhardt to Vienna, 1938 to USA; Arnold Schoenberg to USA; Kurt Schwitters to Norway; Ernst Toller to USA; Kurt Weill to France.

Works
Film   Hans Steinhoff, *Hitlerjunge Quex* (Nazi propaganda film)
Theatre   Kurt Weill, *Seven Deadly Sins*
1934

Walther Gropius leaves Germany for London.

Works
Film   Leni Riefenstahl, *The Triumph of the Will*
1935

Resignation of Richard Strauss as President of Reich Chamber of Music (13 July).
International Film Congress in Berlin (May).
Death of Alban Berg.
'Blood and Soil' art exhibition in Munich.

Works
Literature   Heinrich Mann, *Die Jugend des Königs Henri Quatre* (The Youth of King Henry IV) published in Amsterdam

1936

Käthe Kollwitz expelled from Berlin Academy.
Winter Olympic Games held at Garmisch-Partenkirchen (February).
Summer Olympic Games held in Berlin (August).
Carl von Ossietzky, former editor of *Die Weltbühne* and in a concentration camp since 1933, receives Nobel Peace Prize. Hitler forbids German citizens to accept Nobel prizes. Thomas Mann's first public criticism of the Nazi regime: he is stripped of his citizenship.

Works
Literature   Thomas Mann, *Joseph in Ägypten* (Joseph in Egypt) published in Vienna
Klaus Mann, *Mephisto* (later banned by West German government, 1968)

1937

Degenerate Art exhibition in Munich.
Paul Klee forced to leave his teaching post at
the Düsseldorf Academy.
Gropius appointed to Chair of Architecture at
Harvard.
German National Prize for Art and Science
established (to replace Nobel prizes).
Law passed providing for large-scale
reconstruction of German cities.

Works
Music   Carl Orff, *Carmina Burana*
Painting: Oskar Kokoschka, *Self-Portrait of a Degenerate
               Artist* (after condemnation by the Nazis)

1938

Death of Edmund Husserl.
Suicide of Ernst Ludwig Kirchner.
Death of Ernst Barlach.
Law providing for the confiscation of
'degenerate art' without compensation (31 May).
Sigmund Freud leaves Vienna for London.
John Heartfield emigrates to London.
Oskar Kokoschka moves to London.
Death of Carl von Ossietzky.

1939

Ernst Toller commits suicide in America.
Government auctions 'degenerate art' in
Lucerne.

Works
Film   Karl Ritter, *Legion Condor* (propaganda)
               Willi Forst, *Bel Ami* (popular entertainment)
Architecture: Albert Speer's new Reich Chancellery
Literature   Ernst Junger, *Auf den Marmorklippen* (On Marble
               Cliffs) published in Hamburg
               Thomas Mann, *Lotte in Weimar*, published in
               Stockholm

1940

Thomas Mann begins monthly broadcasts from
London (*Deutsche Hörer*).

Works
Film   Fritz Hippler, *Der ewige Jude* (propaganda
               documentary)

Veit Harlan, *Jud Süss* (anti-semitic propaganda)
Wolfgang Liebeneiner, *Bismarck* (propaganda)
Gustav Ucicky, *Der Postmeister* (popular entertainment)
Willi Forst, *Operette* (popular entertainment)

1941

Government closes down 550 newspaper publishers.

Works
Theatre   Bertolt Brecht, *Mother Courage* (first performance, Zürich)

1942

Erich Kästner banned.

Works
Film   Willi Forst, *Wiener Blut* (popular entertainment)

1943

Works
Film   *Die Abenteuer des Barons Münchhausen* (book by Erich Kästner)
Literature   Robert Musil, *Der Mann ohne Eigenschaften* (The Man without Qualities), Part 3, published in Lausanne
Theatre   Bertolt Brecht, *The Good Person of Sezuan* (first performance, in exile)

1944

Works
Film   Helmut Weiss, *Die Feuerzangenbowle* (popular entertainment)
Helmut Käutner, *Grosse Freiheit Nr 7* (popular entertainment)

1945

Death of Georg Kaiser, Expressionist dramatist.

Works
Film   Veit Harlan, *Kolberg* (premiere, 30 January in Berlin and La Rochelle)

Diplomacy, Rearmament and War, 1918–1945

1. Chronology

1918

8 Jan.	Proclamation of the '14 Points' by US President Woodrow Wilson.
3 Mar.	Treaty of Brest Litovsk.
26 Oct.	Dismissal of Ludendorff. Groener is appointed his successor.
29 Oct.	German naval mutiny at Wilhelmshaven.
3–4 Nov.	Naval mutiny at Kiel.
11 Nov.	Armistice at Compiègne.
12 Nov.	Austria declares itself part of the Reich.

1919

18 Jan.	Opening of the Peace Conference, Paris.
2 Mar.	Founding conference of Third International opens, Moscow.
7 May	Allies inform German delegation of peace terms at Versailles.
28 Jun.	Treaty of Versailles.
Sep.	Allied interventionist forces withdrawn from Russia.

1920

10 Jan.	Treaty of Versailles comes into force.
10 Feb.	Plebiscite in first (northern) zone of Schleswig. 75 per cent majority for Denmark.
14 Mar.	Plebiscite in second (southern) zone of Schleswig. 80 per cent majority for Germany.
6 Apr.	France occupies Frankfurt am Main, Darmstadt and other towns.
5–16 Jul.	Allied Conference in Spa (Belgium) admits German representatives for the first time.
11 Jul.	Plebiscites in Allenstein, East Prussia (98 per cent for Germany) and Marienwerder, West Prussia (92 per cent for Germany).
14 Aug.	Formation of 'Little Entente' (Yugoslavia and Czechoslovakia).
Dec.	Reparations Conference in Brussels.

1921

24–9 Jan.	Paris Conference sets German reparations at 269,000 gold marks.
21 Feb.–14 Mar.	London Conference refuses to accept German counter-proposals on reparations.
8 Mar.	Allied occupation of Düsseldorf and Duisburg.
20 Mar.	Plebiscite in Upper Silesia returns 60 per cent majority for Germany.
5 May	'London Ultimatum' of the Allies, demanding German acceptance of the London reparations payments plan.
24–5 Aug.	USA signs peace treaty with Germany and Austria.
12 Oct.	Silesia partitioned between Germany and Poland.
12 Nov.	Washington Disarmament Conference opens.

1922

6–13 Jan.	Cannes Conference calls a world economic conference in Genoa.
10 Apr.–19 May	Genoa Conference.
16 Apr.	Treaty of Rapallo, providing for economic and military co-operation between Germany and USSR.
7–14 Aug.	London Conference.
28 Oct.	'March on Rome': Mussolini appointed Prime Minister of Italy.

1923

10 Jan.	Lithuanians invade Memel.
11 Jan.	French and Belgian occupation of the Ruhr valley.
13 Jan.	Chancellor Cuno calls for passive resistance in the Ruhr.
26 Sep.	End of passive resistance in the Ruhr.
21 Oct.	Declaration of the Rhenish Republic in Aachen, supported by France.
30 Nov.	Gustav Stresemann becomes Foreign Minister.

1924

21 Jan.	Death of Lenin
22 Jan.	First Labour government elected in Britain.
25 Jan.	France forms alliance with Czechoslovakia.
9 Apr.	Presentation of Dawes Plan to President of Reparations Commission.
16 Apr.	Dawes Plan accepted by German government.

16 Jul.–16 Aug.	Dawes Plan accepted by London Conference.
29 Aug.	Reichstag approves Dawes plan.
24 Oct.	New French government recognises the Soviet Union.
29 Oct.	Conservative government elected in Britain.

1925

5 Jan.	Allies postpone evacuation of Cologne following German failure to abide by terms of disarmament.
21 Jan.	Japan recognises USSR.
7 Jul.	French troops begin to withdraw from the Rhineland.
14 Jul.	Allied evacuation of Ruhr valley begins.
Jul.–Aug.	Expulsions of Germans from Poland and Poles from Germany in disputed territories.
25 Aug.	French evacuation of Düsseldorf and Duisburg.
5–16 Oct.	Locarno Conference. Germany, Britain, France, Belgium, Italy, Poland and Czechoslovakia are participants.
16 Oct.	Locarno Pact guarantees demilitarisation of the Rhineland and Germany's borders with France and Belgium.
27 Nov.	Reichstag approves Locarno Treaties.
30 Nov.	Allied evacuation of Cologne begins.

1926

24 Apr.	Berlin Treaty (of friendship and neutrality) between Germany and USSR.
May	Pilsudski seizes power in Poland.
8 Sep.	Germany is admitted to the League of Nations.
6 Oct.	Dismissal of Seeckt from his post as Chief of Army High Command.
10 Dec.	Stresemann awarded Nobel Peace Prize.

1927

31 Jan.	Inter-Allied Military Commission withdraws from Germany.
17 Aug.	Franco-German commercial treaty.

1928

14 Jan.	Defence Minister Gessler resigns and is succeeded by Groener.

1929

6 Feb.	Germany accepts Kellogg-Briand Pact outlawing war.

9 Feb.	Litvinov Protocol comprising non-aggression pacts between the USSR, Latvia, Estonia, Poland and Romania.
11 Feb.–7 Jun.	Paris Conference for revision of Dawes Plan. President is Owen D Young.
7 Jun.	Publication of Young Plan.
9 Jul.	Alfred Hugenberg and DNVP form 'Reich Committee' against Young Plan with Nazis and Stahlhelm.
6–31 Aug.	First Hague Conference on Young Plan.
4 Sep.	Briand proposes European economic and customs union to League of Nations.
3 Oct.	Death of Gustav Stresemann.
25 Oct.	'Black Friday' in New York.
22 Dec.	Petition against Young Plan fails.

1930

Jan.	Second Hague Conference on the Young Plan.
Jan.–Apr.	London Naval Conference.
12 Mar.	Reichstag adopts legislation for implementation of Young Plan.
30 Jun.	Allied evacuation of the Rhineland completed.

1931

20 Mar.	Government publishes a plan for an Austro-German customs union, leading to protests and economic pressure from France and the Little Entente.
11 May	Collapse of Austrian Credit-Anstalt following French economic pressure.
3 Sep.	Austro-German customs union plan abandoned.
18 Sep.	Japanese occupation of Manchuria.

1932

7 Jan.	Brüning declares Germany's inability to continue reparations payments, and intention to cease paying.
2 Feb.	International Disarmament Conference opens in Geneva.
12 May	Forced resignation of Defence Minister, Wilhelm Groener.
16 Jun.–9 Jul.	Lausanne Conference. Allies officially terminate German reparations.
29 Nov.	Franco-Soviet non-aggression pact.

1933

30 Jan.	Hitler appointed Chancellor.

3 Feb.	Hitler's secret speech to senior *Reichswehr* officers on SA and *Lebensraum.*
13 Mar.	Pope Pius XI praises Hitler's anti-Communism.
8 Jul.	Concordat signed between Germany and the Holy See.
15 Jul.	Rome Pact, binding Britain, France, Germany and Italy to the League Covenant, Locarno Treaties and Kellogg-Briand Pact.
14 Oct.	Germany leaves the League of Nations and the Disarmament Conference.

1934

26 Jan.	Ten-Year Non-Aggression Pact between Germany and Poland.
17 Mar.	Rome Protocols, binding Austria and Hungary to Italy. Mussolini guarantees Austrian independence.
14–15 Jun.	Hitler and Mussolini meet for the first time, in Venice.
25 Jul.	Austrian Chancellor Engelbert Dollfuss murdered in a Nazi putsch in Vienna.
2 Aug.	Death of Hindenburg. *Reichswehr* swears oath of loyalty to Hitler.
18 Sep.	USSR joins the League of Nations.
27 Sep.	Britain and France guarantee Austrian independence.

1935

13 Jan.	Saar plebiscite returns majority in favour of rejoining Germany.
1 Feb.	Anglo-German Conference on German Rearmament.
16 Mar.	Germany restores conscription and repudiates the disarmament clauses of the Treaty of Versailles.
11–14 Apr.	Stresa Conference to establish a common front against Germany by Britain, France and Italy.
17 Apr.	League of Nations censures German rearmament.
18 Jun.	Anglo-German Naval Agreement allows German Navy to rebuild to one third of tonnage of Royal Navy and 100 per cent of British submarine force.
2 Oct.	Italian invasion of Ethiopia.

1936

6 Jan.	Mussolini rescinds guarantee of Austrian independence and leaves the 'Stresa Front' in

	return for German support over Abyssinia.
22 Feb.	Mussolini agrees not to oppose re-militarisation of the Rhineland.
7 Mar.	Germany repudiates Locarno Treaty and German troops reoccupy the demilitarised Rhineland.
9 Jun.	Ciano replaces relatively pro-Western Suvich as Italian Foreign Minister.
11 Jul.	Austro-German Convention.
17–18 Jul.	Spanish Army revolt marks start of Spanish Civil War.
24 Aug.	Two-year compulsory military service introduced.
19 Oct.	Announcement of German Four-Year Plan.
25 Oct.	German-Italian Treaty of Co-operation.
1 Nov.	Rome-Berlin Axis announced.
18 Nov.	Franco regime recognised by Germany and Italy.
25 Nov.	Germany and Japan sign the Anti-Comintern Pact.

1937

27 Apr.	German Condor Legion destroys Basque town of Guernica.
23 Jun.	Germany and Italy withdraw from committee for non-intervention in Spain.
7 Jul.	Outbreak of Sino-Japanese war.
17 Jul.	Anglo-German and Anglo-Soviet naval agreements.
25–29 Sep.	State visit to Germany by Mussolini.
13 Oct.	Germany guarantees inviolability of Belgium.
17 Oct.	Riots in the Sudetenland.
5 Nov.	Meeting between Hitler and his generals (recorded in the Hossbach memorandum) to discuss plans for a future war.
6 Nov.	Italy joins Anti-Comintern Pact.
19 Nov.	Lord Halifax indicates Britain will tolerate a non-violent territorial expansion by Germany.
29 Nov.	Sudeten Germans secede from Czech parliament.

1938

4 Feb.	Joachim von Ribbentrop appointed Foreign Minister. General von Fritsch dismissed from post of commander-in-chief of armed forces; Hitler takes personal command. War Ministry abolished and replaced by OKW.
12 Feb.	Berchtesgaden meeting between Hitler and Austrian Chancellor Kurt von Schuschnigg.

	Austria is forced to appoint a Nazi Interior Minister (Seyss-Inquart), release Nazi prisoners and subordinate Austrian army to Germany.
16 Feb.	Austria declares amnesty for Nazis.
6 Mar.	Austrian President Miklas accepts Schuschnigg proposal for a referendum on Austrian independence scheduled for 13 March.
10 Mar.	Mobilisation of German forces for the invasion of Austria.
11 Mar.	German invasion of Austria.
13 Mar.	Annexation (*Anschluss*) of Austria announced.
24 Apr.	Sudeten Germans demand autonomy.
3–9 May	State visit to Italy by Hitler.
20 May	Hitler presents to generals draft of 'Operation Green' for an attack on Czechoslovakia.
Jun.	Construction of Westwall fortifications begins.
11 Aug.	Czech Prime Minister Beneš opens negotiations with Sudeten Germans.
12 Aug.	German forces mobilise.
18 Aug.	Beck resigns as Chief of Army General Staff. Replaced by Halder.
4 Sep.	Sudeten German leader Henlein rejects Czech offer of full autonomy and breaks off relations.
11 Sep.	USSR denied passage through Poland and Romania to assist Czechs.
15 Sep.	British Prime Minister Neville Chamberlain visits Hitler at Berchtesgaden.
21 Sep.	Czechoslovakia persuaded by Britain and France to cede to Germany territory where over half the population is German.
22 Sep.	Hitler and Chamberlain meet at Godesberg. Germany demands immediate cession of Sudetenland and announces invasion for 28 September. Czech government resigns.
23 Sep.	Czechoslovakia mobilises. USSR promises to support France in protecting Czechoslovakia.
25 Sep.	Britain and France threaten Hitler with force.
26 Sep.	Partial mobilisation in France.
27 Sep.	Mobilisation of Royal Navy.
29 Sep.	Munich Conference (Britain, France, Italy and Germany).
30 Sep.	Munich Agreement: Sudetenland ceded to Germany.
1 Oct.	Czechs cede Těšín (Teschen) to Poland (Cieszyn).

5 Oct.	Resignation of Beneš.
6–8 Oct.	Slovakia and Ruthenia granted autonomy.
21 Oct.	Hitler's secret instruction to prepare for the destruction of the rest of Czechoslovakia.
6 Dec.	Franco-German pact on inviolability of existing frontiers.

1939

14 Mar.	Prompted by Germany, Slovakia declares independence. Catholic Prelate Jozef Tiso becomes President.
15 Mar.	German troops occupy the rest of Czechoslovakia.
16 Mar.	Creation of Protectorate of Bohemia and Moravia.
21 Mar.	Hitler demands return of Danzig and Polish Corridor.
23 Mar.	Germany occupies Memel territory.
28 Mar.	Hitler denounces non-aggression pact with Poland.
31 Mar.	Britain and France guarantee support for Poland if its independence should be threatened. Poland rejects German demands.
7 Apr.	Italy invades Albania.
13 Apr.	Britain and France guarantee independence of Greece and Romania.
16–18 Apr.	Britain and France reject Soviet offer of defensive alliance.
27 Apr.	Britain introduces conscription.
28 Apr.	Hitler denounces Anglo-German Naval Agreement.
17 May	British government further restricts Jewish emigration to Palestine.
22 May	Hitler and Mussolini sign 'Pact of Steel' – a ten-year military and political alliance.
12–21 Aug.	Anglo-Soviet military negotiations fail to reach agreement.
23 Aug.	Nazi-Soviet non-aggression pact, with secret clauses on the partition of Poland.
25 Aug.	Anglo-Polish mutual assistance pact.
1 Sep.	German invasion of Poland and annexation of Danzig.
2 Sep.	Britain introduces National Service Bill.
3 Sep.	Britain and France declare war on Germany.
7 Sep.	Germans overrun western Poland.
17 Sep.	USSR invades Poland.

19 Sep.	Polish government leaves Warsaw.
28 Sep.	Fall of Warsaw.
30 Sep.	Germany and USSR settle partition of Poland.
6 Oct.	End of Polish campaign. Britain and France reject German peace moves.
8 Oct.	Western Poland incorporated into the Reich.
30 Nov.	USSR invades Finland.
13 Dec.	German battleship *Graf Spee* scuttled off Montevideo after Battle of River Plate.

1940

12 Mar.	Finland cedes territory in north-east and Karelia in peace treaty with USSR.
9 Apr.	Germany invades Norway and Denmark.
14 Apr.	British forces land in Norway.
2 May	Evacuation of British forces from Norway.
10 May	Churchill replaces Chamberlain as British Prime Minister. Beginning of German western offensive.
14 May	Dutch army surrenders after bombing of Rotterdam.
28 May	Capitulation of Belgium.
29 May–3 Jun.	Evacuation of over 300,000 British troops from Dunkirk.
Jun.–Sep.	Battle of Britain.
10 Jun.	Italy declares war on Britain and France.
14 Jun.	French government moves to Bordeaux as Germans enter Paris.
16 Jun.	Pétain succeeds Reynaud as head of French government.
17–23 Jun.	USSR occupies Baltic States.
22 Jun.	France and Germany conclude armistice.
24 Jun.	France and Italy conclude armistice.
27 Jun.	USSR invades Romania.
3 Jul.	Britain sinks French fleet at Oran.
5 Aug.	Britain signs agreement with De Gaulle and Free French, and with Polish government in exile.
23 Aug.	Beginning of 'Blitz' (intensive aerial bombardment) of Britain.
7 Oct.	Germany seizes Romanian oilfields.
12 Oct.	Hitler cancels invasion of Britain (Operation Sealion).
28 Oct.	Italy invades Greece.
7 Dec.	Spain refuses to join the war.

1941

6 Jan.	President Roosevelt of USA submits Lend-Lease Bill to Congress.
6 Feb.	German forces under Rommel sent to North Africa after Italian defeats.
11 Mar.	Lend-Lease Bill passed by Congress.
6 Apr.	German invasion of Yugoslavia.
7 Apr.	Rommel launches North African offensive.
10 Apr.	'Independent' Croatian state declared in Zagreb. Ustaša leader Ante Pavelić becomes leader of German puppet government.
11 Apr.	German air attack on Coventry.
13 Apr.	Stalin signs neutrality pact with Japan.
17 Apr.	Capitulation of Yugoslavia.
22 Apr.	German military government established in Serbia under Milan Nedić.
1 May	German occupation government of Greece established under Georgios Tsolakoglu.
10 May	Rudolf Hess flies to Scotland, where he is imprisoned.
13 May	Serbian nationalist 'Chetnik' movement established under Draža Mihailović.
20–31 May	Germans capture Crete.
22 Jun.	Germany invades USSR ('Operation Barbarossa').
27 Jun.	Establishment of Staff of Communist Partisan movement in Yugoslavia under Josip Broz Tito.
6 Jul.	USSR abandons eastern Poland and Baltic States.
10 Jul.	Establishment of staff of Soviet Partisan movement.
12 Jul.	Britain and USSR sign agreement on mutual assistance in Moscow.
16 Jul.	Smolensk falls to Germans.
17 Jul.	Rosenberg appointed Reich Minister for Occupied Eastern Territories.
11 Aug.	Churchill and Roosevelt sign Atlantic Charter.
8 Sep.	Germans besiege Leningrad.
9 Sep.	EDES (Greek Resistance movement) founded.
19 Sep.	Kiev falls to Germans.
2 Oct.–5 Dec.	Battle for Moscow.
16 Oct.	Soviet government leaves Moscow, leaving Stalin behind.
15 Nov.	German advance forces within 20 miles of Moscow.
5 Dec.	USSR launches counter-offensive.

7 Dec.	Japanese bomb Pearl Harbour.
8 Dec.	Britain and USA declare war on Japan.
11 Dec.	Germany and Italy declare war on USA.
16 Dec.	Hitler forbids military retreat, and dismisses General Walther von Brauchitsch.

1942

2 Jan.	Britain, USA, USSR and 23 other states sign Washington Pact.
1 Feb.	Quisling becomes Norwegian Prime Minister.
8 Feb.	Speer becomes Armaments Minister.
14 Feb.	Polish nationalist underground forms 'National Army'.
15 Feb.	Singapore falls to Japan.
10 Mar.	Rangoon falls to Japan.
28 Mar.	RAF destroys much of Lübeck.
12–17 May	Soviets defeated on Kharkov front.
26 May	Anglo-Soviet Treaty for closer co-operation.
6 Jun.	Lidice massacre. Germans murder the entire adult male population of a Czech village as a reprisal for the assassination of Heydrich.
10 Jun.	German offensive in the Ukraine.
21 Jun.	Fall of Tobruk.
25 Jun.	Eisenhower appointed Commander-in-Chief of US forces in Europe.
30 Jun.	Axis troops reach El Alamein.
2 Jul.	Fall of Sevastopol.
28 Jul.	Fall of Rostov. Germans take Caucasus and advance towards Baku oilfields. Zhukov becomes commander of Soviet southern armies.
14 Aug.	Abortive Anglo-Canadian raid on Dieppe.
5 Sep.	Germans enter Stalingrad.
24 Sep.	General Franz Halder replaced by Kurt Zeitler.
11–12 Nov.	German occupation of Vichy France.
19–20 Nov.	Soviet counter-attack at Stalingrad cuts off von Paulus' forces.
27 Nov.	French navy scuttled at Toulon.

1943

2 Jan.	German withdrawal from Caucasus begins.
14–24 Jan.	Casablanca Conference. Britain and USA agree to accept only unconditional surrender.
31 Jan.	Germans under von Paulus surrender at Stalingrad.
2 Feb.	Remaining German forces surrender at Stalingrad.
8 Feb.	Soviet forces take Kursk.

14 Feb.	Soviet forces take Rostov.
16 Feb.	Soviet forces take Kharkov.
15 Mar.	Soviet forces forced out of Kharkov.
20 Apr.	Massacre of Jews in Warsaw Ghetto.
26 Apr.	Discovery of Katyn massacre.
12 May	Axis armies surrender in Tunisia.
17 May	RAF bombs Ruhr dams.
4 Jun.	Formation of French Committee of National Liberation under Jean Moulin.
5 Jul.	Germans launch 'Operation Citadel' offensive on Kursk salient.
10 Jul.	Allies land in Sicily.
12 Jul.	Soviet counter-offensive on Orel salient forces Germans to abandon Kursk offensive.
26 Jul.	Mussolini replaced by General Badoglio. Secret armistice between Italy and Allies.
24–30 Jul.	Allied air attack on Hamburg ('Operation Gomhorrah') kills 30,000 people.
4 Aug.	Soviet forces take Orel.
23 Aug.	Soviet forces take Kharkov.
3 Sep.	Allies land in Italy. Unconditional surrender of Italy.
8 Sep.	German troops occupy northern Italy and Rome. Italian occupation troops in France and the Balkans are disarmed and interned.
25 Sep.	Soviet forces take Smolensk.
27 Sep.	Uprising of Italian resistance in Naples.
10 Oct.	Civil war breaks out in Greece.
2 Nov.	Moscow Declaration of Allied foreign ministers on international security.
6 Nov.	Soviet forces take Kiev.
28 Nov.–1 Dec.	Tehran Conference.
20 Dec.	Britain and USA agree to support Tito's partisans.

1944

22 Jan.	Allied landing at Anzio.
27 Jan.	Relief of Leningrad.
15 Feb.	Allied bombing of Monte Cassino.
1 Mar.	Resistance organises strikes in northern Italy.
18 Mar.	Fall of Monte Cassino.
19 Mar.	German occupation of Hungary.
2 Apr.	Soviet forces enter Romania.
2 Jun.	US forces take Rome.
6 Jun.	'D-Day' landings in Normandy.
10 Jun.	Destruction of French village of Oradour and

	murder of its population as a reprisal for resistance activity associated with Allied invasion.
13 Jun.	'V–1' flying bomb campaign against Britain starts.
30 Jun.	Danish resistance organises general strike.
1 Jul.	Bretton Woods Conference.
9 Jul.	Allied troops take Caen.
20 Jul.	Abortive 'July Plot' to assassinate Hitler.
24 Jul.	Liberation of Majdanek by Soviet forces.
25 Jul.	Goebbels becomes Reich Plenipotentiary for Total War.
26 Jul.	USSR recognises Lublin Committee of Polish Liberation as legitimate government of liberated Poland.
1 Aug.	Rising of Polish Home Army in Warsaw.
11 Aug.	Allies land in south of France.
19 Aug.	Rising of French resistance in Paris.
25 Aug.	Allied troops enter Paris.
29 Aug.	Anti-German uprising in Slovakia.
30 Aug.	Soviet forces enter Bucharest.
4 Sep.	Soviet-Finnish ceasefire.
5 Sep.	Liberation of Brussels by Allied forces.
8 Sep.	Start of 'V–2' rocket campaign against Britain.
17 Sep.	Allied airborne landings at Arnhem.
19 Sep.	USSR and Finland sign armistice.
3 Oct.	Suppression of Warsaw uprising by Germans.
14 Oct.	Athens liberated by British troops.
20 Oct.	Belgrade liberated by Soviet forces and Yugoslav partisans.
21 Oct.	Aachen is the first German city to be captured by the Allies in the West.
23 Oct.	Allies recognise de Gaulle administration as provisional government of France.
3 Dec.	British police action to deal with Athens riots provokes Communist insurrection.
16 Dec.	Germans begin Ardennes offensive ('Battle of the Bulge').

1945

3 Jan.	Beginning of Allied counter-offensive in Ardennes.
17 Jan.	Soviet forces liberate Warsaw.
4–11 Feb.	Yalta Conference.
13 Feb.	Soviet forces liberate Budapest.
23 Mar.	US forces cross Rhine at Remagen.

28 Mar.	End of V-Rocket offensive against Britain.
3 Apr.	Beneš appoints Czech National Front government.
13 Apr.	Fall of Vienna.
20 Apr.	Soviet troops reach Berlin.
25 Apr.	Karl Renner becomes Chancellor in Austrian provisional government. Soviet and American troops meet on the Elbe.
26 Apr.	US and Soviet forces meet up at Torgau.
28 Apr.	Mussolini killed by partisans.
29 Apr.	Surrender of German forces in Italy.
30 Apr.	Hitler commits suicide and is replaced by Admiral Doenitz.
2 May	Surrender of Berlin.
5 May	Rising of Czech resistance in Prague.
7 May	Unconditional surrender of all German forces by Jodl to Eisenhower.
8 May	Keitel surrenders to Zhukov in Berlin. 'VE Day'.
9 May	Soviet forces liberate Prague.
5 Jun.	Allied Control Commission assumes control of Germany.
6 Aug.	Atomic bomb dropped on Hiroshima.
8 Aug.	USSR declares war on Japan.
9 Aug.	Atomic bomb dropped on Nagasaki. Soviet forces enter northern Korea and Manchuria.
14 Aug.	Surrender of Japan.

2. Diplomacy and International Relations

2.1. Major Treaties and Alliances

Treaty of Versailles, 28 June 1919
Between Germany and the Allies.

Section I incorporated the Covenant of the League of Nations.

Sections II and III covered the new frontiers of the German state, arrangements for the Saarland, and provided for plebiscites in disputed territories.

1. Germany surrendered the following territory:
   (a) Alsace-Lorraine to France.
   (b) Eupen-Malmédy to Belgium (plebiscite 1920).
   (c) Northern Schleswig to Denmark (plebiscite 1920).
   (d) Poznania (Posen) and West Prussia to Poland. Upper Silesia to Poland (plebiscite 1921).
2. The Saarland was placed under the control of the League of Nations for 15 years, with mining interests to be controlled by France.
3. Danzig (Gdansk) was placed under League of Nations control.
4. Memel was placed under Allied control and then transferred to Lithuania.
5. Austrian independence was recognised as irrevocable. Any change in Austria's status was subject to approval by the League of Nations.

Section IV dealt with German rights and interests abroad.

1. Germany renounced all her overseas territories. German colonies became mandated territories of the League of Nations.
   (a) German East Africa (to Britain)
   (b) German South West Africa (to South Africa)
   (c) Cameroons, Togoland (to Britain and France)
   (d) Samoa (to New Zealand)
   (e) German New Guinea (to Australia)
   (f) Marshall Islands and Pacific islands north of Equator (to Japan)

2. Germany lost concessions and trading rights in China, Egypt and Middle East.

Sections IV and V contained military conditions.

1. All war *matériel* to be surrendered.
2. Dissolution of the General Staff.
3. Abolition of conscription.
4. The German army limited to 100,000 land and 15,000 marine troops with 4,000 officers. Air force and submarine force prohibited.
5. The Rhineland and Heligoland to be demilitarised.
6. Germany to accept an army of occupation on the west bank of the Rhine and bridgeheads at Cologne, Koblenz and Mainz.

Section VI contained conditions for prisoners of war and war cemeteries.

Section VII contained conditions relating to war criminals and charges against Emperor William II.

Section VIII dealt with reparations.

1. Germany accepted the 'war guilt clause' (Article 231) and responsibility for war damage. Agreed to pay reparations.

Section IX contained financial conditions.

Section X contained economic conditions.

Section XI gave the Allies rights to fly over and land in German air space.

Section XII dealt with harbours, rivers, canals and railways.

1. The Rivers Elbe, Danube, Memel, Oder and Rhine were opened to international traffic, as was the North Sea-Baltic canal.
2. Czechoslovakia was awarded harbour rights in Hamburg and Stettin.

Section XV incorporated German recognition of the treaties with other Axis powers: St Germain (with Austria), Trianon (with Hungary), Sèvres (with Turkey) and Neuilly (with Bulgaria).

Rapallo Treaty, 1922
Signed following diplomatic *rapprochement* between Germany and the USSR, both outcasts from mainstream European international

relations. Germany wanted personnel trained in the Soviet Union, and the Soviet government wanted to enlist German technical expertise to assist armaments production. The treaty regulated Soviet-German relations. It excluded war indemnities and included a most-favoured nation trading clause. Diplomatic relations were resumed.

Locarno Treaties, 1925

The Locarno Treaties were negotiated at the instigation of Gustav Stresemann and the results were a mixture of pragmatism and revisionist aspirations.

1. *Treaty of Mutual Guarantee* (France, Britain, Italy)
   Guaranteed the inviolability of Germany's western border.

2. *Treaties of Arbitration* between
   (a) Germany and Belgium
   (b) Germany and France
   (c) Germany and Poland
   (d) Germany and Czechoslovakia

Although Germany did not accept the eastern borders of the Reich, she undertook not to attempt to alter the boundaries by force, and to respect French treaties in eastern Europe (with Poland and Czechoslovakia).

Berlin Treaty, 1926

A restatement of the conditions of the Rapallo Treaty. The Treaty dealt with political and economic questions and guaranteed neutrality in the event of an attack on the other party by a third power.

German-Polish Non-Aggression Pact, 26 January 1934

Valid for ten years, the pact was intended to damage French interests in eastern Europe, and reflected Hitler's intention to distance Germany from Soviet Russia.

Anglo-German Naval Agreement, 18 June 1935

Germany was to be permitted a surface fleet 35% of the strength of the Royal Navy and a submarine fleet equivalent in size to that of the British. One of the effects of the pact was to undermine the Stresa Front.

Anti-Comintern Pact, 25 November 1936

Agreement between Germany and Japan to co-operate against the USSR and the Communist International. Hitler wanted to involve Britain in this agreement, but failed. Italy joined the pact in

January 1937 after the proclamation of the Rome-Berlin Axis in 1936.

Nazi-Soviet Pact, 23 August 1939

Germany and the Soviet Union agreed to refrain from aggressive action towards each other, and each agreed not to support a third party attacking the other. The Treaty was concluded for ten years. A secret additional protocol specified the signatories' agreed spheres of interest in eastern Europe. The northern border of Lithuania was specified as the limit of Soviet interests in the Baltic, effectively bringing the Baltic states under Soviet control, and Poland was divided along the rivers Narev, Vistula and San. Finally, the USSR emphatically expressed an interest in Bessarabia (now Moldova), and Germany renounced any such interest.

2.2 Reparations

1921

Paris Conference fixed German reparations at 269,000 million gold marks to be paid in 42 annual instalments. In addition 12 per cent of the value of German exports was to be surrendered for a period of 42 years.

London Conference rejected Germany's counter-proposals. Negotiations suspended.

The 'London ultimatum' reduced the amount to 132,000 million gold marks and was accepted by Germany.

1922

Second London Conference rejected further German counter-proposals.

1923

Occupation of the Ruhr after the Reparations Commission claimed Germany had failed to fulfil obligations.

1924

Dawes Plan modified the repayment schedule. Germany's state revenues were to be bonded and a loan made to facilitate a return to the gold standard and enable the German government to make the first payment.

Annual payments of 1,000–1,750 million marks were to be made annually until 1 September 1928. From 1 September 1928 2,500 million marks.

No decision was reached either on the full amount to be paid or the time allowed for repayment. Provisions were made for sanctions in case of a default by Germany.

1930
Young Plan: Germany was to pay 34,500 million gold marks by 1988. The conditions of payment were eased.

1932
Lausanne Conference stipulated one last payment of 3,000 million Reichsmarks to be made by Germany.

2.2. Value of German Reparations (Millions Gold Marks/Reichsmarks)

	Germany	As valued by Reparations Commission
1. To 31 August 1924 (Dawes Plan)	40,689	8,719
Of which:		
Direct payments	1,754	1,710
Coal, coke etc.	2,374	990
Ships	4,542	762
Port goods	80	–
Non-military goods left at front	5,041	140
German private property abroad	10,080	13
State property in ceded territory	9,670	2,781
German POW labour	1,200	–
Navy	1,338	–
2. During occupation of the Ruhr	1,370	921
3. In fulfilment of Dawes Plan	7,993	7,553
4. In fulfilment of Young Plan	3,103	2,800
Total	*53,155*	*19,993*

2.3. Allied Co-operation and War-time Conferences

The Atlantic Charter (August 1941)
This followed the proclamation by the Allies of the 'Four Freedoms' (freedom of speech and expression, freedom of worship, freedom from want and freedom from fear) in January 1941. Drawn up by the United States and Britain, it also repudiated territorial gains for the Allies and reaffirmed the right of the self-determination of peoples. The positive conditions of the Charter were not to apply to Germany.

First Washington Conference (GB, USA: 20 December 1941–14 January 1942)
Churchill (Britain) and Roosevelt (USA) met and convoked an Allied War Council. It was agreed to mount an Allied landing in North Africa. The Washington Pact (1 January 1942) was agreed during the conference. The 26 states at war with the Axis agreed not to conclude a separate peace.

Second Washington Conference (18–26 June 1942)
Agreement to mount a second front in Europe, and to promote research into atomic warfare.

Casablanca Conference (GB, USA: 14–24 January 1943)
Britain and the United States agreed on the Allied landings in Sicily and demanded Germany's unconditional surrender.

Moscow (19–30 October 1943)
Allied foreign ministers agreed on the restoration of democracy in Italy and Austria. It was also agreed that German war criminals were to be put on trial. The talks were also concerned with post-war international relations.

Tehran Conference (GB, USA, USSR: 28 November–1 December 1943)
The decision was taken to move Poland to the west at the expense of Germany. The German-Polish border would be on the Oder, while the Polish-Soviet border would be on the Curzon line. The Allies also decided to invade northern France in preference to the Po Valley. It was agreed that the USSR would liberate the Balkans. No agreement was reached on the future of Germany.

Dumbarton Oaks Conference (GB, USA, USSR, China: 21 August–7 October 1944)
The decision to partition and de-industrialise Germany (the 'Morgenthau Plan', discussed as a possibility by Britain and the USA in Quebec during September) was effectively reversed by the withdrawal of United States support. Plans were made for the foundation of the United Nations Organisation.

Moscow (9–18 October 1944)
Britain and the Soviet Union agreed spheres of interest in eastern Europe. It was agreed that Greece would be a British sphere of influence, while Bulgaria and Romania would effectively become Soviet satellites. Influence was to be shared by Britain and the USSR in Hungary and Yugoslavia.

Yalta Conference (GB, USA, USSR: 4–11 February 1945)

Germany was to be divided provisionally into four zones of occupation with the Soviet Union occupying the territory east of the Elbe. Post-war Germany would be 'de-Nazified' and demilitarised. There was also an agreement in principle that Germany would pay reparations. Foundations were laid for the establishment of an Allied Control Commission, which would govern occupied Germany. The conference also discussed the future of Poland, and it was agreed that members of the London government-in-exile should be admitted to the Lublin Committee, which effectively constituted the Polish government.

Potsdam Conference (GB, USA, USSR: 17 July–2 August 1945)

The 'big three' met once more to work out definitive peace settlements, and agreed to conclude a peace treaty with a united Germany rather than dismember the state permanently. This was, of course, impossible without a German government, and a peace treaty with Germany was signed only in 1990. Divisions widened between the Western powers and the Soviet Union, especially on the question of German reparations. A further problem was the question of the German-Polish border. This too remained unresolved by the conference, and the question of Germany's eastern border was settled only in 1990, after some initial hestitation by the Kohl administration.

3. Rearmament

3.1. German Military Expenditure

	Million marks	% of Net Domestic Product
1913	2,312	4.7
1925	3,933	7.0
1930	4,688	6.8
1932	2,494	5.9
1933	2,772	6.3
1934	6,143	12.0
1935	8,017	14.1
1936	12,325	19.4
1937	13,360	18.7
1938	22,000	25.3
1939	37,340	38.1
1940	66,445	60.4
1941	86,500	72.1
1942	110,400	88.3
1943	132,800	98.4
1944	149,800	115.2

Source: Berghahn, *Modern Germany*

Net domestic product is GNP after social benefits and indirect taxes, but including subsidies.

3.2. Financial Burden of World War II

	Billions[1]	% Financed by Credit		% Tax Increase[2]		% Debt Increase
Germany (1939–45)	414.0	86.0	864	(1940–45)	1,264	(1939–45)
UK (1939–45)	20.5	69.2	336	(1939–45)	294	(1939–45)
USSR (1941–45)	582.3	17.1	141	(1941–45)	262	(1940–45)
USA (1941–45)	306.0	70.5	864	(1940–45)	603	(1939–45)
Italy (1939–43)	278.5	93.0	161	(1939–43)	279	(1939–43)
Japan (1937–45)	174.7	92.0	553	(1938–44)	1,523	(1937–45)

1. In respective local currencies.
2. In other words, increase in total amount of revenue raised by taxation.

3.3. Aircraft Production, 1933–42 (1,000s)

	Germany	UK	USA	USSR
1933	0.37	0.63	0.47	2.59
1934	1.97	0.74	0.44	2.59
1935	3.18	1.14	0.46	3.58
1936	5.11	1.88	1.14	3.58
1937	5.61	2.15	0.95	3.58
1938	5.23	2.83	1.8	7.5
1939	8.29	7.94	2.19	10.38
1940	10.83	15.05		
1941	10.78	20.10		
1942	15.55	23.67		

4. The Consolidation of a Greater Germany

4.1. The *Anschluss* of Austria

On 13 March 1938 the new Austrian federal government led by Seyss-Inquart issued a 'law on the Reunion of Austria with the German Reich'. Article 1 said simply: 'Austria is a state (*Land*) of the German Reich.' A plebiscite was held on 10 April and a corresponding law was enacted in Germany the next day.

4.1.1. Territorial and Name Changes after 1938

Austria retained no separate identity within the Reich. It was divided into seven administrative districts (and corresponding party *Gaue*) which were then incorporated directly into the Reich. The designation 'Austria' was replaced by 'Danube' in the names of Lower and Upper Austria.

Alpen- und Donaugaue		Term used semi-informally to distinguish territory of former Austria from that of former Germany (*Altreich*).
Vienna	(Wien)	*Reichsgau*, enlarged.
Lower Austria	(Niederösterreich)	*Reichsgau* Niederdonau (Lower Danube). Absorbs northern part of Burgenland and, later, part of Sudetenland.
Upper Austria	(Oberösterreich)	*Reichsgau* Oberdonau (Upper Danube). Later absorbs part of Sudetenland.
Salzburg		*Reichsgau* Salzburg.
Tyrol	(Tirol)	*Reichsgau* Tirol absorbs 'administrative district' Vorarlberg.
Vorarlberg		Absorbed by Tyrol.
Styria	(Steiermark)	*Reichsgau* Steiermark.
Carinthia	(Kärnten)	*Reichsgau* Kärnten.

146

Südmark was used to refer to the area covered by Styria and Carinthia together by those organisations with one office in Graz for both *Gaue*: the SA, the Reich Food Estate.

Alpenland was used by the SS and the NSKK to refer to all of Austria except Vienna and Lower Danube; the SA group Alpenland covered Tyrol, Vorarlberg, Salzburg and Upper Austria. The Labour Ministry and the Reich Food estate used it only to refer to Tyrol, Vorarlberg and Salzburg.

Donauland was used by the Reich Food Estate to refer to its district covering Vienna, Lower Danube and Upper Danube. The simpler designation *Donau* was used by the SS for the same area and by the SA group covering Vienna and Lower Danube.

4.2. Czechoslovakia

The Sudeten German territories (population 3.6 million) were ceded to Germany by the Munich Agreement of 29 September 1938, and occupied on 1 October. There were no plans for the organisation or administration of the territories, but they were incorporated directly into the Reich in much the same way as the Austrian *Länder*. In addition the Tešin district (0.25 million inhabitants) was incorporated into Poland in October, and the Feldivék district of southern Slovakia and western Ruthenia was incorporated into Hungary (0.85 million inhabitants). The Czech crisis precipitated the granting of autonomy to Slovakia within a Czecho-Slovak union (6 October 1938). Dr Jozef Tiso, the head of the Slovak People's Party (Hlinka), became Prime Minister.

The military directive for the liquidation of the remaining Czech state was signed by Hitler on 21 October 1938. German troops invaded Czechoslovakia again on 15 March 1939, and established the 'Protectorate of Bohemia and Moravia' (population 7.38 million). Constantin von Neurath was appointed Reich Protector (succeeded by Heydrich, 1941; and Frick, 1942). An 'independent' puppet state was established in Slovakia (population 2.63 million) under Tiso. The Carpatho-Ukraine (population 0.7 million) became a part of Hungary.

The Protectorate of Bohemia and Moravia belonged to a category of 'appended territories' destined for eventual integration into the Reich. The Protectorate retained a nominal autonomy denied other similarly 'appended' territories, but was effectively under the control of the Deputy General of the Reich Protector, Karl Hermann Frank, who was responsible directly to Himmler.

The Czech population was considered assimilable if it could be . dispersed throughout the Reich, and thousands of Czech workers

(244,000 in 1943) were impressed into labour service in Germany and Austria.

4.2.1. Czechs Recruited to the Labour Force of the Reich (1,000s)

1939	95
1940	51
1941	46
1942	135
1943	47

4.2.2. Absorption of GNP generated in the Protectorate (%)

1940	4.6
1941	8.4
1942	11.1
1943	28.7
1944	35.5

4.3. Poland

Poland was divided according to the Nazi-Soviet Pact (1939) into Soviet-occupied territory (201,000 km^2 and a population of 11.9 million), and German-occupied territory (188,000 km^2 and a population of 20.2 million). The latter was subsequently divided into directly incorporated territories and the 'General Government'.

1. *East Prussia* was extended to include Soldau (lost in 1918) in the south, which became part of the administrative district (*Regierungsbezirk*) of Allenstein and the Polish district of Suwalki in the east (appended to the *Regierungsbezirk* of Gumbinnen). Further territory from the Polish district of Warsaw was incorporated into the *Regierungsbezirk* of Zichenau (Ciechanów).

2. *Danzig-West Prussia* was created as a new *Reichsgau*, and included the territory of the Free City and the Polish district (vovodship) of Pomorze. It was divided into three *Regierungsbezirke*. Danzig, Marienwerder and Bromberg (Bydgoszcz), of which only the first had a German majority. The laws applied to the establishment of the Sudetengau were used as a model. Albert Forster was appointed *Gauleiter*.

3. *Posen* (later renamed *Warthegau*) was also a new *Reichsgau* and included Posen (Poznán), lost to Germany in 1918, much of the Polish province of Łodź and part of the province of Warsaw. The *Reichsgau* was divided into the administrative districts of Hohensalza (Inowrocław), Posen (Poznán) and Kalisch (Kalisz).

The laws applied to the establishment of the Sudetengau were used as a model. Arthur Greiser was appointed *Gauleiter*.

4. *Silesia* gained the Polish administrative district of Kattowitz (Katowice) and additional territory from Teschen, Cracow and Kielce. It was divided into Upper and Lower Silesia in 1941. The incorporation of these territories involved a transfer of 22.5 million people.

5. *The Generalgouvernement* (Government-General) was made up of the remaining German-occupied territory: the Polish vovodships of Lublin and Cracow, and the greater part of Radom, Warsaw and Lwów. A Decree for the Administration of the Occupied Polish Territories was issued (12 October 1939) naming Dr Hans Frank, NSDAP *Reichsleiter* and Minister without Portfolio, as Governor-General; and Seyss-Inqart as Deputy Governor-General. The Reich Interior Minister was the ultimate authority in the territories. The decree came into effect on 26 October, with the end of military rule. The territories which came to constitute the Government-General had a population of 10.5 million.

Poland was to be Germanised by selective murder, racial selection (of a 'German' element within the Polish people) and massive resettlement programmes. On 7 October 1939 Himmler was appointed Reich Commissioner for the Strengthening of German Nationality (*Reichskommissar für die Festigung des deutschen Volkstums*) in a decree which provided for the resettlement of Germans (from within and outside the Reich) within the occupied Polish territories.

Non-Germans were to be expelled from the incorporated territories and resettled in the Government-General. Germans from the Government-General and abroad were to be settled in the incorporated territories in turn. In practice the size of the Polish population restricted the implementation of this project. The Germans would have to choose between the absorption, or selective absorption, of the Polish population or mass murder (by direct or indirect means).

By 1941, 200,000 Germans from eastern Poland and the Baltic had been settled in the occupied territories, which had lost about a million Poles and Jews. (The Warthegau had been the most affected area.) Almost a million Germans had been discovered among minorities within the Polish population.

Rural expulsions numbered: 35,000 in Danzig-West Prussia; 15,000 in eastern Upper Silesia; 18,000 in Zichenau (Ciechanów).

149

4.4. Belgium, Alsace, Lorraine and Luxembourg

Eupen, Malmédy and Moresnet were reincorporated into the Reich on 18 May 1941, following the defeat of Belgium.

Civil administrations were established in Alsace, Lorraine and Luxembourg on 2 August 1941. They were made directly accountable to Hitler and incorporated into the Reich in 1942.

Alsace became the responsibility of the Reich Governor and *Gauleiter* of Baden, Robert Wagner. Josef Bürckel, *Gauleiter* of Saar Palatinate, was made responsible for Lorraine, which became part of the enlarged *Gau* Westmark in 1942. Luxembourg became the responsibility of Simon Gustav, *Gauleiter* of Koblenz-Trier, and was united with the latter in 1942 to form the *Gau* Moselland.

4.5. Yugoslavia

On 6 April 1941 Germany invaded Yugoslavia, which surrendered on 17 April. The country was subsequently dismembered as follows.

1. Northern Slovenia (population 0.9 million) was incorporated into the Reich as South Carinthia and Lower Styria.
2. Southern Slovenia and the Dalmatian littoral were incorporated into Italy.
3. An 'independent' Croatian puppet state was established (population 7 million), which included most of Bosnia and Herzegovina, but excluded parts of the Dalmatian coast (ceded to Italy). Power was held by the fascist Ustaša movement led by Ante Pavelić as *poglavnik* (leader). Croatia was assigned to the Italian sphere of influence in the Balkans.
4. Most of Serbia (population 4.8 million) was occupied by Germany.
5. The Vojvodina and parts of Slovenia and Croatia were incorporated into Hungary.
6. South-eastern Serbia and Macedonia were occupied by Bulgaria.
7. Montenegro became an Italian protectorate, and parts of it were incorporated into Albania (along with Kosovo and parts of Macedonia).

5. Defeat and the Division of Germany

No agreement on the future of Germany had been reached by the end of the war, so that the provisional agreements of Yalta became the basis for the occupation of Germany. The Soviet Union took control of an occupation zone between the Elbe-Werra and Oder-Neisse lines. The United States took control of Bavaria, Württemberg and Hesse in the south, and a smaller territory based on Bremen and Bremerhaven in the north. Britain occupied the rest of northern Germany, including the Ruhr valley, and France took control of an occupation zone based on the southern Rhineland, including the Saarland, the Palatinate, Baden and Württemberg-Hohenzollern. Military governors assumed governmental powers in each of the zones: Eisenhower for the USA (succeeded by Clay in 1947); Zhukov for the USSR (succeeded by Sokolovsky in 1946); Montgomery for Britain (succeeded by Robertson in 1947); and Koenig for France. Each administered his zone according to instructions from his own government. Berlin was similarly divided into sectors. All four occupation powers were to act together in the Inter-Allied Control Council where matters affected the whole of Germany (or Berlin). Similar arrangements came into force in Austria.

6. War Losses

6.1. Deaths

	Military	Civilian	Total
Germany	3,250,000	3,600,000	6,850,000
Of which:			
1939–40			88,353
1940–41			160,171
1941–42			485,000
1942–43			464,524
1943–44			573,238
UK	326,000	62,000	388,000
USSR	13,600,000	7,000,000	
USA	500,000		500,000
Japan			2,000,000
Italy	330,000	80,000	410,000

6.2. Germans Missing or Taken Prisoner

1939–40	5,420
1940–41	14,228
1941–42	65,844
1942–43	389,967
1943–44	974,249

7. Maps

7.1. The Versailles Settlement: Territory lost by Germany

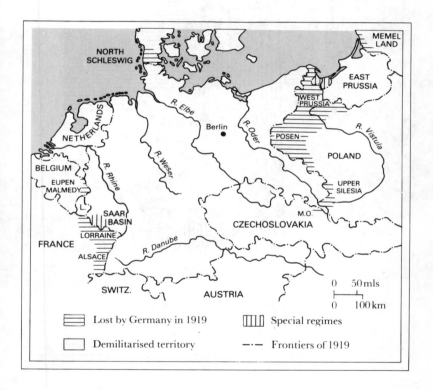

Source: M Freeman, *Atlas of Nazi Germany* (Longman), p. 9.

7.2. Nazi Germany and Europe, 1942

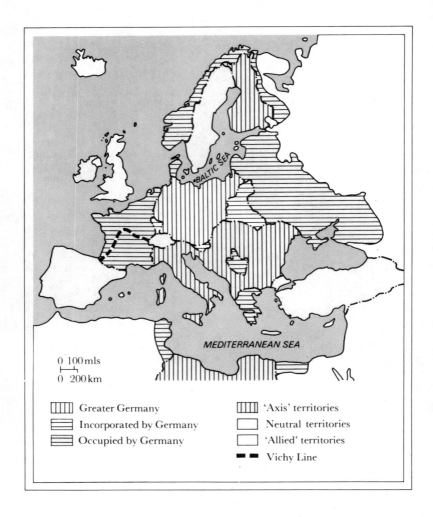

Source: M Freeman, *Atlas of Nazi Germany*, (Longman), p. 135.

7.3. Poland during World War II

Polish boundary before 1.9.39

German-Russian line

Annexed by Germany

Under German civil administration

7.4. Post-war Germany

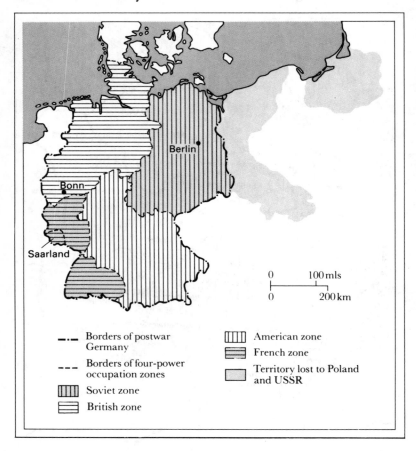

Source: M Freeman, *Atlas of Nazi Germany* (Longman), p. 189.

Anti-semitism, Racial Politics and the Holocaust, 1933–1945

1. Chronology

1933

30 Jan.	Adolf Hitler becomes Reich Chancellor.
Feb.–Mar.	Violence against individual Jews and Jewish shops by members of the NSDAP and the SA.
22 Mar.	Establishment of a department of 'Racial Hygiene' in the Reich Interior Ministry.
1–3 Apr.	Nationwide boycott of Jewish shops.
7 Apr.	'Law for the Restoration of a Professional Civil Service'. Compulsory retirement of Jewish civil servants; supplementary regulations provide for the dismissal of Jewish workers and clerical staff employed in public service.
25 Apr.	'Law against the Overcrowding of German Schools and Universities' limits the proportion of Jewish pupils and students to 1.5 per cent.
7 Jul.	Hess forbids actions against large Jewish department stores which might lead to unemployment.
14 Jul.	'Law on the Repeal of Citizenship and the Removal of German Nationality', affecting 'oriental' Jewish immigrants, above all from Russia and Poland.
14 Jul.	'Law for the Prevention of Hereditarily Sick Offspring': over 360,000 sterilisations carried out by 1945.
29 Sep.	'Reich Entailed Farm Law'. Proof of 'Aryan' ancestry dating back to 1800 is required from entailed farmers.
4 Oct.	An 'Aryan paragraph' in the Editorial Law (*Schriftleitergesetz*) excludes German Jews from journalism.

1934

5 May	Jewish students excluded from medicine and dentistry examinations.
22 Jul.	Jewish students excluded from law examinations.

8 Dec.	Jewish students excluded from pharmacy examinations.

1935

21 May	Army Law excludes Jews from military service.
May–Aug.	Increase in propaganda for the boycott of Jewish businesses.
16 Jul.	Reich Interior Minister Frick instructs registrars not to solemnise any more 'mixed marriages'.
25 Jul.	Jews definitively excluded from all armed forces.
15 Sep.	Nuremberg Laws, announced by Hitler at the Nuremberg party conference, defining 'Jew' and systematising and regulating discrimination and persecution: 'Reich Citizenship Law' deprives all Jews of their civil rights; 'Law for the Protection of German Blood and German Honour' makes marriages and extra-marital sexual relationships between Jews and Germans (*Deutschblütige*) crimes punishable by imprisonment.
14 Nov.	First Supplementary Decree to the 'Reich Citizenship Law'; Jews dismissed from the public service and from all other public offices.
26 Nov.	'Gypsies' and 'Negroes' included in prohibition of racially mixed marriages.

1936

24 Mar.	Benefit payments are withdrawn from large Jewish families.
26 Mar.	Jews no longer permitted to run or lease a pharmacy.
3 Apr.	Jews forbidden to practise as vets.
26 May	Reich Chamber of Fine Arts demands proof of 'Aryan' ancestry from its members.
28 May	'Whitsuntide Memorandum' of the Confessing Church condemns Nazi racial policy.
Jul.	First Sinti and Roma (gypsies) sent to Dachau.
15 Oct.	Jewish teachers forbidden to give private tuition to 'Aryans'.
4 Nov.	Jews are forbidden to use the 'German greeting' (*Heil Hitler!*).

1937

13 Feb.	Jews forbidden to practise as notaries.
15 Apr.	Jews no longer to be awarded doctoral degrees.
12 Jun.	Heydrich orders that after serving their prison sentences Jews guilty of 'racial disgrace'

(miscegenation) are to be sent to a concentration camp, as are female Jewish partners involved in such relationships.

1938

Mar.	Anti-Jewish persecution in Austria following the *Anschluss*, including compulsory 'Aryanisation' of many Jewish firms and expulsion of Jews into neighbouring states.
26 Apr.	All Jewish assets over 5,000 RM to be registered. 'Commissioner for the Four Year Plan' (Goering) is empowered to use such assets 'in the interests of the German economy'.
9 Jun.	Destruction of the synagogues in Munich.
15 Jun.	Some 1,500 Jews arrested and taken to concentration camps: so-called June Operation against 'asocials'.
6 Jul.	Conference on problem of Jewish refugees from Germany and Austria (Evian, France) fails to resolve problem.
23 Jul.	Jews issued with separate identity cards.
25 Jul.	Jewish doctors forbidden to practise. They are restricted to treating only other Jews.
10 Aug.	Destruction of Nuremberg synagogues.
17 Aug.	Jews must take the additional names of Sara and Israel.
27 Sep.	Jewish lawyers restricted to working for Jewish clients, and must refer to themselves as 'consultants'.
5 Oct.	Jewish passports to be stamped with 'J'.
26–8 Oct.	17,000 Jews with Polish citizenship are expelled from the German Reich, and transported to the Polish border.
7 Nov.	Herschel Grynszpan assassinates legation secretary Ernst vom Rath in the German embassy in Paris.
9 Nov.	*Reichskristallnacht*, the 'night of broken glass': a nationwide pogrom. Ninety-one murders; 191 synagogues destroyed. Almost all Jewish cemeteries desecrated. Material damage amounting to 30,000 marks, including cost of ransacking of 7,500 Jewish businesses.
10 Nov.	Mass arrests of Jewish men.
12 Nov.	A compensation fee of a thousand million RM is imposed on German Jews. Jews are forbidden to participate in cultural events.

15 Nov.	Jewish children expelled from German schools.
3 Dec.	Start of compulsory 'Aryanisation' of Jewish businesses.
Dec.	All 'gypsies' to register with the police.

1939

24 Jan.	Goering instructs Frick to establish a Reich Central Office for Jewish Emigration; Heydrich appointed Director.
30 Jan.	In the Reichstag Hitler threatens that another war will mean the 'extermination of the Jewish race in Europe'.
21 Feb.	Jews required to surrender precious metals and jewellery.
30 Apr.	Jews evicted from their homes and forced into designated Jewish accommodation.
21 Jul.	Adolf Eichmann appointed head of Jewish emigration office in Prague.
1 Sep.	Official date for beginning of Euthanasia Programme (authorised retroactively).
20 Sep.	Jews required to surrender radios.
21 Sep.	Decree from Heydrich initiates ghettoisation of Polish Jews; it contains references to a 'final objective' which will require 'a much greater time scale' and must be kept 'strictly secret'. Decision taken to move 30,000 'gypsies' to Poland.
Sep.–Nov.	'*Einsatzgruppen der Sicherheitspolizei*' ('Special units of the Security Police') and other Nazi formations murder large numbers of Jews. Some incidents amount to large scale massacres.
12 Oct.	Jews deported from Austria and Bohemia-Moravia to Poland.
24 Oct.	German occupation authorities in Wloclawec introduce a Jewish identification badge – first such measure in twentieth century.
23 Nov.	General introduction of the 'Yellow Star' for Jews living in the 'Government-General'.
25 Nov.	Sexual relations between foreign workers and Germans forbidden.
Dec.	87,000 Poles and Jews deported from the new *Reichsgau* Wartheland to the 'Government-General'.

1940

Jan.	First gassing of mentally handicapped ('Euthanasia Programme', or 'Operation T4').
23 Jan.	Jews are not issued with ration cards for clothing.
2–13 Feb.	First deportations of Jews from Vienna, Mährisch-Ostrau, and Teschen to Poland; first deportations from Germany (Stettin, Stralsund, Schneidemühl).
Mar.–Apr.	Ghettoes 'closed' in Cracow, Lublin and Łodź
27 Apr.	*Reichsführer* SS Heinrich Himmler orders establishment of a concentration camp at Auschwitz.
30 Apr.	First enclosed Jewish ghetto (Łodź).
Apr.–May	2,500 Sinti and Roma deported from Reich to Poland.
Jun.–Aug.	Plans formulated for the mass deportation of European Jews to Madagascar.
29 Jun.	Jewish telephones are disconnected.
Oct.	Jewish ghetto in Warsaw 'closed'.
22 Oct.	7,500 Jews deported from Saarland, Baden and Alsace-Lorraine to unoccupied France and interned.

1941

1 Mar.	Himmler orders building of extensions to concentration camp at Auschwitz, which is to be ready to receive about 100,000 Soviet prisoners of war.
From Mar.	Jews deployed as forced labour.
Spring	Four *Einsatzgruppen* ('special units') of Security Police and the SD created for attack on Soviet Union.
14 May	3,600 Parisian Jews arrested by French police.
31 Jul.	Goering gives Heydrich the task of the 'comprehensive solution (*Gesamtlösung*) of the Jewish question'.
Summer	Himmler instructs commandant of Auschwitz to prepare the camp to play a central part in the 'final solution' ordered by Hitler; Heydrich orders Eichmann to prepare deportation of European Jews for the 'final solution to the Jewish question in Europe'.
	Special commission from Himmler for the SS and police leader in Lublin, Globocnik, to murder the Polish Jews ('Operation Reinhard');

	the 'Fuhrer chancellery' provides staff from the 'Euthanasia Operation', which has been wound up, though killing continues.
1 Sep.	All Jews in the Reich from the age of six must now wear the 'Yellow Star'.
3 Sep.	First trial gassing with Zyklon B at Auschwitz; around 900 Soviet prisoners of war are victims of further experiments in September and October.
18 Sep.	Jews required to seek permission to use public transport.
Sep.–Nov.	Planning, siting and beginning of construction of death camps at Chelmno, Belzec, Majdanek and Auschwitz-Birkenau in the winter of 1941–42.
14 Oct.	Start of the mass deportation of Jews from the Reich to ghettoes in Kovno, Łodź, Minsk and Riga.
23 Oct.	All Jewish emigration from German-controlled territory is forbidden.
30 Nov.	Around 10,000 deported German and indigenous Jews shot near Riga.
12 Dec.	Jews are prohibited from using public telephones.
Dec.	Use of gas vans for murder of Jews in Chelmno.

1942

20 Jan.	Wannsee Conference in Berlin under Heydrich, for all government departments participating in 'final solution' and administration of Government-General.
Feb.	'Evacuation' of the Polish ghettoes begins; continuous deportations to the death camps.
15 Feb.	Jews are prohibited from keeping pets.
Spring	Camps built at Sobibor and Treblinka for 'Operation Reinhard'.
13 Mar.	Jews are compelled to identify their homes.
24 Mar.	First deportations of south German Jews to Belzec.
26–7 Mar.	First transports of Jewish emigrants from western Europe arrive at Auschwitz.
May–Jun.	Introduction of 'Yellow Star' in occupied western Europe.
12 May	Jews are prohibited from patronising 'Aryan' hairdressers.
11 Jun.	Jews excluded from egg rations.

12 Jun.	Jews must surrender all electrical goods, optical equipment, bicycles and typewriters.
22 Jun.	Jews excluded from tobacco rations.
23 Jun.	Systematic gassing of Jews begins in Auschwitz.
1 Jul.	End of teaching for all Jewish pupils.
15–16 Jul.	First transports of Dutch Jews to Auschwitz.
16–18 Jul.	French police arrest 13,000 'stateless' Jews in Paris, 9,000 (including 4,000 children) deported to Auschwitz.
19 Jul.	Himmler insists Poland must be 'free of Jews' by end of 1942.
22 Jul.	Mass transports from Warsaw ghetto to Treblinka, where 67,000 Jews are gassed immediately after arrival.
Jul.–Sep.	Mass deportations from western Europe to Auschwitz.
Aug.	More than 200,000 Jews gassed at Chelmno, Treblinka and Belzec during last two weeks of the month.
26–8 Aug.	Jews arrested in Vichy France.
9 Oct.	Jews banned from 'Aryan' bookshops.
Nov.	Himmler orders all concentration camps in the Reich to become 'free of Jews'.
19 Nov.	Jews excluded from meat and milk rations.
25–6 Nov.	Beginning of deportations from Norway.

1943

Feb.	Arrest of 'gypsies' remaining in Germany.
27 Feb.	Jewish munitions workers deported from Berlin to Auschwitz.
Mar.	Himmler orders deportation of Dutch gypsies.
Apr.	Beginning of medical experiments in Auschwitz.
7 Apr.	End of mass murder in Chelmno; gas chambers destroyed by SS.
19 Apr.	Beginning of Jewish uprising in the Warsaw ghetto.
30 Apr.	Jews lose German citizenship.
16 May	*SS-Obergruppenführer* Stroop announces destruction of Jewish ghetto in Warsaw.
11 Jun.	Himmler orders liquidation of all Polish ghettoes.
19 Jun.	Goebbels declares Berlin 'free of Jews'.
21 Jun.	Order to liquidate remaining ghettoes on Soviet territory.
1 Jul.	German Jews lose protection of law.

Aug.–Dec.	Liquidation of Russian ghettoes; inhabitants taken to death camps.
2 Aug.	Prisoners' uprising in Treblinka; destruction of gas chambers.
16–23 Aug.	Deportation of about 8,000 Jews from Bialystok and destruction of the ghetto following resistance.
Sep.–Oct.	Around 7,000 Danish Jews smuggled to Sweden.
Oct.–Nov.	Around 8,360 Jews deported from northern Italy to Auschwitz.
14 Oct.	Prisoners' uprising in Sobibor; end of gassing.
19 Oct.	End of 'Operation Reinhard'.

1944

Mar.–Apr.	More than 6,000 Greek Jews deported to Auschwitz. 1,500 escape to Turkey.
Apr.–Jul.	Hungarian Jews ghettoised; 437,000 deported to Auschwitz by July; 280,000 gassed.
May–Aug.	Resumption of mass gassing at Chelmno in connection with the final liquidation of the Łodź ghetto.
24 Jul.	Soviet troops occupy Majdanek.
7 Oct.	Revolt of Jewish 'special unit' in Auschwitz.
27 Nov.	Himmler orders cessation of gassing at Auschwitz.

1945

27 Jan.	Soviet troops reach Auschwitz.
21–8 Apr.	Last gassing of mainly sick concentration camp inmates at Ravensbrück and Mauthausen.
29 Apr.	American troops occupy Dachau.
7–9 May	Unconditional surrender of armed forces of Nazi Germany.

2. Jewish Population of Germany, 1933[1]

		% of Population	% of all German Jews
Prussia	361,826	0.9	72.4
(Berlin)	(160,564)	3.8	32.1
Bavaria	41,939	0.5	8.4
Saxony	20,584	0.4	4.1
Württemberg	10,023	0.4	2.0
Baden	20,617	0.9	4.1
Thuringia	2,882	0.2	0.6
Hesse	17,888	1.3	3.6
Hamburg	16,973	1.4	3.4
Mecklenburg	1,003	0.1	0.2
Oldenburg	1,240	0.2	0.3
Brunswick	1,174	0.2	0.2
Bremen	1,438	0.4	0.3
Anhalt	901	0.2	0.2
Lippe	510	0.3	0.1
Lübeck	497	0.4	0.1
Schaumburg-Lippe	187	0.4	0.0
Reich	*499,682*	*0.8*	*100.0*

1. As defined by religion in the census.

3. Nationality of Jews Resident in Germany, 1933

German	400,935	80.2%
Foreign	98,747	19.8%
of which:		
Polish	56,480	11.3%
Austrian	4,647	0.9%
Czech	4,275	0.9%
Hungarian	2,280	0.5%
Romanian	2,210	0.4%
Soviet	1,650	0.3%
Dutch	1,604	0.3%
Lithuanian	903	0.2%
Latvian	827	0.2%
British	532	0.1%
Turkish	753	0.2%
Other European	1,692	0.3%
US	536	0.1%
Other non-Eur.	398	0.1%
Stateless	19,746	4.0%
Unknown	214	0.0%
Total	**499,682**	

4. Jewish Population of Germany by Economic Sector, 1933

	Employed Population	%	Total	%
Agriculture	4,167	1.7	5,124	1.0
Industry and Crafts	55,655	23.1	95,472	19.1
Trade and Transport	147,314	61.3	262,223	52.5
Services	29,974	12.5	53,443	10.7
Domestic Service	3,377	1.4	3,494	0.7
Total employed	240,487	100.0		
Independent	60,941		79,926	6.0
Total			*499,682*	*100.0*

5. Jewish Emigration from Germany, 1937–39

	1937	1938	1939
Prussia	4,248	9,393	14,671
(of which from Berlin)	948	2,901	6,987
Bavaria	776	1,547	1,169
Saxony	104	229	496
Württemberg	350	600	442
Baden	624	950	654
Hamburg	429	1,620	2,187
Hesse	386	566	381
Bremen	59	189	141
Austrian *Gaue*		1,193	1,915
Other parts of the Reich	179	274	650
Reich	*7,155*	*16,561*	*22,706*

6. Destination of Jewish Emigrants from the Reich, 1937–39

	1937	1938	1939
Europe	4	159	4,520
British North America	19	29	203
USA	5,040	10,173	6,325
Mexico and Central America	68	604	2,828
Argentina	913	1,956	869
Brazil	325	254	1,245
Rest of South America	679	2,592	2,698
South Africa	77	265	700
Rest of Africa	12	48	290
Asia	7	202	2,572
Australia	11	279	456
Total	*7,155*	*16,561*	*22,706*

7. Mass Murder

The Holocaust

Country	Jewish Population	Estimates of Number of Jews Killed		
		Lowest	Highest	% of Jewish Population
Poland	3,300,000	2,350,000	2,900,000	88
USSR	2,100,000	700,000	1,000,000	48
Romania	850,000	200,000	420,000	49
Czechoslovakia	360,000	233,000	300,000	83
Germany	240,000	160,000	200,000	83
Hungary	403,000	180,000	200,000	50
Lithuania	155,000		135,000	87
France	300,000	60,000	130,000	43
Holland	150,000	104,000	120,000	80
Latvia	95,000		85,000	89
Yugoslavia	75,000	55,000	65,000	87
Greece	75,000	57,000	60,000	80
Austria	60,000		40,000	67
Belgium	100,000	25,000	40,000	48
Italy	75,000	8,500	15,000	26
Bulgaria	50,000		7,000	14
Denmark		(less than 100)		
Luxembourg		3,000		
Norway		1,000		
Total		**4,194,200**	**5,721,000**	**68**

According to Noakes and Pridham, more recent research puts the estimated number of Jews in the Soviet Union in 1941 at 4.7 million, of whom an estimated 2.2. million were killed (Jeremy Noakes and Geoffrey Pridham, *Nazism*, p.1208).

Glossary of Terms and Abbreviations

Abschnitt Division of territorial organisation of the *SS* (q.v.) immediately below *Oberabschnitt* (q.v.).

Abwehr Section of military service dealing with espionage, counter-espionage and sabotage.

Action Française Radical right-wing French political movement: royalist, clerical and anti-semitic.

Agram German name for Croatian Zagreb.

Agrarian League See *Landbund.*

Ahnenerbe Ancestral Heritage: SS agency founded in 1935 to promote racist view of world history through archaeological research and the promotion of mystic theories of the origins of the 'Aryan race'.

Aktion T4 Nazi euthanasia programme. Named after the organisation's Berlin headquarters at Tiergartenstrasse 4.

Alltagsgeschichte 'Everyday history'.

Alte Kämpfer Literally 'old fighters'; Nazi Party veterans.

Altreich German Reich within the borders of 1937.

Amt Office.

Amtsleiter Official with special duties.

Anordnung Order, instruction.

Anschluss Unification of Germany with Austria, sought by both sides after World War I, effected with German invasion and annexation, 1938.

Anti-Comintern Pact German-Japanese anti-Soviet pact of 1936. Signed by Italy in 1937.

Appeasement Term used to describe British foreign policy under Prime Minister Neville Chamberlain, which sought to avoid war by placating Hitler with concessions.

Arbeitsdienst Labour service.

Arbeitseinsatz Labour allocation.

Arbeitserziehungslager Labour Education Camp. Work camp used to punish workers for infringements of labour discipline.

Arrow Cross Virulently anti-semitic Hungarian fascist movement. Its leader, Ferenc Szalasi, became puppet Prime Minister following a German-backed coup in 1944, and the movement assisted in rounding up Jews for deportation.

Asocial Category of concentration camp prisoners deemed 'biologically criminal', including beggars, vagrants and the 'workshy' as well as 'habitual criminals'.

Austrofascism Term used by contemporaries and historians to describe variously the Austrian *Heimwehr* (q.v.) movement and the Dollfuss-Schuschnigg dictatorship. Political rival on the right to Austrian Nazism.

Autarky 'Economic self-sufficiency'.

Axis War-time alliance of Germany with Italy and Japan.

Babi Yar Site of SS massacre of 30,000 Ukrainian Jews in 1941.

Bann Division of Hitler Youth.

Barbarossa Codename for invasion of Soviet Union.

Battle of Britain Decisive Anglo-German air conflict of 1940, when the RAF frustrated the attempt of the *Luftwaffe* (q.v.) to establish air supremacy over the English Channel after the fall of France.

Bauernpartei Farmers' Party: Weimar splinter group.

Bauhaus Avant-garde school of design and architecture in Weimar Germany.

BDM *Bund deutscher Mädel* (League of German Girls). Girls' equivalent of the Hitler Youth for those aged 14 to 18. See also *Jungmädelbund*.

Beamter Official, civil servant.

Beauftragter Commissioner; official charged with specific task.

Bekennende Kirche 'Confessing church' of German Protestants opposed to the effective Nazification of the German Evangelical church.

Berchtesgaden Bavarian location of Hitler's 'Eagle's Nest' retreat.

Betriebsrat Works council.

Bevollmächtigter Plenipotentiary.

Bezirk Administrative district.

Blitz Term used to describe heavy bombing attacks on British cities by the *Luftwaffe*.

Blitzkrieg Literally 'lightning war'; rapid attacks on limited battle fronts.

Blubo Abbreviation of *Blut und Boden* used to describe Nazi films idealising rural life.

Blut und Boden 'Blood and Soil': slogan of propaganda idealising and mythologising the countryside.

Borchardt thesis Argument advanced by Knut Borchardt that Brüning could not save Weimar because political choices were constrained by the state of the economy, and in particular the burden of the wages of industrial labour; i.e., that social welfare undermined liberal democracy.

Breslau German name for Polish (and formerly German) city of Wrocław.

Bürgermeister Mayor.

Burgfrieden Literally 'fortress peace'. Refers to the domestic political truce at the outbreak of World War I.

BVP *Bayerische Volkspartei,* (Bavarian People's Party).

CdZ *Chef der Zivilverwaltung,* Head of Civilian Administration (of occupied territories).

Central Powers (Ger. *Mittelmächte*). Term applied to Germany and her allies, above all Austria-Hungary, during World War I.

charismatic leadership Weberian model applied by historians of Nazi Germany to the type of authority exercised by Hitler.

Chetniks Serbian nationalist anti-German partisans.

Christian Social Party Austrian clerical-conservative party whose anti-semitic platform attracted popular support in Vienna at the turn of the century. The success of its leader, Dr Karl Lueger, is held to have impressed the young Hitler.

Comintern 'Communist International'. The Third International established by the Bolsheviks in 1919. Its interpretation of fascism as the political expression of monopoly capital posed problems for Marxists; its hostility to anti-fascist collaboration with the Social Democrats divided the German left during the Depression. After Hitler came to power it supported Popular Front co-operation.

commissar Soviet term for a leading political official, particularly those with the Red Army. Political commissars were identified by the SS for 'liquidation'.

concentration camps Large internment camps erected by Nazis on coming to power and used in the first instance for the mass imprisonment of left-wing political opponents. Jews, 'asocials', gypsies and homosexuals were also interned in them. Some, particularly in Poland, were transformed into 'death camps' with the mass murder of Jews and others.

Continentalists School of foreign policy historians who place emphasis on Hitler's programme but argue that his final aim was the conquest of *Lebensraum* (q.v.) in eastern Europe.

corporatism Political doctrine which sought to transcend class conflict in modern industrial societies by means of a system of 'corporations' or 'estates'. Such ideas, originally propagated by the Roman Catholic church, contributed to fascist social thought, and were more explicit in Italy and Austria than in Germany.

Council of People's Representatives See *Rat der Volksbeauftragten*.

Creditanstalt Leading Austrian bank whose collapse in 1931 precipitated a financial crisis whose effects were also felt in Germany.

DAF *Deutsche Arbeitsfront* (German Labour Front).

Danzig German name for Gdansk, now in Poland. It was separated from Germany in 1918 and designated a Free City to be administered by the League of Nations. German irredentist claims constituted the ostensible reason for the invasion of Poland in 1939.

DAW *Deutsche Ausrüstungswerke GmbH* (German Armaments Works). An SS subsidiary organisation.

Dawes Plan Revised reparations plan presented to Germany by Entente powers in 1925.

D-Day 'Deliverance Day'. Codename for first day of Allied landings in Normandy: 6 June 1944.

Degenerate art Term applied to modernist and non-representational art deemed by the Nazis to be unsuitable and racially contaminated.

DEST *Deutsche Erd-und Steinwerke GmbH* (German Earth and Stone Works). An SS subsidiary organisation.

Deutsches Frauenwerk 'German Women's Enterprise'. Nazi organisation set up in 1933 as umbrella for all existing German women's organisations.

Deutsches Jungvolk Pre-Hitler Youth organisation for small boys (aged 10–14).

Dienststelle Administrative HQ.

DNVP *Deutschnationale Volkspartei* (German National People's Party).

Dolchstosslegende 'Stab-in-the-back myth'. Widespread belief on the nationalist right that Germany was betrayed by Socialists and Jews and not militarily defeated in 1918.

Donau German name for Danube.

Drang nach Osten Literally 'push to the east'. Term used to describe Nazi aim of winning *Lebensraum* (q.v.) in eastern Europe and USSR. It originally referred to mediaeval settlement of the Baltic by Germans.

Dulag *Durchgangslager* (transit camp).

Edelweiss Pirates Oppositional youth group in Nazi Germany.

EHER-Verlag Central NSDAP publishing house in Munich.

Einheit Unit.

Einsatz Deployment, operation, action.

Einsatzgruppe Special task force of Security Police *Sipo*, (q.v.) or *SD* (q.v.) in occupied territories.

ELAS Greek abbreviation of People's Liberation Front (*Ellenikon Laikon Apeleutherikon Straton*) formed by the Greek Communist Party after the German invasion of 1941.

Endlösung See 'final solution'.

Erbkrank 'Hereditarily ill': sufferers from mental and physical disabilities deemed by Nazi medicine to be hereditary.

Erlaß Decree.

Fasci di combattimento Early Italian fascist squads.

final solution (Ger. *Endlösung*). Nazi euphemism for the elimination by mass murder of European Jews.

Fischer controversy Debate sparked in 1960s by Fritz Fischer's *Griff nach der Weltmacht,* which argued that there were long-term continuities in German foreign policy between and during the two world wars. Fischer's thesis, re-stated more radically in his later book *Krieg der Illusionen* (War of Illusions) undermined the notion that World War I was a consequence of the mismanagement of a diplomatic crisis in 1914. Instead he argued that Germany had deliberately sought war. In such a context Hitler's aggression appears less anomalous, and World War II less convincingly attributable entirely to Nazism.

Four Year Plan Plan to co-ordinate German economic resources in preparation for war, announced in 1936 against the background of gathering economic (and potentially political) crisis. The plan, overseen by Goering, was intended to resolve conflicts of interest in the allocation of currency reserves between the demand for raw materials imports for the arms industry and food imports to meet the shortfall which German agriculture was unable to cover. The emphasis of the plan was on increased self-sufficiency, and the production of synthetic raw materials was encouraged. Wages, prices and labour mobility were made subject to stringent controls in an attempt to contain inflationary pressures. The Plan had limited success and was superseded from 1938 by the systematic plunder of the reserves of annexed territories.

Free French (*Forces Françaises Libres*). French army, navy and air force personnel led by de Gaulle in opposition to Vichy France and the Nazis.

Free Trades Unions Trades unions associated with the labour movement rather than sponsored by the Roman Catholic church or employers.

Freikorps Free Corps. Right-wing German paramilitary units active in the early years of the Weimar Republic, largely manned by ex-officers and often financed by industry. They were used to help suppress the Communist uprising by the Spartacist League (q.v.) in 1919.

Führer Leader. Title adopted by Hitler during the early years of the Nazi Party, and after the death of Hindenburg to denote the fusion of the offices of Chancellor and President.

fulfilment policy (Ger. *Erfüllungspolitik*). German foreign policy based on adherence to the Treaty of Versailles.

Functionalists See structuralists.

Gau (pl. *Gaue*) Main territorial division of NSDAP (q.v.).

Gauleiter Leader of *Gau* (q.v.), responsible directly to Hitler. The party office usually coincided with the state office of *Reichstatthalter* (Reich Governor).

GBA *Generalbevollmächtigter für den Arbeitseinsatz* (Plenipotentiary General for the Allocation of Labour).

Gdansk See Danzig.

Gefolgschaft Literally 'retinue'. A medieval term used in Nazi ideology to describe industrial workforce, which was to follow the 'factory leader'.

geheim secret (adj.).

Gemeinde Administrative division, community.

Gemeinschaftsfremde 'Community aliens'. People deemed outside the 'national racial community' of Nazi Germany by virtue of their character, behaviour or other 'defects'.

Generalbevollmächtigter Plenipotentiary general.

Generalgouvernement 'Government-General'. That part of Poland not directly incorporated into the Reich, but governed as a satellite territory by a German civilian administration in Cracow.

Generaloberst German military rank with no British or US equivalent; literally 'Colonel General'.

Gericht Court of law.

German Revolution Political upheaval of 1918–19 during which the constitutional reforms were accompanied by the more radical councils movement.

Gestapa *Geheimes Staatspolizeiamt.* (Gestapo HQ in Berlin).

Gestapo *Geheime Staatspolizei* (Secret State Police). Established by Goering in Prussia in 1933, it came increasingly under the control of Himmler in 1934. It was involved in the surveillance of political and ideological opponents and the maintenance of industrial discipline.

Glaube und Schönheit 'Faith and Beauty'. Youth organisation for 17–21-year-old girls.

Gleichschaltung 'Co-ordination'. The Nazification of German institutions and society.

Globalists Historians who emphasise the existence of a Hitler plan for world domination.

Grenzpolizei Border police.

Grepo See *Grenzpolizei.*

Grossraumwirtschaft Greater economic sphere of interest. Notion of European economic integration under German leadership.

Gruppe Literally 'group'; unit of SA or SS; department within a ministry.

Gruppenführer SS rank equivalent to Lieutenant General.

HA *Hauptamt* (Head Office).

Hakenkreuz Swastika.

Heer Army.

Heimwehr Right-wing Austrian paramilitary movement with increasingly Austrofascist tendencies in the late 1920s and 1930s. Some branches, particularly the Styrian *Heimatschutz*, were closer to the Nazis.

Herrenvolk 'Master race'.

Hirsch-Dunker Unions Employer-sponsored trades unions.

Historikerstreit Debate among German historians in the 1980s which followed attempts to relativise the Holocaust.

Hitler Jugend (HJ) Hitler Youth. Established in 1926 and still insignificant in terms of membership by 1933, it expanded during the Third Reich. Membership became compulsory in 1939. See also *BDM, Deutsches Jungvolk, Glaube und Schönheit, Jungmädelbund.*

Holocaust Term used to describe the mass murder of the Jews by the Nazis.

Hossbach memorandum Controversial minutes of meeting of Hitler, armed forces chiefs, War Minister and Foreign Minister in 1938. The 'memorandum' was used at Nuremberg as evidence of Nazi plans to wage aggressive war.

IG Farben Giant chemicals cartel involved in attempts to manufacture synthetic materials for Four Year Plan; developed Zyklon B gas.

Intentionalists Historians placing greater emphasis on Hitler's personal power and determination to implement a preconceived programme than on 'structures' of power in the Third Reich.

Iron Front Movement set up by the SPD in 1932 to defend the Weimar Republic.

Jungmädel-Bund Nazi girls' organisation for those aged between 10 and 14.

Junker Member of Prussian landowning aristocracy.

Kapp putsch Attempt by right-wing conspiracy with support of army officers to seize power in Germany (in March 1920).

Kärnten German name for Carinthia.

KdF Kraft durch Freude (Strength through Joy). Nazi leisure organisation, a division of the *DAF* (q.v.).

Kdo Kommando. (Military unit or authority, commando).

Königsberg German name for Kaliningrad, part of USSR from 1945.

KPD Kommunistische Partei Deutschlands (German Communist Party).

Kreis Administrative district.

Kripo Kriminalpolizei, (criminal police).

KZ Konzentrationslager, (concentration camp) (q.v.).

Lagebericht Situation report (compiled by *SD*, q.v., Gestapo, q.v. or other body used for surveillance).

Lager Camp.

Land (pl. *Länder*) Province, (federal) state, e.g., Bavaria.

Landbund Agrarian League. Weimar splinter party close to DNVP.

Landtag Diet, or assembly of a *Land* (q.v.); e.g., Prussia.

Lebensborn Literally 'fountain of life'. SS society founded to promote doctrines of racial purity.

Lebensraum Literally 'living space'. Term used to describe territory to be gained for German settlement in eastern Europe and Russia from Slavs and Jews.

Little Entente Originally pejorative term for alliances between Czechoslovakia, Yugoslavia and Romania in 1920 and 1921 against the possibility of Austrian or Hungarian revisionism.

Litzmannstadt German name invented during Third Reich for Polish town of Łodź.

Luftwaffe German air force.

Machtergreifung 'Seizure of power' (by the Nazis).

Madagascar Plan Plan to deport all European Jews to Madagascar and create a Jewish colony there under an SS governor.

Maquis French resistance guerilla groups.

Mein Kampf *My Struggle*. Hitler's political *magnum opus*, originally written as two separate books while Hitler was in prison and published (by Max Amann) in two volumes: *Eine Abrechnung* (*A Reckoning*, 1925) and *Die Nationalsozialistische Bewegung* (*The National Socialist Movement*, 1926). About half a million copies had been sold by the time of Hitler's appointment as Chancellor. Sales were then boosted by the semi-official status of the book, and bulk purchases by government departments and institutions. Total sales are estimated at some eight or nine million by the time of Hitler's death. *Mein Kampf* has been reprinted in English since the war, but is banned in both Germany and Austria. Hitler dictated a second book to Amann, which was published only posthumously in 1961 as *Hitlers Zweites Buch* (*Hitler's Secret Book*).

Mitbestimmung Co-determination or participatory decision making, generally used in context of economic matters.

Mittelstand Literally 'middle estate'. Lower middle class of small farmers, small businessmen and white collar workers.

Modernisation theory General explanatory model of transformation of 'traditional' societies into 'modern' ones; applied by some non-Marxist historians to Nazi Germany.

Morgenthau Plan   Plan proposed by Henry Morgenthau of the US Treasury at the Quebec Conference of 1944 to de-industrialise the defeated Nazi Germany after the end of the war. The plan was considered unrealistic by Britain and the USA.

Munich Agreement   Agreement between Britain, Germany, France and Italy to partition Czechoslovakia by forcing the cession of the Sudetenland to Germany, as Hitler had demanded. The agreement was the culmination of British Prime Minister Neville Chamberlain's Appeasement (q.v.) policy.

Munich putsch   Abortive attempt by a group of Nazis and German Nationalists, including Hitler and Ludendorff, to seize power in 1923. The authorities were sympathetic but reluctant to back the putschists without clearer evidence of support in northern Germany. All the conspirators were treated leniently, the trial was a propaganda coup for Hitler, and the putsch marked a turning point in Hitler's strategic thinking.

Nachrichtendienst   Intelligence or signals service.

Nahrungsfreiheit   'Nutritional freedom'. Nazi term for agricultural self-sufficiency.

Neue Sachlichkeit   'New Objectivity'. Weimar art movement.

New Order   Economic and political integration of Europe under German domination planned by the Nazis.

Niederdonau   Nazi name for Niederösterreich (Lower Austria).

NSBO Nationalsozialistische Betriebszellen-organisation (National Socialist Factory Cell Organisation).

NSDAP Nationalsozialistische Deutsche Arbeiterpartei (National Socialist German Workers' Party).

NS Frauenschaft   Nazi women's organisation, intended to recruit an elite cadre of Nazi women.

NSKK Nationalsozialistische KraftfahrerKorps. (Nazi motor corps).

NSV Nationalsozialistische Volkswohlfahrt. (Nazi 'welfare' organisation).

Oberabschnitt   Major regional division of SS, corresponding roughly with a *Wehrkreis* (q.v.).

Oberdonau   Nazi name for Oberösterreich (Upper Austria).

Oberstes Parteigericht   Supreme Party Court of NSDAP.

OKW *Oberkommando der Wehrmacht.* (High Command of the Armed Forces).

Operation Citadel Defensive German strategy of latter war years (after the failure of Operation Barbarossa) which aimed to create a 'Fortress Europe' whose exploitation by Germany would enable a renewed attack on the USSR following a 'breathing space'.

Orgesch *Organisation Escherisch.* Right-wing paramilitary organisation in Weimar Republic.

Osthilfe 'Eastern aid'. Economic assistance for rural German Nationalist areas east of the Elbe.

Pact of Steel Term used for military alliance between Germany and Italy concluded in 1939.

Paragraph 175 Section of Reich legal code used by Nazis for persecution of homosexuals, reinforced by the more draconian Paragraph 175a in 1935.

partisans Term used above all in the USSR and Yugoslavia to describe Communist guerillas operating behind enemy lines.

Parteikanzlei Party Chancellery.

pluralists Historians opposing 'Hitler-centric' interpretations of the Third Reich in favour of more 'polycratic' interpretations.

pogrom Attacks on Jews (originally in Tsarist Russia) such as that of November 1938.

Polish Corridor Land transferred from Germany to Poland after World War I to give the Poles access to the sea.

Polykratie 'Polyocracy'. Term used to refer to nature of government in Nazi Germany by historians who emphasise importance of institutional rivalry rather than the role of Hitler.

Preussenschlag Term used to refer to constitutional coup whereby Papen deposed elected Social Democratic government of Prussia.

Pressburg German name for Bratislava.

RAD *Reichsarbeitsdienst.* (Reich labour service).

Rat (pl. Räte) Council. Particularly the councils formed by soldiers, sailors and workers in 1918. Their opponents believed the councils were intent on a Soviet (Russian word for council) style proletarian dictatorship, but the politics of German council members were significantly more moderate.

Rat der Volksbeauftragten Council of People's Deputies. National assembly of workers' and soldiers' councils during the revolution.

Reich Empire. Used to refer to state in successive German constitutional arrangements including the Holy Roman Empire, the German Empire of 1871 ('Second Reich') and in certain contexts the Weimar Republic, as well as the 'Third Reich'.

Reichsbanner Social Democratic paramilitary formation.

Reichskrisstallnacht 'Night of Broken Glass'. Pogrom of 9 November 1938.

Reichsnährstand Reich Food Estate. Corporate organisation for German agriculture established in 1933 by the Nazis.

Reichsrat Federal Council. Upper house of Reich parliament.

Reichsstatthalter Reich governor (government official) of *Land* (q.v.) or *Gau* (q.v.), often the same person as the *Gauleiter* (q.v.).

Reichstag Parliament of German Reich established by the North German Confederation in 1867. Its powers were limited until after World War I, when the Weimar constitution made ministers accountable. It was retained by the Nazis, but was functionally without power.

Reichstreuhänder der Arbeit Reich Trustees of Labour: twelve regionally based state officials responsible for the regulation of industrial relations and accountable directly to the Ministry of Labour. Established by Law on Trustees of Labour, 1933.

Reichswehr German army. It became the *Wehrmacht* (q.v.) in 1935.

Revisionism Foreign policy which sought to 'revise' the Treaty of Versailles.

RFSS *Reichsführer SS* (*und Chef der deutschen Polizei*), Reich Leader SS (and Head of the German Police): Himmler's official title.

RKFDV *Reichskommissar für die Festigung des deutschen Volkstums* (Reich Commissar for the Strengthening of German Nationhood).

Roma Minority ethnic group which Nazis sought to 'eradicate'; with Sinti, generally known as gypsies.

RSHA *Reichssicherheitshauptamt.* Reich Security Head Office formed in 1939 with the merger of the head office of the SS and the head office of the *Gestapo* (q.v.) under Heydrich.

RUSHA *Rasse und Siedlungs-Hauptamt.* (Race and Settlement Head Office) (SS organisation).

SA *Sturmabteilung,* 'storm division'. Nazi stormtroopers' organisation: the party's paramilitary force, founded in 1921 and effectively without a role once Hitler was in power. The SA was effectively neutralised by the Night of the Long Knives in 1934.

Scharführer Minor SS rank.

Schönheit der Arbeit German Labour Front (*DAF* organisation established by the Nazis to encourage German employers to improve working conditions).

Schutzpolizei Uniformed police.

SD *Sicherheitsdienst,* Security Service of SS. Founded 1932, it became Nazi Party intelligence service.

Sinti Minority ethnic group which Nazis sought to 'eradicate'; with Roma, generally known as gypsies.

Sipo *Sicherheitspolizei,* Security Police, comprising *Gestapo* and *Kripo* (q.v.).

Sondergerichte (pl.) Special courts set up by the Nazis to deal with special crimes.

Sonderweg Term used by some historians to describe Germany's 'peculiar route' to modernity.

SOPADE German Social Democratic Party in Exile.

Spartacist League Radical left-wing political group within the *USPD* (q.v.), led by Rosa Luxemburg and Karl Liebknecht. Its members formed the basis of the German Communist Party (*KPD*), formed in December 1918.

SPD *Sozialdemokratische Partei Deutschlands* (German Social Democratic Party).

SS *Schutzstaffeln,* (literally 'guard unit'). Founded in 1925 to protect leading Nazis. Under Himmler (from 1929) it became the most powerful affiliated organisation of the *NSDAP* (q.v.), establishing control over the entire police and security systems, and forming the basis of the Nazi police state, and the major instrument of racial policy in the camps and in occupied Europe.

Stab Staff (in an organisational or military sense).

Stahlhelm Largest and most important *Freikorps* (q.v.) formation in Weimar Republic.

Stalag *Stammlager.* (A permanent POW camp).

Stalingrad, Battle of Most important battle on the eastern front during World War II, and a turning point in German military success and civilian morale.

Stapo *Staatspolizei* (state police). Prussian political police before 1933, subsumed in *Gestapo* (q.v.).

Stettin Formerly German town, now Szczecin in Poland.

Stresa Front   Term used for the agreements reached at the Stresa Conference of 1935 by Britain, France and Italy. The last common front against German rearmament and Nazi expansionism, it was undermined by the separate naval agreement between Britain and Germany the following year and Italy's invasion of Ethiopia.

Structuralists   Those espousing a 'structural' or 'functional' interpretation of the politics of Nazi Germany, placing emphasis on the polycratic nature of the regime, as opposed to 'intentionalists', who emphasise the role of Hitler.

Sturm   *SA* or *SS* (q.v.) unit equivalent to a company.

successor states   States formed from the territory of the defeated Habsburg Empire after World War I.

Sudetenland   Formerly Austrian German-speaking territories in Bohemia which were incorporated into Czechoslovakia after World War I. The Nazis financed a Sudeten German Party from 1935, which agitated for secession from Czechoslovakia, providing popular support for Hitler's irredentist claim on the region. It was transferred to Germany in 1938 by the *Munich Agreement* (q.v.), considerably weakening Czechoslovakia's border defences and industrial strength.

Terezín   Czech name for Theresienstadt.

Third Reich   Term for the Nazi dictatorship. The Hitler Regime was portrayed as the successor to the mediaeval empire and the German Empire founded in 1871. The term was popularised on the German right by Moeller van den Bruck's book of the same name, published in 1923, and was quickly appropriated by the Nazis.

Tripartite Pact   Military agreement between Germany, Japan and Italy, signed in Berlin in 1940 for ten years.

U-Boat   *Unterseeboot* (submarine).

USCHLA   *Untersuchungs- und Schlichtungs-Auschuss.* Investigation and Arbitration Committee (of NSDAP).

USPD   *Unabhängige Sozialdemokratische Partei Deutschlands* (Independent Social Democratic Party of Germany). Radical splinter group from the *SPD* (q.v.) after 1917 (the latter was referred to as the Majority SPD or MSPD). It split in October 1920 when the majority of its members joined the *KPD* (q.v.). The rest returned to the *SPD* in 1922.

Vaterlandspartei   Right-wing party formed in 1917 to oppose *Reichstag* (q.v.) peace initiative. It disbanded in December 1918.

Vergangenheitsbewältigung   'Mastering the past'. A term used to denote post-war Germany's attempts to come to terms with the Nazi past by overcoming it.

Vichy France   Authoritarian German puppet state in unoccupied France. It was occupied directly by the Germans following the Allied landings in North Africa in 1942.

V-Mann   *Vertrauensmann.* (Informer or intelligence agent).

Volk   Literally 'people', a term which also contains the meaning of nation or race.

völkisch (adj.)   Designation containing the meaning of nationalist where nationalism is racist.

Völkischer Beobachter   Nazi newspaper.

Volksgemeinschaft   'National community'. Nazi notion of a harmonious society which transcended class conflict and was founded on racial exclusivity.

Volksgenossen   'National comrades'. Term used to describe members of the *Volksgemeinschaft.*

Volksgericht   'People's Court', set up after the Reichstag fire to deal with treason.

Volkssturm   Militia of all able-bodied German males between the ages of 16 and 60, formed in September 1944 and deployed, without training or adequate arms, against the invading Allied armies.

Volkstum   Term denoting ethnicity or national cultural identity.

V-Weapons   *Vergeltungswaffen* (revenge weapons). The V1 was an unmanned aircraft carrying an explosive warhead, and was used against Britain after, and ostensibly as revenge for, the '*D-Day*' landings in 1944 (q.v.). The V2 was a rocket, which was used against Britain and France from September.

Waffen-SS   Term introduced in 1940 to designate militarised units of SS.

Wehrkreis   'Defence district'.

Wehrmacht   Armed forces. The term refers to army, navy and air force.

Wehrwirtschaft Defence economy: term used to refer to mobilisation of nation's resources for war during peace-time.

Wilhelmstrasse   Site of German Foreign Office in Berlin.

WVHA   *Wirtschafts- und Verwaltungshauptamt.* (Head Economic and Administrative Office) (of SS).

ZAG *Zentralarbeitsgemeinschaft* (Central Working Association). Formal forum for negotiation of agreements between employers and workers in German industry during Weimar Republic. Agreements negotiated in November 1918, and subsequent legislation, introduced modern liberal industrial relations system into German industry.

Z Plan Shipbuilding programme of 1939 giving battleship construction top military and economic priority.

SECTION VII
Biographies

Abetz, Otto (1903–58): Diplomat and Nazi politician. Born in Schwetzingen and educated in Karlsruhe, Abetz was a Nazi supporter from the early 1930s, joined the diplomatic service in 1935, and specialised in French affairs under Ribbentrop before the war. Deported from Paris in 1939 he returned after the invasion in 1940 and in November of that year became ambassador to the Vichy puppet regime. He was sentenced to twenty years' imprisonment by a French military tribunal in 1949, but served only five years and was killed in a motor accident in Germany.

Albers, Hans (1892–1960): Film star. Born in Hamburg, Albers became involved with circus and variety theatre before serving in World War I. After the war he established a successful career in the Berlin theatre, and was one of the first actors to appear in sound films. He was one of the most popular film actors of the 1930s and 1940s. Often cast in the role of heroic patriot, he also appeared in lighter films such as *Die Abenteuer des Barons Münchhausen*. Albers' film career continued after World War II.

Amann, Max (1891–1957): Nazi politician and press baron. Born and educated in Munich, Amann took over the business management of the NSDAP in 1921, and its publishing house (Eher) in 1922. He was elected to Munich city council in 1924, and to the Reichstag in 1933. He was appointed President of the Reich Press Chamber the same year, and used this position to establish party control of the press. Amann oversaw Hitler's personal finances, ensuring that he benefited from the royalties of *Mein Kampf* and from his journalism. He also made immense personal profits from his publishing interests. At Nuremberg he claimed to be a businessman without political motivation, lost all his property and was sentenced to two-and-a-half years' imprisonment.

Axmann, Artur (b.1913): Reich Youth Leader. Born in Hagen, Axmann studied law and founded a Nazi youth group in Westphalia in 1928. He succeeded Baldur von Schirach (q.v.) as Reich Youth Leader in 1940. He escaped arrest at the end of the war and organised a Nazi underground movement, but was captured in December 1945 and sentenced in 1949 to three years and three months' imprisonment.

Bach-Zelewski, Erich (1892–1972): SS general. Born in Lauenberg, Pomerania, Bach-Zelewski served in World War I and in a *Freikorps* unit before joining the Nazi Party in 1930. He represented Breslau in the Reichstag from 1932. Promoted to SS General in 1939, he was responsible for large-scale atrocities in Estonia and Belorussia. From 1943 he was responsible for anti-partisan operations in the occupied Soviet Union and was decorated for his part in the suppression of the Warsaw rising of 1944. He subsequently testified against Himmler and other senior SS officers at Nuremberg, and was sentenced to ten years' house arrest in 1951. He was never tried for the massacre of Jews in the East, but was sentenced in 1961 for his part in the Night of the Long Knives, and in 1962 (for life) for the murder of German Communists in 1933. He died in prison.

Backe, Herbert (1896–1947): Nazi Minister of Food and Agriculture. Born and educated in Russia, Backe studied at Göttingen University and went on to teach at the Technical University in Hanover. He joined the NSDAP after becoming a farmer and was a Nazi member of the Prussian *Landtag* in 1932 and 1933. Appointed Reich Food Commissioner for the Four Year Plan in 1936, he succeeded Darré (q.v.) as Food and Agriculture Minister and Reich Farmers' Leader in 1942. He committed suicide in prison at Nuremberg.

Baeck, Leo (1873–1956): Jewish leader. Born in Lissa, Prussia, Baeck trained as a rabbi in Berlin and established a reputation as a rabbinical scholar before World War I. He was elected President of the Union of German Rabbis in 1922 and Chairman of the central Jewish Welfare Organisation in 1926. He was chairman of the leading Jewish organisations in Nazi Germany until he was sent to Theresienstadt in 1943. Baeck survived to preside over the World Union for Progressive Judaism after the war, and to found the Leo Baeck Institute. He died in London.

Barth, Karl (1886–1968): Protestant pastor and theologian. Born in Basel, Switzerland, Barth established his reputation in 1919 with an attack on liberal Protestant theology. He held chairs in Göttingen, Münster and Bonn during the Weimar Republic. In 1933 he took issue with Hitler's Protestant supporters, the German Christians, was dismissed from his post at Bonn in 1935 and returned to Switzerland.

Beck, Ludwig (1880–1944): German general. Born in Biebrich, Beck served in Alsace-Lorraine before 1914 and in World War I. He was promoted through the ranks of the *Reichswehr* during the Weimar Republic, and was Head of General Staff of the German Army between 1935 and 1938. Beck sought to win a role in political decision-making for military leaders. He resigned in August 1938 in opposition to Hitler's planned invasion of Czechoslovakia, believing Germany to be militarily unprepared for the general war he thought would inevitably follow. He was succeeded by General Halder (q.v.). Beck continued to be associated with oppositional circles in the armed forces, including the bomb plot of July 1944, and committed suicide when the assassination attempt failed.

Beckmann, Max (1884–1950): Graphic artist. Born in Leipzig, Beckmann studied in Weimar and was a member of the Berlin and Dresden Secessions. He moved to Frankfurt am Main in 1915 and taught at the art school there during the Weimar Republic. He was associated with the *Neue Sachlichkeit* movement in the 1920s. He moved to Paris and then Amsterdam in 1933 and died in New York. His works include: *Die Nacht* (1919), *Gesichter* (1919), and *Die Enttäuschten* (1922).

Behrens, Peter (1868–1940): Industrial architect and designer. Born and educated in Hamburg, Behrens also studied in Karlsruhe, Düsseldorf and Munich. As architect to AEG he designed a turbine factory in Berlin (1909) and the IG Farben office in Höchst (1920). He subsequently taught at the Vienna Academy (1922–36) and at the Berlin Academy under the Nazis.

Benn, Gottfried (1886–1956): Poet. Born in Mansfeld, Benn studied theology and philosophy at Marburg and then medicine at Berlin. His first collection of poems, *Morgue*, was published in 1912. A military doctor in World War I, he went on to practise in Berlin in the 1920s. Benn was on the political right and initially supported Nazism, but was condemned as degenerate himself in 1933 and expelled from the Nazi writers' organisation in 1937. He renounced his sympathy with the Nazis and received the Georg Büchner Prize in 1951. He died in Berlin.

Berg, Alban (1885–1935): Austrian composer. Born in Vienna, Berg studied with Schoenberg (q.v.) and became one of the leading composers to use twelve-tone music. His opera *Wozzeck* was staged by the Berlin State Opera in 1925. His next opera, *Lulu*, was unfinished and remained unperformed until 1979.

Best, Werner (b.1903): Reich Commissioner for occupied Denmark. Born in Darmstadt, Best was brought up and educated in Dortmund and Mainz. He was implicated with plans for a coup with the discovery of the Boxheim Documents in 1931 and forced to resign from his position in the Hesse Justice Ministry. He was appointed Police Commissioner in Hesse when the Nazis came to power and later became Governor. Best was promoted rapidly during the 1930s and worked closely with Heydrich in building up the Gestapo and SD in the RSHA in Berlin. He was Chief of the Civil Administration and head of the SD in occupied France until 1942, when he became Reich Plenipotentiary for occupied Denmark. He was imprisoned after the war, first in Denmark, and then in Germany.

Blaskowitz, Johannes (1883–1948): Born in Peterswalde, Blaskowitz served in World War I and later took part in the invasions of Austria, Czechoslovakia and Poland. He became military governor in Warsaw in 1939. As Commander-in-Chief in the East he complained to his superior, von Brauchitsch (q.v.), about German atrocities and was transferred to the western front. He subsequently served on several fronts without again resorting to criticism of excesses, and surrendered to the British in the Netherlands in 1945. He committed suicide while awaiting trial in Nuremberg.

Blomberg, Werner von (1878–1946): Minister of War, 1935–38. Born in Stargard, Pomerania, Blomberg became head of the *Reichswehr* troop office in 1927 and head of Defence District I (East Prussia) in 1929. He was appointed Minister of Defence in January 1933 and promoted to Infantry General. He became War Minister and Commander-in-Chief of the Wehrmacht in 1935, and was further promoted to Field Marshal in 1936. Blomberg was an important member of the conservative faction in Hitler's government until 1938. His downfall was prepared by Himmler and Goering shortly after his marriage to Eva Gruhn, a former prostitute, in January of that year. The Berlin Police prepared a dossier on his wife's past, and he was dismissed and ordered to spend a year abroad. His departure, accompanied by those of Fritsch (q.v.) and Neurath (q.v.), constituted something of a purge of leading conservatives. The War Ministry was abolished and replaced by the OKW under Keitel. Hitler himself became Supreme Commander of the *Wehrmacht*.

Blunck, Hans Friedrich (1888–1961): Nazi functionary. Born in Altona, Blunck studied at Kiel and Heidelberg, and published folk tales and historical novels in the 1920s. He was a firm supporter of the Nazis and was appointed President of the Reich Chamber of Literature in 1934.

Bonhoeffer, Dietrich (1906–45): Protestant pastor and theologian. Bonhoeffer studied theology at Tübingen and Berlin and worked as a pastor in Barcelona and London. In 1934 he signed the founding 'Barmen declaration' of the confessing church ('*bekennende Kirche*'), a conscientious reaction to the Nazification of the Protestant church in Germany. At the beginning of World War II he became involved with conspirators in the military resistance to Hitler, and went to Stockholm in 1942 to attempt to mediate with the Allies on their behalf. He was arrested in 1943 and subsequently imprisoned in a concentration camp, where he was murdered by the Gestapo shortly before the camp was liberated.

Bormann, Martin (b: 1900): Hitler's private secretary and Head of the Party Chancellery. Bormann was born in Halberstedt, served in World War I and then joined a *Freikorps* unit and got involved in politics. He joined the NSDAP in 1925 and was attached to the Supreme Command of the SA between 1928 and 1930. He became Chief of Staff and Secretary to Rudolf Hess (q.v.) in 1933. His personal power within the Nazi political system increased after the flight of Hitler's deputy to Scotland in 1941, when he was appointed Head of the Party Chancellery with ministerial rank. From 1943, when he became Hitler's secretary, he was the pivotal figure in both party and state and used Hitler's increasing isolation to his political advantage, ultimately undermining the influence of Hitler's closest associates, including Himmler and Goering. Bormann was a radical Nazi himself and his increasing influence reflected the accelerating radicalisation of the regime. He disappeared in 1945, and reports of his death have never been unequivocally confirmed. He was sentenced to death in his absence at Nuremberg the following year, and pronounced dead by the West German authorities in 1973.

Born, Max (1882–1970): German physicist. Born in Breslau, Born was Professor of Physics at Göttingen from 1921. Dismissed by the Nazis in 1933 on account of his Jewish ancestry, he moved to Cambridge and then in 1936 to a Chair at Edinburgh. He continued his work on quantum physics and was awarded the Nobel Prize for physics in 1954. He retired to Bad Pyrmont, near Göttingen, where he died.

Bosch, Carl (1874–1940): German chemist. Born in Cologne and educated at Leipzig, Bosch joined BASF in 1898 and worked on the practical application of Fritz Haber's process for the synthesis of ammonia. He was an expert witness at the Versailles negotiations after World War I. He became Chairman of the managing board at IG Farben (successor to BASF) in 1925 and was Chairman of its supervisory board until his death. Bosch was awarded the Nobel Prize for chemistry in 1931 (with Friedrich Bergius).

Bouhler, Philipp (1899–1945): Head of the Nazi Euthanasia programme. Born in Munich, Bouhler served in World War I before studying philosophy at Munich. He left without completing his studies to work on the *Völkischer Beobachter*. He was the paper's business manager from 1925 to 1934, when he became Police President of Munich. In 1934 he also became head of the Führer Chancellery, which Hitler set up by decree after taking over the office of Reich President ('Bouhler Bureau'). It was this office which organised the Euthanasia programme in 1939. The programme was halted in 1941. Bouhler committed suicide in Zell-am-See in 1945.

Brack, Viktor (1904–48): SS officer. Brack was born in Haaren and studied economics at Munich. He was appointed to the Health Department in 1936 by Philipp Bouhler (q.v.) and became the latter's deputy in the Führer Chancellery. Brack's office (T4) was directly responsible for the Euthanasia programme of 1939–41, and Brack himself subsequently assisted in the construction of death camps in Poland. He was tried by an American military court and hanged at Landsberg prison.

Brauchitsch, General Walter von (1881–1948): Commander-in-Chief of the Germany Army, 1938–41. Born into a military family in Berlin, von Brauchitsch was a professional soldier, and was awarded the Iron Cross in World War I. He was promoted to General in 1938 when he succeeded Werner von Fritsch as Commander-in-Chief of the *Wehrmacht,* and to General Field Marshal in 1940 after the successful campaigns in Poland and the West. He was retired on health grounds in 1941, when Hitler himself became Commander-in-Chief. Von Brauchitsch was compliant in his relations with Hitler, and opposed none of his military plans. He died of a heart attack in Hamburg before he could be tried by a British military court.

Braun, Eva (1912–45): Hitler's mistress. Eva Braun was born in Munich and met Hitler in 1929, and moved into his flat after the death of his niece. She moved to Berchtesgaden in 1936. The exact nature of Hitler's relationship with her is unknown, but the two were married on 29 April 1945, the day before they both committed suicide.

Braun, Otto (1872–1955): Leading Social Democrat in Weimar Germany. Elected to the party leadership in 1911 he was a member of the National Assembly in 1919 and a member of the Reichstag from 1920 to 1933. From 1921 to 1933 he was also a member of the Prussian *Landtag,* and served as Prussian Minister President from 1920 until the *Preussenstreich* of 1932 (apart from brief periods in 1921 and 1925). He was also Prussian Agriculture Minister from 1918 to 1921. He emigrated to Switzerland when the Nazis came to power.

Braun, Werner von (1912–77): German rocket engineer. Braun was born in Wirsitz, Prussia, and studied at the Charlottenburg Institute of Technology in Berlin. He was appointed Technical Director at the rockets research base at Peenemünde in 1937, and worked there on the V2 rocket, a prototype of which was developed in 1938. Braun gave himself up to the Americans in 1945 and continued his research in the USA where he contributed to the American space flight programme.

Brecht, Bertolt (1898–1956): Marxist playwright and theatre director. Brecht was born in Augsburg, studied medicine at Munich and served as a medical orderly in World War I. He worked at the Munich Kammerspiele from 1921 and at the Deutsches Theater in Berlin from 1924, and worked with Erwin Piscator and Kurt Weill. He married Helen Weigel in 1928 and founded the Berliner Ensemble with her. He fled to Switzerland in 1933, and then to the United States via Scandinavia and the USSR. He was called before the House Committee on Un-American Activities in 1947 and soon afterwards left the USA. He returned to Germany in 1949 to found the 'Berliner Ensemble' in East Berlin. His early work reflected expressionist and anarchist influences (*Baal*, 1918) but he later became committed to Marxism and was the chief exponent of documentary theatre. His best known work is the 'Threepenny Opera' (*Die Dreigroschenoper* 1928); others include *Das Leben des Galilei* (1938–39), *Mutter Courage und ihre Kinder* (1939) and several propagandistic 'didactic' plays (*Lehrstücke*).

Breitscheid, Rudolf (1874–1944): Weimar politician. Born in Cologne, Breitscheid joined the SPD in 1912, and left with the USPD in 1917. He served as Prussian Interior Minister (1918–19) and was elected to the Reichstag in 1920 and joined Germany's League of Nations delegation in 1926. He fled to Switzerland in 1933, and later to France, where the Vichy government deported him to Germany. He was murdered in Buchenwald.

Brockdorf-Rantzau, Ulrich Graf von (1869–1928): German diplomat and Weimar politician. Born in Schleswig, he entered the diplomatic service in 1894 and was ambassador to Denmark during World War I. He led the German delegation at Versailles, and was Foreign Minister (non-party) from February to June 1919. He was ambassador to the USSR from 1922 to 1928, and died in Berlin.

Brüning, Heinrich (1885–1970): Weimar Chancellor. Born in Münster, Brüning studied at Bonn and worked as a functionary in the Christian trades union movement from 1920 to 1930. He was elected to the Reichstag for the Centre Party in 1924 and to the Prussian *Landtag* in 1928. As Chancellor from 1930 to 1932 he was responsible for the introduction of rule by presidential decree, and his own memoirs reveal him to have been fundamentally anti-democratic and authoritarian. His deflationary economic policies, intended not least to demonstrate Germany's inability to pay reparations, fuelled the rise in unemployment which did much to undermine popular support for his government. He emigrated to Britain in 1934 and from there to the United States where he pursued an academic career at Harvard University.

Buch, Walter (1883–1949): President of Nazi Supreme Court. Born in Bruchsal, Buch was a professional soldier who served in World War I. He joined the Nazi Party in 1922 and in 1927 became Chairman of the party tribunal USCHLA (Investigation and Arbitration Board), which carried out surveillance of party personnel and organisations. He was involved in the executions following the Night of the Long Knives, and as President of the Party Supreme Court acquitted those involved in the 1938 pogrom. He committed suicide after his second de-Nazification trial.

Bürckel, Josef (1894–1944): Nazi politician and Reich Commissioner for the Re-Unification of Austria with the German Reich. Born in Lingfeld, Bürckel was a teacher before he became *Gauleiter* of the Rhineland Palatinate in 1926. He was elected to the Reichstag in 1930. After the plebiscite in the Saarland he was appointed Reich Commissioner there, and remained until his appointment as *Gauleiter* of Vienna and Reich Commissioner for Austria in 1938. He later returned to the Saarland, and committed suicide in 1944.

Canaris, Wilhelm (1887–1945): German admiral. Born in Aplerbeck, Canaris joined the navy in 1905, commanded submarines in World War I, and became involved in counter-revolutionary politics (including the Kapp putsch) during the Weimar Republic. He was appointed head of the counter-intelligence service in 1935 and remained there until 1944, reconciling close co-operation with the security service with a sympathy for military and conservative resistance circles. He was dismissed in February 1945 and became more closely involved in the July bomb plot, and was executed for treason in April 1945.

Curtius, Julius (1877–1948): Weimar politician. Born in Duisburg, Curtius served in World War I and was elected to the Reichstag for the DVP in 1920. He served as Economics Minister (1926–29) and Foreign Minister (1929–30), resigning after opposition to the Austro-German customs union project. He died in Heidelberg.

Dagover, Lil (1897–1980): German film star, born in Java. She appeared in *The Cabinet of Doctor Caligari*, and worked in German cinema throughout the Weimar Republic, the Nazi dictatorship and the war. Her career continued until the late 1970s and she died in Munich.

D'Alquen, Gunter (b.1910): SS officer. Born in Essen. He joined the Hitler Youth in 1925 and the SS in 1931. He was appointed editor of the anti-semitic SS paper *Das Schwarze Korps* in 1935. After the war he was fined by de-Nazification courts in 1955 and 1958.

Daluege, Kurt (1897–1946) SS officer. Born in Kreuzburg, Upper Silesia, he served in World War I and studied at the Technical High School in Berlin. He joined a *Freikorps* unit, and then the Nazi Party (1922), becoming leader of the Berlin SA in 1928, before moving to the SS. Daluege became a powerful figure in the SS and was Deputy Protector of Bohemia and Moravia (q.v.) after the death of Heydrich. He was executed by the Czechs in 1946.

Darlan, François (1881–1942); French politician. Naval Chief of Staff from 1936 and Commander-in-Chief from 1939, Darlan became Navy Minister in the Pétain (q.v.) government of Vichy France after the German invasion. He was appointed Deputy Prime Minister in 1942 but was subsequently eclipsed by Pierre Laval (q.v.). He decided to collaborate with the Allies after the invasion of Algeria in 1942, but was assassinated the same year.

Darré, Richard-Walther (1895–1953): Nazi politician. Born in Buenos Aires, Darré attended school in Germany and England, and served in World War I. After the war he joined first a *Freikorps* unit and then the NSDAP, and was appointed Reich Farmers' Leader and Minister for Food and Agriculture in 1933. A proponent of 'blood and soil' ideology, he published a number of racist works on the land and the peasantry. His inefficiency led to his marginalisation and removal from office during the war. He was tried and sentenced to five years' imprisonment by the Americans after the war, and died in Munich after his release.

de Gaulle, Charles (1890–1970): Leader of the Free French. Born in Lille, de Gaulle was a professional soldier who served in World War I. In 1940 he escaped to England, where he became leader of the opposition to the Germans and the Pétain (q.v.) regime. He became head of the French Committee of National Liberation in 1943. After the war he was elected President, but resigned in 1946. In 1958 he returned to power in the terminal political crisis of the Fourth Republic and promulgated a new constitution, establishing the Fifth Republic. He remained in office until 1969.

Delp, Alfred (1907–45): German priest. Delp was a member of the Kreisau circle, and opposed the Nazis on religious grounds. He was arrested after the July bomb plot in 1944 and hanged the following year.

Diels, Otto (1900–57): First head of the Gestapo. Diels was born in Berghaus and studied law at Marburg after serving in World War I. He became a civil servant in the Prussian Interior Ministry in 1930 under Severing, and was charged with undertaking police measures against political extremists. After the Nazi takeover of power he became head of section IA of the Prussian State Police and was active in the purge of republican public servants. He was dismissed amid the power struggle between Himmler and Goering for control of the police. He held other minor posts, and continued a career in local and national administration in the early years of the Federal Republic. He accidentally shot himself in 1957.

Dietrich, Marlene (1901?–92): German film actress. Born Maria Magdalene von Losch, Marlene Dietrich studied with Max Reinhardt and pursued a career in the German theatre in the 1920s. She established her reputation with Josef von Sternberg's *The Blue Angel* in 1930. She then moved to America where she made a number of films into the 1960s. During the war she made propaganda films in German.

Dietrich, Otto (1897–1952) Reich press chief. Born in Essen, Dietrich served in World War I and was awarded the Iron Cross. He studied political science after the war and went into journalism. He was appointed Reich Press Chief in 1931, organised the propaganda campaigns for the 1932 elections, and mediated between the party and business circles. He was State Secretary in the Propaganda Ministry from 1937 to 1945. In April 1949 he was sentenced to seven years' imprisonment, but was released the following year.

Dietrich, Sepp (1892–1966): SS officer. Born in Hawangen, Dietrich joined the NSDAP early and took part in the Munich putsch. He was elected to the Reichstag in 1930 and promoted to SS General after 1934 for his part in the Night of the Long Knives. Dietrich pursued a successful military career on several fronts during World War II. He had been responsible for atrocities in the Soviet Union and the execution of American prisoners of war, and was tried and sentenced for life for the latter. Released in 1955 he was imprisoned again in 1956 after a trial for the murder of Röhm (q.v.) and others. He was finally released in 1959.

Dimitrov, Georgi (1882–1949): Bulgarian Communist. Born in Pernik, he was one of the founder members of the Bulgarian Communist Party in 1919, but fled to the USSR in 1923. He was arrested and tried by the Nazis in 1933 for complicity in the Reichstag fire, but conducted a defence which put Goering firmly on the defensive and led to his acquittal. Subsequently an architect of the Comintern's 'popular front' strategy (1934), he went on to become the first Prime Minister of Bulgaria after the war. He died in Moscow.

Dix, Otto (1891–1969): German artist. After art school in Dresden (1910–14) Dix served in World War I, an experience which radically affected his work. In the early 1920s he produced works depicting the victims of war and capitalism, including *War*

Cripples (etching and painting exhibited at the Berlin Dada fair, 1920) and *Two Victims of Capitalism* (drawing, 1923). He was a leading figure in the *Neue Sachlichkeit* movement. In 1927 he was appointed Professor at the Dresden Academy. He was dismissed by the Nazis in 1933 and his work was banned in 1934. He remained in Germany during the Nazi dictatorship and the war, living in obscurity near Lake Constance.

Djilas, Milovan (b.1911): Yugoslavian communist. Djilas was born in Montenegro and joined the Communist Party while a student. He was a partisan leader and close friend of Tito during World War II, and held office after the war. He was dismissed in 1955 and imprisoned as a dissident from 1956 to 1961 and from 1962 to 1966.

Döblin, Alfred (1878–1957): Modernist writer. A doctor by profession, Döblin was a member of the USPD until 1920, and of the SPD from 1921 until 1930. He emigrated to France in 1933, went on to the USA in 1940, and returned to Germany after the war. His best known work is the novel *Berlin Alexanderplatz* (1929).

Doenitz, Karl (1891–1980): German admiral and Chancellor, May 1945. The son of a civil servant, Doenitz joined the navy in 1910 and served in World War I, where he was responsible for submarines. He became a rear admiral in 1935 and was given responsibility for the development and deployment of the German submarine fleet. In 1943 he succeeded Admiral Raeder as Commander-in-Chief of the German navy, and was appointed to succeed Hitler shortly before the end of World War II. As German Chancellor he surrendered unconditionally to the Allies in May 1945. He was tried at Nuremberg and sentenced to ten years' imprisonment.

Dollfuss, Engelbert (1892–1934): Austrian dictator, 1932–34. A conservative politician from a farming background, Dollfuss became Chancellor and leader of the Christian Social Party in 1932 after serving as Agriculture Minister. He suspended parliament in 1933, and ordered the brutal suppression of a Socialist uprising in 1934. He was assassinated by disaffected Austrian Nazis in July 1934.

Dorpmüller, Julius (1869–1945): Nazi Transport Minister. Born in Elberfeld, Dorpmüller pursued a career in the Prussian railway service and became Director General of the German State Railways in 1926. He collaborated closely with the Nazis before his appointment as Transport Minister. He died at home in Schleswig-Holstein shortly after the end of the war.

Drexler, Anton (1884–1942): German nationalist politician. Born in Munich, Drexler was one of the founders of the *Deutsche Arbeiterpartei*, forerunner of the NSDAP. Although he remained a party member until his death, he was rarely involved actively in Nazi politics after 1921.

Duesterberg, Theodor (1875–1950): German nationalist politician. Born in Darmstadt, Duesterberg served in World War I, before founding the *Stahlhelm* (with Franz Seldte, q.v.), the largest paramilitary organisation in Weimar Germany. An important figure in the Harzburg Front, Duesterberg nevertheless turned down an offer of a post in the Hitler cabinet of 1933, was briefly arrested after the Röhm (q.v.) purge of the following year, but survived the Nazi dictatorship.

Duisberg, Carl (1861–1935): German chemist. Duisberg was born in Leverkusen, and joined Bayer in 1884, where he undertook research. He became Director General of Bayer in 1912, and was Chairman of the supervisory board of IG Farben from 1925.

Ebert, Friedrich (1871–1925): Leading Social Democrat and first President of the Weimar Republic (1919–25). He pursued a career in left-wing journalism and local politics in Bremen before World War I and was elected to the Reichstag in 1912 and President of the SPD in 1913. On the right of the party he led the 'Majority Socialists' after the 1917 party split, and was instrumental in the marginalisation and suppression of the left in the early years of the Weimar Republic. He became Chancellor following the resignation of Prince Max von Baden in 1918, and President of the Council of People's Deputies in the same year. He was elected President by the National Assembly in 1919.

Eckart, Dietrich (1868–1923): Bavarian journalist and writer. Eckart was a close companion of the young Hitler and the first editor of the *Völkischer Beobachter*. He died of a heart attack shortly after release from imprisonment for participation in the Munich putsch.

Eichmann, Adolf (1906–62): SS officer responsible for the implementation of the 'final solution'. Eichmann was born in Solingen but grew up in Linz, Austria, and was educated in Thuringia. He joined the Austrian Nazi Party in 1932 and moved to Berlin after its prohibition the following year. In 1934 he joined the SD and in 1935 became head of the 'Office for Jewish Emigration'. During 1938 and 1939 Eichmann was charged with the expulsion of Jews from Austria and Bohemia. Following the Wannsee Conference of 1942 he was then charged with the implementation of the 'final solution'. In 1944 he supervised the deportation of Hungarian Jews. Although he was captured at the end of World War II, he escaped and fled to Argentina, where he lived in obscurity until he was kidnapped by Israeli agents. He was tried in Israel in 1962 for crimes against humanity, found guilty and executed.

Eicke, Theodor (1892–1943): SS officer. An anti-republican political activist who had been convicted of bomb attacks in 1932 and ordered to a psychiatric clinic by Bürckel (q.v.) in 1933, he was reinstated to the SS and appointed Commandant of Dachau by Himmler in 1933. In 1934 he became Inspector of Concentration Camps and SS Death's Head formations. He executed Röhm (q.v.) in 1934. From 1939 he led Death's Head formations in Poland, and was promoted to General in the *Waffen SS* in 1943. He was killed the same year.

Einstein, Albert (1879–1955): German physicist. Born in Ulm, Einstein studied in Zürich and became a Swiss citizen in 1901. He published his *General Theory of Relativity* in 1916. He won the Nobel Prize for physics in 1921. He was subjected to anti-semitic attacks by the Nazis, who also refused to accept his work, and he fled to the USA in 1933, where he participated in the development of atomic weapons.

Epp, Franz Xaver Ritter von (1868–1947): Right-wing Bavarian general. He was decorated during World War I and returned to his native Munich to found a *Freikorps* unit which was responsible for the murder of a number of Socialists there in 1919. The Epp unit was also deployed against Communists in the Ruhr. He was actively involved in right-wing politics in the early 1920s. He was Nazi Governor of Bavaria from 1933 to 1945. He died in American detention in 1947.

Ernst, Max (1891–1976): German painter. Ernst served in World War I and led the Cologne branch of the Dada movement in 1919. He moved to Paris in 1922 where he did most of his best-known work. He joined the Surrealists in 1924 and pioneered *frottage*, the technique of applying brass rubbing to rough natural surfaces. He was imprisoned by the Nazis after the fall of France, and went to America in 1941. He returned to France in 1949.

Erzberger, Matthias (1875–1921): Weimar politician. A Roman Catholic journalist by profession, he was elected to the Reichstag for the Centre Party in 1903, entered Prince Max von Baden's government in 1918, and led the German delegation to Compiègne where he signed the armistice agreement on behalf of Germany. As Finance Minister from 1919 to 1921 he instituted major financial reforms. He was assassinated by radical right-wing paramilitaries in 1921.

Esser, Hermann (1900–81): Co-founder of the Nazi Party. Esser co-founded the DAP with Drexler (q.v.) in 1919 and became the editor of the *Völkischer Beobachter* in 1920. Esser quarrelled with several other leading party members, including the Strasser brothers, Goebbels, Julius Streicher and Adolf Wagner (q.v.). He was elected to the Reichstag in 1933 and was briefly Bavarian Economics Minister (1933–35). During the war he held obscure or honorary posts. In 1947 the US authorities released him from detention, but he was imprisoned by a German de-Nazification court in 1950.

Falkenhausen, Alexander Freiherr von (1878–1966): Military Governor of occupied Belgium and France, 1940–44. A Prussian career soldier, Falkenhausen was decorated in World War I and served in World War II after being recalled from China by Hitler. As Governor of Belgium he had hostages executed and Jews expropriated and deported. He was imprisoned on suspicion of complicity in the July plot, and remained in Dachau until the end of the war. He was sentenced to twelve years' imprisonment by the Belgian authorities in 1951, but was released after three weeks.

Falkenhorst, Nikolaus von (1885–1968): Commander of German forces in Norway. A career soldier who served in World War I, and *Freikorps* member during the early years of the Weimar Republic, he was later attached to the War Ministry and the German embassies in Prague, Belgrade and Bucharest. He took part in the Polish campaign, and was appointed Commander of German troops in Norway in 1940. He was dismissed after coming into conflict with Terboven (q.v.). Initially sentenced to death after the war by a British tribunal, he eventually served six years of a twenty-year sentence.

Fallada, Hans (1893–1947): German novelist. Fallada was born in Greifswald and established his reputation with popular novels about the Depression, above all *Kleiner Mann – was nun?* (What Now, Little Man?), published in 1931. He remained in Germany after 1933 and died in Berlin after the war.

Faulhaber, Cardinal Michael von (1869–1952): Archbishop of Munich. Successively Professor of Theology at Strasbourg (1903), Bishop of Speyer (1911), Archbishop of Munich (1917), and Cardinal (1921), Faulhaber was an anti-republican Bavarian legitimist who defended the church against Nazi incursions after 1933 and preached against ideological 'neo-paganism'. His criticism of the regime and its racial policies was intermittent, partial and indirect and his attitude was also characterised by partial approval. Faulhaber was not involved in the July plot, which he denounced.

Feder, Gottfried (1883–1941): Influential figure in the early NSDAP. Born in Würzburg, Feder became involved in right-wing Bavarian politics after World War I, propounding anti-capitalist policies which were later rejected by the party leadership in the more pragmatic electioneering of the Depression. Feder was given a minor position in the Economics Ministry in 1933, but was dismissed in 1934 after provoking powerful opposition to his rural settlements policy. He took no further part in politics.

Fehrenbach, Konstantin (1852–1926): Weimar Chancellor. Born in Wellendingen, Fehrenbach was a lawyer by profession. He was a Centre Party member of the Bavarian *Landtag* from 1901 to 1913 and was elected to the Reichstag in 1903. He served as Chancellor from June 1920 until May 1921. He died in Freiburg.

Flick, Friedrich (1883–1956): German industrialist. A leading Ruhr businessman, Flick made donations to the Nazis (among other political parties) in 1932 and 1933, and to the SS on an annual basis. He joined the party in 1937. Flick's concerns were major employers of slave labourers during the war, the majority of whom died. Flick was sentenced to seven years' imprisonment in 1947, but released in 1951. Some assets were confiscated, but the Flick business was rebuilt after the war. Flick consistently refused to pay compensation for the exploitation of slave labour.

Forster, Albert (1902–54): Born in Fürth, Forster was elected as a Nazi to the Reichstag for Franconia in 1930 and became *Gauleiter* of Danzig the same year. The Poles sentenced him to death (commuted to life imprisonment) for war-time atrocities.

Franck, James (1882–1964): German physicist. Born in Hamburg, Franck was educated at Heidelberg and Berlin and was decorated with the Iron Cross in World War I. Appointed Professor of experimental physics at Göttingen in 1920, he was awarded the Nobel Prize for physics in 1925 (with Gustave Herz) for work on the quantum theory. He resigned in 1933 in protest at Nazi legislation excluding Jews (although he was exempted), and moved to America, where he worked on the development of atomic weapons. The recommendations of the Franck report of 1945, which suggested international controls, were ignored.

Frank, Anne (1929–45): Anne Frank was a German Jewish girl, born in Frankfurt-am-Main. Her family moved to Amsterdam in the 1930s to escape from the Nazis and went into hiding there after the occupation of the Netherlands. Anne kept a diary of her time in hiding up to the family's arrest by the Gestapo. All the members of the family except Anne's father, Otto Frank, were murdered in concentration camps. Her diary was published after the end of the war.

Frank, Hans (1900–1946): Nazi lawyer and Governor-General of Poland. Born in Karlsruhe, Frank was active in the *Freikorps* and became an early member of the DAP. He practised as a lawyer in Munich from 1926, and became head of the NSDAP legal office in 1929. In 1933 he became Bavarian Minister of Justice, the Reich Ministry remaining with Franz Gurtner of the DNVP, and in 1934 Reich Minister without Portfolio. From 1939 to 1945 he was Governor-General of occupied Poland. He retained the post until the end of the war despite being stripped of his party and legal positions in 1942, when he made a call for a return to constitutional rule following the execution of a friend. He was tried and hanged at Nuremberg.

Freideburg, Hans Georg von (1895–1945): German admiral. Promoted to Supreme Commander of the navy at the end of World War II, he was responsible for its surrender in May 1945. He committed suicide shortly afterwards.

Freisler, Roland (1893–1945): Nazi Deputy to the Reichstag from 1932, and President of the Berlin *Volksgericht* from 1942, Freisler was the prosecutor in the trials of conspirators involved in the 1944 bomb plot. He was killed during an air raid in 1945.

Freud, Sigmund (1856–1939): Austrian psychologist. Born in Moravia, Freud studied medicine at Vienna and subsequently practised psychiatry in the Vienna hospital. He developed his psychoanalytical theories in Vienna at the turn of the century, and had established an international reputation by 1923, when he was appointed Professor of neurology at Vienna, a position he held until the *Anschluss*. He fled to London in 1938.

Frick Wilhelm (1877–1946): Nazi Interior Minister. Born in Alsenz, Frick studied law and worked in the Munich police department from 1904 to 1924 when he was elected to the Reichstag. He was the first Nazi minister (in Thuringia from 1930) and was Reich Interior Minister from 1933 to 1943, when he was replaced by Himmler (q.v.) and appointed Protector of Bohemia and Moravia. He was hanged at Nuremberg.

Fritsch, Werner Freiherr von (1880–1939): Head of the Army High Command, 1934–38. Born in Benrath into a military family, Fritsch served in World War I, and was promoted during the Weimar Republic. He reached the rank of Lieutenant General and was placed in command of Defence District III (Berlin) in 1932. Three years later he became Commander-in-Chief of the *Wehrmacht*. A conservative critic of Nazi foreign policy, he was effectively dismissed in 1938 (as a result of false accusations of homosexuality) along with Werner von Blomberg (q.v.).

Fritzsche, Hans (1900–53): Nazi head of radio broadcasting. Fritzsche joined the DNVP in 1923 and the NSDAP in 1933, on being appointed head of the news service in the Propaganda Ministry's press section. He moved to the radio section in 1942 after five years as a political commentator on radio. He was acquitted of war crimes at Nuremberg and released in 1950 after a further trial by a German de-Nazification court.

Funk, Walther (1890–1960): Nazi economics minister. Funk was born in East Prussia and studied law at Berlin and Leipzig. In 1916 he became a journalist on the conservative *Börsenzeitung,* which he edited from 1922 to 1932. He joined the Nazi Party in 1931, and mediated between the party leadership and business interests. Appointed government press chief in 1933, he succeeded Schacht (q.v.) as Economics Minister in 1937, a post he held until the end of the war. He was given a life sentence at Nuremberg, not least for his part in the banking of the valuables of murdered Jews on behalf of the SS, and was released in 1957.

Galen, Clemens Graf von (1878–1946): Cardinal Archbishop of Münster. Born in Dinklage, he served as a bishop's chaplain in Münster and as a priest in Berlin before returning to Westphalia in 1939. He became Archbishop in 1933. His attitude to the Nazi regime was ambiguous: he swore an oath of allegiance and approved of Hitler's foreign policy from the occupation of the Rhineland to the invasion of the Soviet Union, but opposed anti-Christian elements in Nazi ideology (taking issue with Rosenberg in 1934) and defended the interests of the church. His reputation as a leading opponent of Nazism rests on his sermon of 1941 against the Euthanasia programme, which was suspended shortly afterwards, arguably as a consequence of his criticism. Galen was arrested after the July bomb plot in 1944 and sent to Sachsenhausen, where he survived the remainder of the war.

Geiger, Hans Wilhelm (1882–1945): German physicist. Educated at Munich and Erlangen, Geiger moved to Manchester. Here he worked with Schuster and Rutherford on the alpha particle and instruments, used to detect it, from which Geiger counters were later developed. He moved to Berlin in 1912 and then to Chairs at Kiel, Tübingen and the Technical University in Berlin (1936).

George, Heinrich (1893–1946): German film star. George's reputation was established with his parts in *Metropolis* (1926), *Dreyfus* (1929) and *Berlin Alexanderplatz* (1931). He became a Nazi supporter in 1933 and appeared in propaganda films such as *Hitlerjunge Quex* (1933), *Jud Süss* (1940) and *Kolberg* (1945). He was arrested by Soviet troops in East Prussia and died while in detention.

Gessler, Otto (1875–1955): Weimar defence minister (1920–28). Born in Ludwigsburg, Gessler was Mayor of Regensburg and Nuremberg before World War I and a co-founder of the left-liberal DDP in 1918. He served as Weimar Germany's Defence Minister from 1920 to 1928, when he was replaced by Wilhelm Groener (q.v.). He was imprisoned in Ravensbrück in 1944 by the Nazis.

Globocnik, Odilo (1904–45): Austrian Nazi and SS officer responsible for 'Operation Reinhard'. Globocnik was born in Trieste and was an early party member. He was appointed *Gauleiter* of Vienna in 1938 and SS and Police leader of Lublin in 1941. Under the patronage of Himmler he was given responsibility for the mass murder of European Jews and was responsible for the construction and operation of Chelmno, Belzec, Sobibor and Treblinka. He was captured by British troops in Carinthia in 1945, and apparently committed suicide shortly after his arrest.

Goebbels, Paul Joseph (1897–1945): Reich Propaganda Director of the NSDAP and Reich Minister of Public Enlightenment and Propaganda. Goebbels was born in Rheydt, in the Rhineland and became involved in Nazi politics after receiving a doctorate from Heidelberg in 1921. He joined the NSDAP in 1924 and edited the Nazi *Völkische Freiheit*. He became a fervent supporter of Hitler during the factional in-fighting within the party during the mid-1920s and remained loyal to the end of the war. He was appointed *Gauleiter* of Berlin in 1926, and Reich Propaganda Director in 1929. Elected to the Reichstag in 1933, he became Minister of Enlightenment and Propaganda the same year. As Minister he exercised an unprecedented control over Germany's mass media, cultural life and education system. His power and influence in the Nazi state increased during the war, and his appointment as Reich Plenipotentiary for Total War, in 1944, effectively placed him in overall command of the domestic war effort. Shortly after Hitler's suicide in the bunker, he killed his wife and family and then committed suicide.

Goerdeler, Carl (1884–1945): Conspirator in the 1944 bomb plot. Goerdeler was a conservative civil servant and Mayor of Königberg (1920–30) and Leipzig (1930–37). He was the leading civilian in the July conspiracy, but envisaged a post-Nazi Germany which retained Hitler's territorial gains. He was arrested after the failure of the assassination attempt and executed in 1945.

Goering, Hermann (1893–1946): Leading Nazi, Minister of Aviation and Plenipotentiary for the Four Year Plan. Goering was born in Bavaria and served as a pilot in the Richthofen Squadron in World War I. He left Munich University without graduating to

the SA the following
...ich putsch. Elected to
...dent in 1932; and Prime
...ussia in 1933. He was
... Hitler came to power and
...f the air force, of which he
...5. As head of the Prussian
...Gestapo and the first concen-
...ost control of the Third Reich's
...o Himmler. In 1936 he was made
...tation of the Four Year Plan, and
...sation for that purpose which rapidly
..., Economics and Labour Ministries.
...e in the many elements of the radical-
... the late 1930s, assisting in the downfall of
... in 1938, and the expropriation of Jewish
p... ...ustrial empire expanded into Austria and
Czec... ...d he made a forthright economic case for their
annexatio... ...ough he was promoted to Reich Marshal in 1940,
his influence ...eclined after the Battle of Britain, and he was even
expelled from the party in 1945. He was captured and tried at
Nuremberg, but committed suicide in his prison cell.

Greiser, Arthur (1897–1946): *Gauleiter* of the Wartheland. Greiser
joined the Nazi Party in 1929 and the SS in 1931, and succeeded
Rauschning (q.v.) as President of the Danzig senate in 1934. He
was appointed Chief of the Civil Administration in Posen and
Gauleiter and Reich Governor of the Wartheland in 1939. He was
tried in Poland after the war and hanged in 1946.

Grimm, Hans (1875–1949): German Nationalist writer. Grimm
spent fourteen years in South Africa as a young man and wrote a
semi-autobiographical novel based on his experiences (*Volk ohne
Raum*) which was both anti-British and imbued with 'blood and
soil' ideology. Published in 1926, it was an enormous success.
Grimm never joined the NSDAP but was a staunch supporter of
Nazism.

Groener, Wilhelm (1867–1939): German officer. Responsible for
war production from 1916, Groener was second-in-command of
the German army at the end of World War I, and supported the
establishment of the Weimar Republic in return for the suppression of the revolutionary left. He promoted the growth of the
Freikorps movement which was used as an instrument of the state in
violent political conflicts. He served as Transport Minister
(1920–23) and Defence Minister (1928–32) and sponsored the rise
of General Kurt von Schleicher who subsequently conspired with
the Nazis against him when, as Brüning's Interior Minister (1930–

32), he banned the SA (1932). His attempts to defend the Republic and keep the army out of politics were unsuccessful and he resigned in 1932.

Gropius, Walter (1883–1969): Architect and founder of the Bauhaus. Gropius was born in Berlin, and practised as an architect before serving in World War I. In 1918 he was appointed head of the *Kunstgewerbeschule* in Weimar. The Bauhaus was founded there the following year, and moved to Dessau in 1925. He retired as the school's director in 1928 and emigrated to Britain in 1933 (when the Bauhaus was closed down by the Nazis). He moved to the United States in 1937, where he pursued an academic career at Harvard University.

Grosz, George (1893–1959): German artist noted for his satirical work and caricature. Grosz studied in Dresden and Berlin and became a leading member of the Berlin Dada movement after World War I, and of the New Objectivity (*Neue Sachlichkeit*) school of the mid-1920s. He moved to the United States in 1932, where he remained almost to the end of his life. He died shortly after returning to Berlin in 1959.

Grynszpan, Herschel (b.1921): Grynszpan was a German Jew of Polish extraction who left Germany to stay with relatives in Brussels and Paris in 1936. He shot and mortally wounded a German legation secretary in the Paris embassy after hearing that 17,000 Jews, including his own family, had been deported to Poland and left stranded in the no-man's-land of the border by a Polish government which was unwilling to accept them. His act was the ostensible cause for the organised pogrom which followed, initiating a radicalisation of anti-Jewish policy. Grynszpan was handed over to the Nazis by the Vichy authorities, but survived in a Berlin prison, pending a criminal trial.

Guderian, Heinz (1888–1945): German general. A professional soldier, Guderian served in World War I and specialised in the development of communications techniques and tank warfare between the wars. He became Commander-in-Chief of Panzer troops in 1939 and directed *Blitzkrieg* on both the eastern and western fronts, but was dismissed in 1941 after a difference of opinion with Hitler. After reverses on the eastern front he was recalled as Inspector General of Armoured Forces in 1943, was promoted to Chief of General Staff in the OKW after the July bomb plot of 1944, and purged the army of hundreds of officers. Dismissed again in March 1945 over a further disagreement with Hitler, he was captured in May and died a few days later.

Gürtner, Franz (1881–1941): Nazi justice minister. Born in Regensburg, Gurtner studied law before serving in World War I. A

German Nationalist, he became Bavarian Justice Minister in 1922, a position he held until he became Reich Justice Minister under Papen in 1932. He remained in post until his death in 1941, alternately collaborating with the Nazis in the fusion of state and party organisations, and protesting at excesses.

Hahn, Otto (1879–1968): German nuclear scientist. Educated at Marburg, Hahn subsequently worked with Rutherford in Canada, returning to Germany in 1907. He was appointed Professor of chemistry in 1910 and moved to the Kaiser Wilhelm Institute of Chemistry in 1912. With Lise Meitner he discovered the element protactinium (1917) and carried out research on uranium with Meitner and Fritz Strassmann in the 1930s, contributing to the discovery of nuclear fission. He remained in Germany during the war, and was awarded the Nobel Prize for chemistry in 1944.

Halder, Franz (1884–1972): German general. Born in Würzburg and a Roman Catholic, Halder was a career soldier who served in World War I and then joined the *Reichswehr* Ministry (1919). He replaced Beck (q.v.) as army Chief of Staff in 1938. His initial opposition to a European war had waned by 1939 and he remained involved in military planning until 1942 when he disagreed with Hitler over the diversion of troops to Stalingrad and was dismissed.

Hanfstaengl, Ernst (1887–1975): Head of NSDAP Foreign Press Section. Born in Munich into a wealthy family, Hanfstaengl spent ten years in America before returning to Bavaria after World War I. He was an early associate of Hitler whose loans to the party were used – among other things – to buy the *Völkischer Beobachter*. He took part in the Munich putsch and was Head of the Foreign Press Department from 1931 to 1937 when he fled to Britain and then the US. He returned to Germany after the war, following internment in the US.

Harlan, Veit (1899–1963): German film director. A Berlin actor, Varlan moved into films in 1934. He was a staunch Nazi supporter and directed *Jud Süss* (1940) and *Kolberg* (1945). He continued his film career after the war.

Hassell, Ulrich von (1881–1944): German career diplomat. Ambassador to Italy from 1932 to 1938, when he was dismissed during the general purge of conservatives from office. Hassell was involved in the bomb plot conspiracy and was hanged in 1944.

Heartfield, John (1891–1968): German satirical artist. Born Helmut Herzfeld, he changed his name as an act of political protest. He collaborated in the establishment of the Malik publishing house (from 1917) and the Berlin Dada group (1919), and was scenic director for Max Reinhardt (1920–23). Among his best-known work is his series of satirical photomontages directed against Hitler and the Nazi movement.

Heidegger, Martin (1889–1976): German philosopher. Heidegger was born in Baden-Württemberg and educated at Freiburg University, where he studied under Husserl. His best-known works are probably *Being and Time* (1927) and *Existence and Being* (1929). He was appointed Professor of philosophy at Freiburg in 1928, and Rector in 1933 by the Nazis, for whom he expressed his support. He was dismissed in 1945 by the Allies, and prohibited from teaching until 1951.

Heisenberg, Werner (b.1901): German physicist. Heisenberg worked with Niels Bohr in Copenhagen before his appointment to the Chair of physics at Leipzig in 1926. His work furnished the basis of quantum mechanics, and his uncertainty principle is still accepted by modern physicists. Politically, Heisenberg was a Nationalist and was appointed Director of the German nuclear weapons programme during World War II. It remains unclear whether the programme failed due to the exodus of Germany's Jewish scientists, or due to the reluctance of those remaining to develop such a weapon. He remained a leading West German research scientist after World War II.

Henlein, Konrad (1898–1945): Leader of the Sudeten Germans. Born in Bohemia, Henlein served in World War I and founded the Sudeten German *Heimatfront* in 1933 (the Sudeten German Party from 1935). With financial support from Nazi Germany, Henlein and the Sudeten German Party agitated against the Czech state. After the occupation of the Sudetenland he was appointed Chief of the Civil Administration and *Gauleiter* (1939). He committed suicide in 1945 after his capture by the Americans.

Hess, Walther Richard Rudolf (1894–1987): Deputy leader of the NSDAP. Hess was born in Alexandria, Egypt, and served in the same regiment as Hitler in World War I. Hitler's secretary from 1920, he took part in the Munich putsch and was imprisoned with Hitler in Landsberg. He became Deputy Party Leader in 1932, and Minister without Portfolio in 1933. As Führer's Deputy for Party Affairs, Hess (and increasingly his deputy, Bormann, q.v.) played a pivotal role in party-state relations during the 1930s. In 1938 he became one of only six standing members of the Ministerial Council for the Defence of the Reich. In 1941 he flew to Scotland, ostensibly to negotiate peace, but was interned until 1945, then tried and sentenced to life imprisonment at Nuremberg. He remained the sole prisoner in Spandau prison, Berlin, from 1966 until his death in 1987.

Hesse, Herman (1877–1962): German writer. Author of *Siddhartha* (1922), *Der Steppenwolf* (1927), *Narziss und Goldmund* (1930) and *Das Glasperlenspiel* (*The Glass Bead Game*, 1943), Hesse lived in Switzerland from 1912 and was a critic of the Nazis. His interests in oriental philosophy and psychoanalysis ensured a resurgence of his work's popularity in the 1960s and 1970s.

Heydrich, Reinhard (1904–1942): Head of the RSHA. Born in Halle into a conservative middle class family, Heydrich became a naval cadet in 1922 and was promoted to Lieutenant in 1928. He joined the NSDAP and the SS in 1931 after some involvement with the *Freikorps* and *völkisch* organisations. He became head of the SD in 1932 and was promoted to SS Lieutenant-General in 1934 after the Night of the Long Knives and the purge of the SA. Himmler's deputy from 1933, he was appointed head of the Reich Central Office for Jewish Emigration in January 1939 and head of the Reich Security Head Office (RSHA) in September of the same year. He was responsible for the deportation of Jews to the Government General and the briefing of the *Einsatzgruppen*. In 1941 Goering gave him overall responsibility for the mass murder of the Jews. Reich Protector of Bohemia and Moravia from 1941, he was assassinated by the Czech resistance in 1942.

Hilferding, Rudolf (1877–1941): Social Democratic Finance Minister (1923 and 1928–29). Viennese by birth, Hilferding moved to Berlin before World War I where he became an editor of *Vorwärts* and published his major scholarly work *Das Finanzkapital* in 1910. A member of the USPD between 1919 and 1922, he was a member of the Reichstag from 1924 to 1933. He fled to France after the Nazis came to power but was arrested there in 1941, and died in the hands of the Gestapo.

Himmler, Heinrich (1900–1945): *Reichsführer SS* and head of the German Police; Minister of the Interior, 1943–45. Himmler was born in Munich and served in World War I from 1917. A poultry farmer in Bavaria after the war, he became involved in right-wing politics and participated in the Munich putsch in 1923. In 1929 he was appointed head of the SS, in 1933 he became police chief in Munich, and by the end of the year was commander of the political police in all states except Prussia. In 1934 he took over as head of the Prussian police and the Gestapo. By 1936 he was in control of the entire German police apparatus, a position which he used as a power base. In 1939 he was appointed Commissar for the Consolidation of German Nationhood, and was in ultimate command of the Nazi racial extermination campaign, including the mass murder of European Jews. Himmler seems to have taken seriously the 'racial' pseudo-science propagated by 'academic' institutes and, although unable to witness violent murder himself (as at Minsk in 1941), was indifferent to the consequences of his policies. In 1943 he became Interior Minister, an index of the expansion of the power of the SS within Germany itself. He lost influence towards the end of the war, and when he advocated surrender in 1945 Hitler ordered his arrest. He fled from Berlin and was captured by British troops, but committed suicide before he could be brought to trial.

Hindemith, Paul (1895–1963): Hindemith was a distinguished composer and viola player in Weimar Germany. He became leader of the Frankfurt Opera orchestra in 1915 and in 1921 formed the Amor Quartet, which performed mainly contemporary works. Appointed Professor of music in Berlin in 1929, he fled Nazi Germany in the 1930s, and settled first in Turkey and then the US. He returned to Europe in 1953 and settled in Switzerland.

Hindenburg, Paul von Beckendorff und von (1847–1934): After serving in the campaigns against Austria (1866) and France (1870–71), Hindenburg retired a general in 1911. He came out of retirement in 1914, and with Erich von Ludendorff repelled the Russian invasion of 1914 at Tannenberg and the Masurian Lakes. He was promoted to Field Marshal. His collaboration with Ludendorff continued on the western front, and the partnership became a political one towards the end of the war, when the two officers ran Germany as a virtual military dictatorship. Hindenburg again retired from private life after the war, until he was elected President in 1925 and again in 1932. His authority guaranteed the governments of Brüning, Papen and Schleicher, who ruled largely by presidential decree, and his consent was decisive in the appointment of Hitler. He remained in office until his death.

Hitler, Adolf (1889–1945): Leader of the NSDAP and Chancellor of Germany (1933–1945). Adolf Hitler was born in 1889 in Braunau am Inn, Upper Austria, the fourth child of Alois Hitler, a civil servant. After a short spell in Passau, Bavaria (1892–95), the family moved back to Upper Austria on the retirement of Hitler's father and he was educated in Linz and Steyr. His father died in 1903 and he left school in 1905, having failed to make adequate progress, and moved to Vienna. Here he was rejected twice by the Academy of Arts and subsequently lived as a vagrant. He finally left Vienna for Bavaria in 1913 in order to avoid Austrian military service, but volunteered for a Bavarian regiment shortly before the outbreak of war in 1914. He spent the war on the western front, where he was wounded twice, temporarily blinded by poison gas and decorated for bravery. In 1919 Hitler was appointed to a post in the army political department in Munich, where he joined the German Workers' Party (DAP), one of a number of small political groups on the radical right. The party was subsequently refounded as the National Socialist German Workers' Party and Hitler became Chairman in July 1921. With Erich von Ludendorff he led an unsuccessful putsch in Munich in November 1923, and served a term of imprisonment at Landsberg in Bavaria, where he dictated *Mein Kampf.* After his release in 1924 he transformed the Nazi Party into a mass organisation employing legalistic methods to come to power.

Despite a massive gain in electoral support in 1930, consolidated and extended in July 1932, the NSDAP consistently failed to win either a majority of seats in the Reichstag or a place in the successive right-wing coalitions of the Depression years. It was only in January 1933, after electoral losses in the general election of the previous November, that Hitler was appointed Chancellor at the head of a minority right-of-centre coalition government. This administration, like its predecessors, was dependent on rule by presidential decree until Hitler acquired unlimited powers for a year by means of an Enabling Act. He then suppressed all political opposition, and after the death of President Hindenburg styled himself leader (*Führer*) of the German Reich, and elicited a personal oath of loyalty from the German armed forces. During the 1930s he worked with Germany's traditional ruling elites on a rearmament programme enforced by an authoritarian dictatorship. From the re-occupation of the demilitarised Rhineland in defiance of the Treaty of Versailles (1936), the Hitler government undertook a programme of military aggression in central Europe which resulted in the annexation of Austria (1938), Czechoslovakia (1938–39) and much of Poland (1939), before Europe was finally plunged into a general war. Much of Europe was occupied or dominated by Nazi Germany between 1940 and 1943, when the tide was turned by the Red Army at Stalingrad. The domestic policies of the Nazi state also underwent an accelerating radicalisation from the mid-1930s. In 1935 the Nuremberg Laws initiated a persecution of the Jews which culminated in the Holocaust; leading conservative politicians, public servants and army officers were purged from high office in 1937 and 1938, when Hitler made a decisive break from his conservative nationalist allies shortly before the start of Germany's aggressive territorial expansion.

The extent to which this radicalisation was a consequence of Hitler's own intentions and actions, or of the structure and policy-making procedures of the Nazi state, remains a matter of debate among historians. Except in the fields of anti-semitism and foreign policy, Hitler himself paid little attention to the details of policy-making, and research has revealed organisational chaos behind the monolithic facade of the Third Reich. Bureaucratic norms in government and administration were undermined by

Hitler's 'charismatic' legitimation of his political authority; while the leadership cult established in the party's early days, and built up by Goebbels' (q.v.) propaganda apparatus, created the myth of the 'man of the people' become heroic leader, and humble corporal become military genius. The myth endured as long as Germany's military success, but was undermined as public morale collapsed in the later war years. Hitler survived an assassination attempt by disaffected army officers and leading conservatives from Germany's pre-Nazi elites (the July bomb plot) in 1944, and committed suicide less than a year later with the Allied armies occupying Germany. His political testament, written shortly before his death, reaffirmed his radical nationalism and rabid anti-semitism.

Hoess, Rudolf (1900–1947): Commandant of Auschwitz. Hoess served on the Turkish front in World War I and received the Iron Cross, joined a *Freikorps* unit after the war, and was imprisoned for violent murder (1923–28). He joined the SS in 1934 and was posted to Dachau, Sachsenhausen (1938) and Auschwitz (1940), where he was appointed Commandant. Hoess lived at Auschwitz with his wife and family, prided himself on the efficiency of the extermination camp, and was commended as a model death camp commandant. He was captured by military police in Germany in 1946, and executed by the Polish authorities in 1947.

Hossbach, Friedrich (1894–1980): Infantry general and author of the 'Hossbach memorandum', the record of a secret meeting between Hitler, the Foreign Minister and the Commanders-in-Chief of the armed forces in 1938. Hossbach's account, based on his minutes of the meeting, was used in evidence at the Nuremberg Trials.

Hugenberg, Alfred (1865–1951): Born in Hanover, Hugenberg was a civil servant, banker, company director (of Krupp) before World War I, and press baron during the Weimar Republic. He was a co-founder of the Pan-German League in 1894, and a DNVP deputy to the National Assembly in 1919 and the Reichstag from 1920. A key figure in the 'National Unity Front' of German Nationalists and Nazis against the Young Plan in 1929, and the Harzburg Front of 1931, his press empire was instrumental in Hitler's rise to power. He was Minister for Economics and Food in Hitler's first cabinet, but was forced to resign in June 1933. (The DNVP was dissolved the following day.) Although he remained a member of the Reichstag until 1945, he took no further active part in politics, profiting only from the sale of a publishing house to the Nazis in 1943. He retained this property after the war.

Husserl, Edmund (1859–1938): German philosopher. Husserl taught at Halle 1887–1901), Göttingen (1901–16) and Freiburg (1916–28), where he was succeeded by his student Heidegger (q.v.). Husserl is considered the founder of the modern school of phenomenology.

Itten, Johannes (1888–1967): German artist. Itten taught at the Bauhaus from 1919 and ran his own school from 1926 to 1934. He founded the school for textile design at Krefeld, before returning to Switzerland where he was Director of the Arts and Crafts School and Museum of the Zürich Textile School (1938–54). His most important book, *The Art of Colour* was published in 1944.

Jodl, Alfred (1890–1946): Head of OKW Operations Staff during World War II and Hitler's closest military adviser. Jodl served as a staff officer in World War I after being wounded in 1914. He became head of the national defence department in the War Ministry in 1939, and was appointed head of OKW operations staff in 1939. He was tried for war crimes at Nuremberg, found guilty of complicity in Nazi atrocities and hanged.

Joyce, William (1906–46): American-born Nazi collaborator: 'Lord Haw-Haw'. Joyce was born in New York to Irish Protestant parents who moved back to Ireland in 1909, and to England after independence. Educated at Birkbeck College, Joyce joined the BUF, but left to form his own National Socialist League before moving to Berlin to avoid arrest in 1939. He was employed by the Nazi Propaganda Ministry to broadcast to Britain, and was hanged for treason after the war.

Jünger, Ernst (b.1895): German writer. Born in Heidelberg, Jünger served in World War I and remained in the *Reichswehr* until 1923. His war experience was recorded in his book *In Stahlgewittern* (1920), which established his literary reputation. A nationalist and Nazi sympathiser who also flirted with the idea of Bolshevism, he never joined the NSDAP, but served on the staff of the German military commander in Paris until 1944, when he was dismissed. His later work *Auf den Marmorklippen* (*On Marble Cliffs*, 1940) has been read as a critical allegory of despotism. He continued to write after the war.

Kaiser, Georg (1878–1945): Expressionist playwright. Author of *Von Morgen bis Mitternachts* (1916), and a trilogy on capitalism: *Die Koralle* (1917), *Gas I* (1918) and *Gas II* (1920). He emigrated to Switzerland in 1933.

Kaltenbrunner, Ernst (1903–1946): Austrian Nazi and Head of the RSHA. Born near Braunau and educated in Linz, where he became a friend of Eichmann, Kaltenbrunner studied law at Graz, subsequently practised law in Linz, and joined the NSDAP in 1932.

Imprisoned briefly in 1934 and 1935, he was appointed Austrian Minister of State Security by Seyss-Inquart in 1938. He took charge of the SS in Vienna and succeeded Heydrich as head of the RSHA in January 1943. He was captured in Austria after the war, tried at Nuremberg, and hanged in 1946.

Kandinsky, Wassily (1866–1944): Russian born painter, based in Munich from 1897. A pioneer of abstract painting, he published his *Treatise on the Spiritual in Art* in 1912 and was a founding member of the *Blaue Reiter* group before World War I. In 1914 he returned to Russia, where he worked with the Bolsheviks after the revolution, returning to Germany to teach at the Bauhaus in 1926. He left for Paris in 1933, and became a French citizen in 1939.

Karajan, Herbert von (1908–89): Austrian conductor. He became general musical director at Aachen in 1934, joined the NSDAP and continued to work in Germany throughout the Third Reich. His association with the Nazis prevented his resuming work after the war until he was appointed conductor of the Vienna Symphony Orchestra in 1947.

Kaufmann, Karl (1900–69): *Gauleiter* of Hamburg. Born in Krefeld, he was a co-founder of the NSDAP in the Ruhr (1921) and was *Gauleiter* of the Rhineland in 1928, when he was sacked for corruption. He was rehabilitated in 1933 and appointed Governor of Hamburg, a position he retained until 1945. He was temporarily detained several times after the war before his final release in 1953.

Kautsky, Karl (1854–1938): Marxist theoretician. A contributor to the anti-revisionist Erfurt Programme of the SPD (1891) and editor of the Social-Democratic journal *Die Neue Zeit* (1883–1917), Kautsky became one of the party's leading theorists before leaving to join the USPD (1917). A deputy foreign office minister (1918–20), he lived in Vienna in the 1920s and 1930s, and fled to the Netherlands in 1938.

Keitel, Wilhelm (1882–1946): General Field Marshal and Chief of Staff, OKW, 1938–45. Keitel served in World War I, and then pursued a career in administration in the War Ministry where he was appointed Chief of Staff to War Minister Werner von Blomberg in 1935. He was head of the OKW from its inception in 1938. Promoted to Field Marshal in 1940, he was loyal to Hitler throughout the war and retained his post until 1945. He was tried at Nuremberg, found guilty of war crimes and hanged.

Keppler, Wilhelm (1882–1960): Nazi politician. An early Nazi Party member, Keppler was elected to the Reichstag in 1933 and appointed Reich Commissioner for Economic Affairs in the same year. He was an important mediator between the party and big business during the Depression, an adviser to Goering at the Four Year Plan Office in 1936, briefly Reich Commissioner for Austria in 1938, and administered property expropriated by the SS in Poland and the USSR. He was sentenced to ten years' imprisonment in 1949, but released in 1951.

Kerrl, Hanns (1887–1941): Nazi Minister for the Churches. Kerrl became a Reich Commissioner in the Prussian Justice Ministry in 1933, Minister without Portfolio in 1934, and Minister for Ecclesiastical Affairs in 1935. He died in office.

Kesselring, Albert (1885–1960): German Field Marshal. Kesselring served as an officer in World War I and moved from the army to the new Nazi Air Ministry in 1933. He commanded the air force in Poland, the Battle of Britain and the Soviet Union before his promotion to Commander-in-Chief of land and air forces in the south in 1941. He was moved to the western front shortly before the end of the war. Kesselring was sentenced to death for war crimes by a British military court in Venice in 1947 but his sentence was commuted to life imprisonment. He was released in 1952 and was later President of the *Stahlhelm.*

Kirchner, Ernst Ludwig (1880–1938): German expressionist painter. An important member of the expressionist group *Die Brücke*, Kirchner suffered a nervous breakdown shortly after his mobilisation in 1914. He spent the rest of his life in Switzerland and committed suicide after his work was condemned by the Nazis.

Klee, Paul (1879–1940): Swiss-born artist classified as degenerate by the Nazis. A member of the *Blaue Reiter* group before World War I, he taught at the Bauhaus (1921–31) and at the Düsseldorf Academy. He was dismissed in 1933 and returned to Switzerland when the Nazis came to power.

Koch, Erich (1896–1986): Nazi politician. Koch joined the NSDAP in 1922 and became *Gauleiter* of East Prussia in 1928. He was elected to the Reichstag in 1930 and was appointed Chief of the Civil Administration in Bialystok in 1941, and Reich Commissar of the Ukraine the same year. A committed advocate of Nazi racial policies in the East, he was captured after the war and tried by the Poles in 1958. His death sentence was commuted to life imprisonment for health reasons.

Kokoschka, Oskar (1886–1980): Austrian expressionist painter. Kokoschka moved to Berlin in 1910, served in World War I, and was wounded in battle. He moved to Dresden after the war and then spent several years travelling. He fled to London in 1938 after the condemnation of his work as degenerate (*Self-Portrait of a Degenerate Artist*, 1937) by the Nazis, and finally settled in Switzerland in 1953.

Kollwitz, Käthe (1867–1945): German artist. Born in Königsberg, Kollwitz was a committed Socialist whose subjects were poverty and the horror of war. She was Professor at the Berlin Academy from 1919 to 1933. She remained in Germany but was prohibited from exhibiting her work.

Kramer, Josef (1907–45): Commandant of Birkenau and Bergen-Belsen concentration camps. Kramer served in a number of camps (Auschwitz, Dachau, Esterwagen, Sachsenhausen, Mauthausen and Natzweiler). He was condemned to death by a British military court in 1945.

Krüger, Friedrich Wilhelm (1894–1945): SS *Obergruppenführer* and police chief in the *Generalgouvernement* (Poland) during World War II.

Krupp Von Bohlen Und Halbach, Alfried (1907–67): German arms manufacturer. The son of Gustav Krupp (q.v.), Alfried studied engineering at Aachen Technical Institute before joining the family business. He joined the NSDAP in 1936 and took over the Krupp empire in 1943. Under his direction the company plundered the industrial plant of occupied Europe and exploited concentration camp labour. He was tried at Nuremberg as a war criminal and sentenced to twelve years' imprisonment, but was released in 1951 following American intervention and his estate was restored to him.

Krupp Von Bohlen Und Halbach, Gustav (1870–1950): German arms manufacturer and 'Leader of the Reich Estate of German Industry' during the Third Reich. Tried as a war criminal at Nuremberg.

Lammers, Hans Heinrich (1879–1962): Head of the Reich Chancellery, 1933–45. Lammers was born in Upper Silesia and studied law at Breslau and Heidelberg before serving in World War I. After the war he joined the Interior Ministry and was appointed head of the Reich Chancellery by 1933. He became Minister without Portfolio in 1937 and a member of the Ministerial Council for the Defence of the Reich in 1939. An honorary SS General from 1940 he controlled access to Hitler (along with Bormann, q.v.) and chaired the cabinet in his absence. He lost favour in 1945 by supporting Goering (q.v.) in a bid to assume the leadership. After the war he was sentenced to twenty years' imprisonment, but the sentence was reduced (twice) and he was released in 1951.

Lang, Fritz (1890–1976): Austrian film director. Lang was born in Vienna and served in the Austrian army in World War I. He was wounded several times and discharged in 1916. He directed a number of important silent films between the end of the war and the release of his best-known film, *Metropolis*, in 1927, which was followed by his other well-known film, *M*, in 1931. He left Germany when Hitler came to power, and was divorced by his wife who stayed behind to work for the Nazis. He settled in America in 1935.

Laval, Pierre (1883–1945): French politician and collaborator. Elected to the Chamber of Deputies as a Socialist in 1914 he served in a number of governments and became Prime Minister in 1935, when he was forced to resign for appeasing Mussolini. He was Foreign Minister for the Vichy regime briefly in 1940, and then Prime Minister and Foreign Minister from 1942 to 1944. He was tried for treason and executed in 1945.

Leber, Julius (1891–1945): German socialist. An SPD journalist and Reichstag deputy, he was imprisoned in concentration camps between 1933 and 1937 and became involved with resistance circles after his release. He was close to the Kreisau circle and Claus von Stauffenberg, but was arrested before the assassination attempt of July 1944 and executed in October of that year.

Leers, Johann von (1902–65): Anti-semitic writer. A member of the NSDAP from 1929 Leers was employed by the Nazi regime to write crude anti-semitic propaganda for popular consumption. He was also appointed Professor at Jena. After the war he fled to Italy and Argentina, was employed by Nasser and died in Cairo.

Lenya, Lotte (1905–81): Austrian actress. Lotte Lenya studied ballet and drama in Zürich (1914–20) and established a reputation in the German theatre during the Weimar Republic. She was most closely associated with the works of Brecht and Weill. In 1933 she moved to Paris.

Leuschner, Wilhelm (1888–1944): German trades unionist. Hessian Interior Minister for the SPD from 1929, he was arrested by the Nazis in May 1933 and sent to a concentration camp. After his release he became involved with resistance circles around Beck and Stauffenberg (q.v.). He was arrested after the failure of the July plot and hanged in September 1944.

Ley, Robert (1890–1945): Leader of the German Labour Front (DAF). A chemistry graduate and World War I pilot, Ley worked for IG Farben after the war and joined the NSDAP in 1924. He was elected to the Prussian *Landtag* in 1928 and the Reichstag in 1930. He became Reich Organisation Leader in 1932 and leader of the German Labour Front, created to replace the Free Trades Unions, in 1933. He committed suicide in 1945.

Liebermann, Max (1847–1935): German artist. Born in Berlin, Liebermann spent several years in Paris in his youth and returned to Germany in 1878 to establish a reputation as a leading German impressionist. A co-founder of the Berlin Secession, he was President of the Academy of Arts from 1920 to 1930. He was forced to resign in 1933 and died two years later in Berlin. His work was categorised as 'degenerate' by the Nazis.

Liebknecht, Karl (1871–1919): Revolutionary Socialist. Elected to the Reichstag for the SPD in 1912 he was the only member to vote against war credits in 1914. A co-founder of the Spartacus League in 1918 with Rosa Luxemburg (q.v.), he helped organise the January 1919 uprising in Berlin. At the instigation of the government he was murdered by members of a *Freikorps* to suppress the uprising.

Löbe, Paul (1875–1967): Socialist journalist. Editor of *Die Volkswacht* from 1899, he was elected to Weimar's Constituent Assembly (1919) and the Reichstag (1920–33) for the SPD. Imprisoned by the Nazis briefly in 1933 and in a concentration camp from 1944, he resumed his political career after the war and served in the *Bundestag* from 1949 to 1953.

Lohse, Heinrich (1896–1964): Reich Commissioner for the Baltic and Belorussia. *Gauleiter* of Schleswig-Holstein from 1945 and *SA-Gruppenführer* from 1944, he was Reich Commissioner for the *Ostland* from 1941 to 1944. He was sentenced to ten years in 1948, but was released in 1951.

Lubbe, Marinus van der (1909–1934): Dutch Communist. Lubbe was found in the burning Reichstag building in 1933. He was charged with starting the fire, found guilty of high treason in an unconvincing show trial, and executed.

Ludendorff, Erich von (1865–1937): German military leader during World War I and supporter of the radical right during the Weimar Republic. Ludendorff pursued a military career before the outbreak of World War I and led the assault and capture of Liège in 1914. He was then moved to the east where his expertise was invaluable to Hindenburg in the German victories of Tannenberg and the Masurian Lakes. Along with Hindenburg he began to extend his power into the political sphere, and was instrumental in the overthrow of the Chancellor, Bethmann-Hollweg. At the end of the war Ludendorff suffered a nervous breakdown and resigned. He subsequently took part in the Munich putsch of 1923, sat as a Nazi Reichstag deputy from 1924 to 1928 and stood against Hindenburg in the 1925 presidential election. His politics became increasingly eccentric and he was estranged from most of his former colleagues before his death.

Luther, Hans (1879–1962): Non-party politician during the Weimar Republic. After a career in municipal politics and ministerial appointments under Cuno, Stresemann and Marx, he served as Chancellor from January 1925 to May 1926. He joined the DVP in 1926 and subsequently became President of the *Reichsbank* (1930–33) and ambassador to the United States under the Nazis (1933–37).

Luxemburg, Rosa (1870–1919): Revolutionary socialist and theoretician. Luxemburg was born at Zamość in Russian Poland and studied law and political economy at Zürich University, where she gained a doctorate in 1898. In this year she also acquired German citizenship through marriage. A co-founder of the Polish Social Democratic Party (in Switzerland) and participant in the Russian revolution of 1905, she spent World War I in prison. As a member of the Spartacus League (which she founded with Karl Liebknecht, q.v.), and of the KPD, she was a participant in the January 1919 uprising in Berlin. She was murdered, along with Liebknecht, by radical right-wing members of the government's security troops.

Mann, Heinrich (1871–1950): Liberal writer and publicist, brother of Thomas Mann, with whom he quarrelled on political grounds. His best known works are *Professor Unrat* (1905), on which the film *The Blue Angel* was based, *Der Untertan* (1918), translated into English as 'Man of Straw', and *König Henri Quatre* (1935–38). He fled first to Czechoslovakia in 1933, and then via France to the United States.

Mann, Thomas (1875–1955): German writer. Politically conservative before and during World War I, he wrote an essay on Frederick the Great which served as an apologia for the violation of Belgian neutrality. A post-war convert to republicanism he won the Nobel Prize in 1929 (for *The Magic Mountain*). He fled to Switzerland in 1933 and subsequently to the United States. His best known works are *Buddenbrooks* (1901), *Der Zauberberg* (*The Magic Mountain*) (1924), *Josef und seine Brüder* and *Doktor Faustus* (1947).

Marx, Wilhelm (1863–1946): German politician. Member of the Reichstag for the Centre Party (1910–18 and 1920–33), and of the National Assembly (1919), he served as Chancellor twice (1923–25 and 1926–28).

Meinecke, Friedrich (1862–1954): German historian. Meinecke was editor of the *Historische Zeitschrift* from 1893 to 1933, Professor of History at Strasbourg (1901–6), Freiburg (1906–14) and Berlin (1914–28). A conservative nationalist, he was an 'intellectual republican' under Weimar and was dismissed from the *Historische Zeitschrift* by the Nazis. He was appointed Rector of the Free University of Berlin in 1948 and published a critical book on the Nazi dictatorship, *Die deutsche Katastrophe* in 1950.

Mengele, Josef (b.1911): Extermination camp doctor. Appointed chief doctor at Auschwitz in 1943 after a career at the Institute of Hereditary Biology and Racial Hygiene in Berlin, he conducted medical experiments on the victims of the Nazis. He fled to South America after the war and in 1959 became a citizen of Paraguay, whose government refused to agree to his extradition.

Mies Van Der Rohe, Ludwig (1886–1969): German architect. With Gropius (q.v.), Mies was an assistant of Behrens (q.v.) before World War I and became an original and acclaimed architect in his own right during the Weimar Republic. He succeeded Gropius as Director of the Bauhaus in 1930 and remained until it was closed by the Nazis in 1933. He emigrated to the USA in 1937.

Müller, Heinrich (b.1901): Head of the Gestapo. Born in Munich, Müller served in World War I and then pursued a career in the Bavarian police. He was head of the Gestapo from 1935 until the end of the war. He was closely involved in the routine administration for the implementation of the 'final solution'. He disappeared at the end of the war and was never found.

Müller, Hermann (1876–1931): Weimar politician. Elected to the SPD leadership in 1906 and to the Reichstag in 1916, he became Foreign Minister in 1919 and was Chancellor twice (1920 and 1928–30).

Nebe, Arthur (1894–1945): Head of the Criminal Police (*Kripo*) from 1933 to 1945. Commander of *Einsatzgruppe B*, operating from Minsk in 1941, and responsible for 46,000 executions.

Neurath, Constantin Freiherr von (1873–1956): Foreign Minister, 1932–38. He began his career as a diplomat and served in Copenhagen (1919–21), as ambassador in Rome (1921–30), and in London (1930–32). He was appointed Foreign Minister in 1932 and remained in office until Hitler's purge of the conservatives in 1938. He subsequently became Reich Protector of Bohemia and Moravia (1939–43; on leave after 1941).

Niemöller, Martin (1892–1984): Anti-Nazi Protestant pastor. Niemöller was awarded the *Pour le Mérite* for his service as a U-boat commander in World War I. He studied theology after the war and was a pastor in Berlin when the Nazis came to power. An anti-republican nationalist, he was initially approved of by the Nazis, but was a co-founder of the *Pfarrernotbund* (Pastors' Emergency League) and leader of the Confessing Church. He spent seven years in Sachsenhausen and Dachau for outspoken criticism of the Nazis, and was elected President of the Protestant church in Hesse and Nassau after the war, and was active in the peace movement.

Nolde, Emil (1867–1956): Expressionist artist. Born near Nolde (Schleswig-Holstein) as Emil Hansen, Nolde studied in Munich, Paris and Copenhagen. He was a member of *Die Brücke* before World War I, and one of the leading exponents of expressionist painting in Weimar Germany. His work was prohibited in 1941 and categorised by the Nazis as 'degenerate'.

Orff, Carl (1895–1982): German composer. Orff was born in Munich and worked in musical education after World War I and co-founded the Günther School for gymnastics, dance and music in Munich in 1924. His most famous work is the *Carmina Burana* (1937), based on mediaeval poetry found in a Bavarian monastery.

Ossietzky, Carl von (1889–1938): Left-wing German journalist. A member of the German peace movement, Ossietzky was an editor on a number of publications in the 1920s, including the *Berliner Volkszeitung* and *Das Tagebuch*, and from 1927 was editor-in-chief of *Die Weltbühne*. Gaoled in 1931 and released the following year, he was re-imprisoned under the Nazis and died as a consequence of his treatment in prison. He was awarded the Nobel Peace Prize in 1935.

Papen, Franz von (1879–1969): German Chancellor (1932). Following a military and diplomatic career before and during World War I, he was elected to the Prussian *Landtag* for the Centre Party in 1920. He was appointed Chancellor in 1932 at the head of the so-called 'cabinet of barons'. During his short term in office he sought to undermine the power of the labour movement, not least through his illegal removal of the government of Prussia. He returned as Deputy Chancellor in Hitler's first cabinet, but was sent as minister to Vienna (1934–38) after the Night of the Long Knives. After the *Anschluss* he was appointed ambassador to Turkey (1938–1944). He was sentenced to eight years' imprisonment by a German court in 1947, but released in 1949.

Paulus, Friedrich von (1890–1957): German officer. Paulus was born in Breitenau, joined the army as a cadet in 1910 and served in World War I. In 1939 and 1940 he served in the Polish, French and Belgian campaigns and was appointed Deputy Chief of Staff in 1940. In 1942 he was promoted to General and appointed

Commander-in-Chief of the Sixth Army, which was defeated at Stalingrad. Against Hitler's wishes, Paulus surrendered his army to the Soviets in 1943. He remained in prison in the USSR until 1953, and settled in East Germany after his release.

Pétain, Philippe (1856–1951): French collaborator. A national military hero for his service during World War I, Pétain retired from the army in 1931 and entered politics. He was appointed War Minister in 1934 and Prime Minister in 1940, a short time before the defeat of France. He immediately negotiated peace with the Germans and established an authoritarian puppet regime in unoccupied France, whose government was based at Vichy. Civil rights were removed, trades unions abolished and political opposition prohibited. Pétain's regime also passed anti-semitic legislation and its leaders assisted in the deportation of French Jews. 'Vichy France' was directly occupied by Germany in 1942 and Pétain himself was taken to Germany in 1944. He was tried as a traitor in 1945, but his death sentence was commuted to life imprisonment.

Piscator, Erwin (1893–1966): German dramatist. Piscator joined the KPD after serving in World War I. He was involved with the Berlin Dada movement and the Proletarian Theatre, and was director of the *Volksbühne* (1924–27) before forming his own company. He went to the USSR in 1931 and Paris in 1938, before emigrating to America.

Planck, Max (1858–1947): German physicist who developed the quantum theory. Educated at Munich and Berlin Universities, Planck was appointed Professor of physics at Berlin in 1887. He was awarded the Nobel Prize in 1918. Planck opposed Nazi racial policies, and defended Einstein, but failed to slow the process of dismissal on racial grounds.

Preuss, Hugo (1860–1925): Liberal constitutional lawyer at the Commercial University in Berlin. Preuss was a co-founder of the DDP, and as Reich Interior Minister (1918–19) was commissioned by Ebert to work on the new constitution. His original radical draft was altered under pressure from sectional and particularist interests.

Quisling, Vidkun (1887–1945): Norwegian collaborator. As leader of the Norwegian fascist movement *Nasjonal Sammling*, Quisling assisted the German invasion of Norway and was appointed head of the puppet government installed there by the Nazis (1940–45). He was executed for treason after the war.

Raeder, Erich (1876–1960): German admiral and Commander-in-Chief of the German navy to 1943. Raeder served in World War

I, and took part in the Battle of Jutland. He was promoted to Rear-Admiral in 1922, and Commander-in-Chief of the navy in 1928. He was promoted to Grand Admiral in 1939 and led the naval offensive against Britain from the north European coast. He resigned in 1943 and was replaced by Doenitz. He was sentenced to life imprisonment at Nuremberg, but released in 1955.

Rathenau, Walther (1867–1922): Industrialist and politician, president of AEG. A physicist and chemist by training, in 1914 Rathenau was appointed Director of the raw materials department in the Prussian War Ministry. In 1919 he joined the DDP and became Minister for Reconstruction in 1921 and Foreign Minister in 1922. Rathenau was conciliatory in his dealings with the West, and recommended fulfilment of the Treaty of Versailles. He was also responsible for the concluding of the Treaty of Rapallo with the USSR. He was assassinated in Berlin by right-wing extremists in 1922.

Rauschning, Hermann (1887–1982): Nazi politician. Born in West Prussia, Rauschning served in World War I and moved to Danzig in 1926. Appointed President of the Danzig Senate in 1933 after a Nazi election victory, he fled to Switzerland in 1935, renounced his previous political convictions and published books seeking to warn the outside world against the dangers of Nazism (*Revolution of Nihilism*, and *Hitler Speaks*).

Reichenau, Walter von (1884–1942): German officer. Reichenau was born in Karlsruhe, joined the army in 1903 and served in World War I. He was a supporter of Nazism and was appointed Chief of Staff in 1933 and Commander of the Tenth Army in 1939. He endorsed both Hitler's war plans and the racial atrocities in the east.

Reinhardt, Max (1873–1943): Austrian actor and director. From the 1890s Reinhardt lived and worked in Berlin, where he was director of the Deutsches Theater from 1894. He returned to Vienna when the Nazis came to power, and emigrated to the USA in 1938.

Remarque, Erich Maria (1898–1970): German novelist. Born in Osnabrück, Remarque served in World War I and was wounded twice. His novel *Im Westen nichts Neues* (*All Quiet on the Western Front*), a realistic depiction of the experience of war published in 1927, sold millions of copies, and was burnt by the Nazis in 1933. His other works were banned and he left Germany for the USA in 1939, where he remained after the war.

Renteln, Theodor Adrian von (1897–1946): Commissioner-General of Lithuania during World War II. Born in Russia and educated in Berlin and Rostock, von Renteln joined the Nazi Party in 1928 and was appointed Reich Youth Leader and Students' Leader in 1931. He was appointed Commissioner-General of Lithuania in 1941 and hanged by the Russians in 1946.

Ribbentrop, Joachim von (1893–1946): Nazi Foreign Minister, 1938–45. Ribbentrop returned to Germany from Canada in 1914 and served in the cavalry regiment during World War I. He joined the NSDAP in 1932 and became Hitler's foreign affairs adviser in 1933. He was appointed Reich Commissioner for Disarmament at Geneva in 1934, and ambassador to Britain in 1936. He was appointed Foreign Minister in 1938 in place of von Neurath and negotiated the German-Soviet non-aggression treaty of the following year. He was less influential during the later war years, and was tried and hanged at Nuremberg.

Riefenstahl, Leni (b:1902): Nazi film director. Born in Berlin, Riefenstahl began her career as a dancer and actress there. She was chosen personally by Hitler to make propaganda films for the Nazi regime, including *Reichsparteitag* (1935) and *The Triumph of the Will* (1935) and *Olympia* (1938). She continued her career after the end of the war.

Röhm, Ernst (1887–1934): Leader of the Nazi stormtroopers (*Sturmabteilung*, SA). Born in Munich, Röhm served in World War I, and met Hitler in 1919. He participated in the abortive putsch of 1923. In 1930 he was appointed head of the SA, whose street violence and intimidation were central to the terminal political crisis of the Weimar Republic and the rise of the Nazi Party to power. After 1933 the stormtroopers were not only regarded as dispensable, but also, in so far as their persistent violence alienated conservative support, as a threat to the consolidation of Nazi power. Röhm was murdered in the purge known as the 'Night of the Long Knives' in 1934.

Rommel, Erwin (1891–1944): Field Marshal. Rommel was commissioned as a lieutenant in 1912 and was decorated for valour in World War I. In World War II he took part in the invasion of France before his transfer to North Africa, where he reversed the disastrous military position of the Axis following the collapse of the Italian campaign. He was Commander of the Afrika Korps from 1941 to 1943. After the German withdrawal from Africa he commanded the Army Group in France (1943–44). Rommel was implicated in the Stauffenberg plot to assassinate Hitler, but his prestige in Germany prevented the Nazis from publicly humiliating him with a trial and execution. He was forced to poison himself, and then buried with full military honours.

Rosenberg, Alfred (1893–1946): Nazi ideologue. Born in Estonia, Rosenberg fled to Bavaria during the Russian revolution, took part in the 'Beer Hall' putsch in Munich, and provisionally took over the party leadership during Hitler's imprisonment. His racist ideology was formulated in his *Myth of the Twentieth Century* (1930), which was enormously influential on the German right. He was in charge of ideological training within the party from 1934 and was appointed Minister for Occupied Eastern Territories in 1941. He was tried and hanged at Nuremberg.

Rust, Bernhard (1883–1945): Nazi Education Minister. Rust was born in Hanover and studied German and classics before serving in World War I. After the war he worked as a schoolmaster until he was sacked for molesting a pupil in 1930. He joined the NSDAP in 1922, was *Gauleiter* of Hanover and Braunschweig (Brunswick) from 1925, and was elected to the Reichstag in 1930. In 1933 he was appointed Prussian Minister of Science, and in 1934 Reich Minister of Education. He committed suicide in 1945.

Salomon, Erich (1886–1944): German photo journalist. Born in Berlin, the son of a banker who was subsequently ruined by the 1923 inflation, Salomon studied law and worked in the publishing department of the publishing house Ullstein. He became a freelance photo journalist in 1928, working in Berlin. In 1931 he published his collection *Berühmte Zeitgenossen in Unbewachten Augenblicken (Famous People in Unguarded Moments)*. Salomon fled to the Netherlands in 1933, but was sent to Auschwitz with his family in 1943 and murdered in 1944.

Salomon, Ernst von (1902–72): German nationalist writer. Sentenced to five years for his part in the murder of Rathenau, he was released in 1928 and became a popular writer of *völkisch* fiction. During the Nazi dictatorship he wrote mainly film scripts and apolitical fiction, but published a popular right-wing critique of de-Nazification after the war.

Sauckel, Fritz (1894–1946): Nazi *Gauleiter* of Thuringia and Plenipotentiary-General for Labour Mobilisation. Sauckel was a merchant seaman before World War I and was imprisoned in France during the war. He joined the Nazi Party in 1923. In 1927 he was elected to the Thuringian *Landtag* and appointed *Gauleiter*. During the war Sauckel was responsible for the mobilisation of foreign slave labour for the war effort, and the murder of Jews in Poland. He was tried and hanged at Nuremberg.

Schacht, Hjalmar (1877–1970): President of the *Reichsbank* and Economics Minister under the Nazis. Schacht was brought up in America, returning to Germany to study economics and take up a career in banking. Appointed Reich Currency Commissioner, and subsequently head of the *Reichsbank* in 1923, he was an important participant in the Dawes Plan and Young Plan negotiations. Initially a DDP supporter he joined the nationalist Harzburg Front in 1931 and supported Hitler's claim to the chancellorship the following year. The Nazis reappointed him head of the *Reichsbank* in 1933 and Economics Minister in 1934, and he devised the economic strategies which financed Germany's rearmament. He was appointed Plenipotentiary-General for the War Economy in 1935, but the economic crisis of 1936, the increasing influence of the autarky lobby, and the establishment of the Four Year Plan under Goering contributed to his eclipse. He was removed from the Economics Ministry in 1937 and from the Presidency of the *Reichsbank* in 1939, but remained a Minister without Portfolio until 1943. He was cleared at Nuremberg and resumed his career after the war.

Scheidemann, Philipp (1865–1939): Leading Social Democrat politician. Born in Kassel, Scheidemann was a printer by trade who joined the SPD in 1883, pursued a career in Socialist journalism and was elected to the Reichstag in 1903. In 1919 he was a member of the Council of People's Deputies, and as Minister President of the Provisional Government was effectively the first Weimar Chancellor. He was subsequently Mayor of Kassel until 1925. Scheidemann fled when the Nazis came to power and died in exile in Copenhagen.

Schellenberg, Walter (1910–52): Head of the Nazi intelligence service. Born in Saarbrücken, Schellenberg studied law at Bonn and joined the Nazi Party and SS in 1933, and the Gestapo in 1934. He organised SS 'special units' for the occupation of Czechoslovakia, and was later responsible for establishing the autonomy of the same units in their actions in the occupied eastern territories. He was promoted rapidly within the SS and RSHA, and was appointed Supreme Head of Military and SS Intelligence in 1944. He was acquitted of complicity in genocide, but sentenced to six years for the murder of Soviet prisoners of war and released after serving only half his sentence.

Schirach, Baldur von (1907–74): Nazi Reich Youth Leader and Governor of Vienna. Born in Berlin, Schirach joined the Nazi Party in 1924 while a student at Munich. He was head of the National Socialist German Students' League from 1929 and Nazi Youth Leader from 1931 (Reich Youth Leader from 1933) to 1940. After a brief spell of military service, Schirach was appointed *Gauleiter* and Governor of Vienna in 1940. He was sentenced to twenty years' imprisonment at Nuremberg and was released in 1966.

Schleicher, Kurt von (1882–1934): General and last Chancellor of the Weimar Republic. Following a military career before and during World War I, and a civil service career in the Defence Ministry during the 1920s, Schleicher was appointed Chancellor in 1932 after considerable intrigue against his predecessors. After only a few weeks in office he was replaced by Hitler. He was murdered during the 'Night of the Long Knives' (30 June 1934).

Schlemmer, Oskar (1888–1943): German artist. Schlemmer served in World War I and worked at the Bauhaus from 1920 to 1929, where he ran the theatre. In 1929 he moved to the Breslau Academy and from 1932 worked in schools in Berlin. He was dismissed in 1933.

Schmitt, Carl (1888–1985): Conservative German jurist and constitutional theorist. Born in Westphalia, Schmitt was an academic lawyer and Professor of law at Greifswald, Bonn, Cologne and Berlin, where he held the Chair from 1933 to 1945. Schmitt was an anti-republican figure opposed to political pluralism, parliamentary politics and conventional notions of the rule of law. He joined the Nazi Party in 1933 and became the Third Reich's principal legal and constitutional apologist. He accepted the Enabling Act and its implications as a valid constitutional starting point, promoted the notion of a 'legal revolution', argued that the will of the 'Führer' was law, and approved of the Nuremberg laws.

Schoenberg, Arnold (1874–1951): Austrian composer. Born in Vienna, Schoenberg was a pioneer of modern music, establishing his reputation with *Verklärte Nacht* (Transfigured Night, 1899). From 1910 he taught at the Vienna Academy, where his students included Berg and Webern (q.v.). He fled to the United States in 1933.

Scholtz-Klink, Gertrud (b.1902): Leader of the Nazi Women's League. Scholtz-Klink was an early member of the Nazi Party, women's leader in her native Baden from 1929, and Reich Women's Leader from 1933. She was also head of the *Deutsches Frauenwerk*, and from 1934 head of the women's section of the DAF. She went into hiding after the war but was tried by the French in 1948 and sentenced to eighteen months' imprisonment.

Schröder, Kurt (1889–1966): Nazi banker. Born in Hamburg, Schröder studied at Bonn, served in World War I and subsequently pursued a banking career in the Rhineland. An early contributor to the NSDAP who also directed funds to the party from the business community, he arranged the meeting between Papen and Hitler in January 1933, where the fall of Schleicher was planned. Schröder pursued a successful business career under the Nazis and received a nominal prison sentence in 1947.

Schrödinger, Erwin (1887–1961): Austrian physicist. Schrödinger studied at Vienna and served in World War I before taking up university teaching posts at Stuttgart and Kiel. In 1927 he succeeded Planck (q.v.) as Professor of physics at Berlin, and was awarded the Nobel Prize for physics in 1933 for his work on the wave equation. He fled Germany when the Nazis came to power, returning to Austria briefly (1936–38) before the *Anschluss*. He settled at the Institute of Advanced Studies in Dublin in 1939 and remained there until 1956.

Schultze, Walther (1894–1979): Nazi Leader of the Association of University Lecturers. A party member from 1919, he participated in the Munich putsch and was elected to the Bavarian *Landtag* in 1936. He became Leader of the University Teachers' Association in 1935. He was sentenced to four years in 1960 for complicity in the Euthanasia programme.

Schuschnigg, Kurt von (1897–1977): Chancellor of Austria from 1934 until the Nazi invasion (*Anschluss*) of 1938. Schuschnigg was born at Riva on Lake Garda, then lived in Austria and served in the Austrian army during World War I. He was elected to parliament for the Christian Socialist Party in 1927 and, after serving as Minister of Justice and Minister of Education, was appointed Chancellor following the assassination of his predecessor Engelbert Dollfuss. He was imprisoned by the Germans following the *Anschluss* and pursued an academic career in the United States for twenty years after the end of the war.

Schwarz, Franz Xaver von (1875–1947): NSDAP treasurer. Schwarz joined the NSDAP in 1922 and became treasurer in 1925. He died in an internment camp after the war.

Schwerin von Krosigk, Lutz Graf (1887–1952): German finance minister. Born in Anhalt and educated at Oxford and Lausanne, Schwerin von Krosigk served in World War I and was an anti-republican civil servant during the 1920s. Although unaffiliated to a political party he was a conservative with German nationalist and anti-semitic sympathies. He was appointed Finance Minister by Papen in 1932, a post he retained until 1945, when he was appointed Foreign Minister by Doenitz (q.v.). He was sentenced to ten years at Nuremberg in 1949 but released in 1951.

Schwitters, Kurt (1887–1948): German artist. Schwitters, a Hanover draughtsman and naturalistic painter, turned increasingly to expressionism towards the end of World War I. He began to make collages from refuse. This technique, which he called 'Merz' was his distinctive creative form. His own house became a *Merzbau* and he published a journal under the name *Merz* from 1923. In 1927 he organised a retrospective touring exhibition of his work.

Clearly a degenerate to the Nazis, he nevertheless remained in Hanover until 1937, when he moved to Norway.

Seeckt, Hans von (1886–1936): German officer. Born in Schleswig, Seeckt was a career officer who served in World War I and was a member of the German delegation to Versailles. He was Commander of the Reichswehr from 1920 to 1926, when he was dismissed for offering a post to a member of the former royal family. He was a DVP member of the Reichstag (1930–32) and supporter of Hitler during the Depression. He acted as a military adviser to Chiang Kai-Shek (1934–35) shortly before his death in Berlin.

Seldte, Franz (1882–1947): Founder of the *Stahlhelm* and Reich Minister of Labour, 1933–45. Born in Magdeburg, Seldte served in World War I before taking over the family chemicals business. He founded the *Stahlhelm* on Christmas Day in 1918 and ran it jointly with Duesterberg (q.v.) from 1924. He was appointed Reich Labour Minister by Hitler in 1933, and became head of the German Veterans' Organisation the following year.

Severing, Carl (1875–1952): German Socialist and minister. Severing was born in Herford, trained as a fitter, and joined the SPD in 1893. He edited the Social Democratic *Volkswacht* from 1912 and was elected to the Reichstag for the first time in 1907, serving as a deputy until 1912, and again from 1920 to 1933. He was Prussian Interior Minister from 1920 until 1926 and again from 1930 to 1932, and Reich Interior Minister in the intervening period (1928–30).

Seyss-Inquart, Arthur (1892–1946): Austrian Nazi. Seyss-Inquart was leader of the 'moderate' faction of Austrian Nazism during the 1930s, and was appointed to the Austrian State Council in 1937 by Schuschnigg (q.v.), who hoped to win their support for the government. The Chancellor was then forced by Hitler (q.v.) to appoint him Interior Minister in February 1938, a position which he used to undermine the Austrian state from within. He was briefly Chancellor, then Governor of Austria, and subsequently Reich Commissioner of the occupied Netherlands. He was tried and executed at Nuremberg.

Spann, Othmar (1878–1950): Austrian writer of the radical Right. Spann was born in Vienna, and held a Chair at Brünn (Brno) University until the fall of the Habsburg Empire, when he was dismissed by the Czechs. A clerical proponent of the 'corporate state' and opponent of parliamentarism and Marxism, he was an unofficial philosopher of Austrofascism and an important influence on European fascist ideology more broadly. Nevertheless, his relationship with Nazism was ambiguous, and he was arrested and imprisoned after the *Anschluss*.

Speer, Albert (1905–81): Reich Minister for Armaments and War Production, 1942–45. Born in Mannheim, Speer studied architecture and joined the NSDAP in 1931. He stage-managed the Nuremberg rallies and designed the new Reich Chancellery in Berlin and Party Headquarters in Munich. He was appointed Armaments Minister on the death of Fritz Todt in 1942, and was responsible for a sharp increase in arms production during the later war years. Despite clashes with other centres of influence within the regime, his responsibilities were extended and his influence increased until his eclipse by Goebbels during the last twelve months of the war. He was sentenced to twenty years at Nuremberg, and was released in 1966. He published two volumes of apologetic memoirs before his death.

Spengler, Oswald (1880–1936) German writer. Spengler studied at Munich, Berlin and Halle and worked as a schoolmaster until 1911. His major work, *Der Untergang des Abendlandes (The Decline of the West)*, was an emotive discussion of the imminent fall of modern European civilisation, based on literary allusion and mixed metaphors rather than historical analysis; but it was popular and influential on its publication after World War I. In it he elaborated a cyclical theory of history founded on the then fashionable pseudo-biological theories. He welcomed Nazism but remained a conservative elitist in his last years.

Srbik, Heinrich Ritter von (1874–1951): Austrian historian and collaborator. Educated at Theresianum and Vienna University, Srbik taught at the Austrian Institute of History and at Vienna University before World War I and held Chairs at Graz and Vienna. Austrian Education Minister (1928–32) during the First Republic, he welcomed the *Anschluss* and was elected to the Reichstag and appointed head of the German Historical Commission in 1938. He died in retirement in the Tyrol.

Stangl, Franz (1908–71): Commandant of Treblinka death camp, 1942–43. An Austrian policeman from 1931, Stangl joined the Euthanasia Institute in 1940 and was appointed to run the death camp at Sobibor in 1942. He was transferred to Treblinka the same year, where he remained until the camp revolt of August 1943, when he was transferred to Trieste. After the war he was sent to an open prison by the Austrians and escaped with the assistance of the Vatican to Syria and then to Brazil. Despite his active leading role in the Holocaust he was not pursued by Austria until 1961, was finally arrested in 1967, and tried and sentenced to life imprisonment for the murder of 900,000 Jews by a German court in 1970.

Stauffenberg, Claus Schenk Graf von (1907–44): German officer and leader of the 1944 plot by senior officers to assassinate Hitler (the 'Stauffenberg Plot'). He was born in Jettingen, attended military schools, and was commissioned as an officer in 1930. He served in Africa in World War II, and was wounded there and posted back to Berlin where he recruited support for an assassination attempt on Hitler, to be followed by a coup. The plotters failed to win Allied support, not least because they proposed to retain many of Hitler's territorial gains and an authoritarian system of government within Germany. The assassination attempt itself failed, and Stauffenberg and others were arrested and executed after show trials.

Stegerwald, Adam (1874–1945): Christian trades unionist and Centre Party politician. A member of the National Assembly (1919) and the Reichstag (1920–33), he was appointed Transport Minister in 1929 and was subsequently Minister of Labour (1930–32). After the war he was a co-founder of the CSU.

Stinnes, Hugo (1870–1924): German industrialist. Stinnes was a Ruhr businessman who was born in Mühlheim and whose interests included coal, iron, steel, energy, catering and the press. He was chief negotiator for the industrialists in the drawing up of a social and economic settlement with the trades unions after World War I.

Strasser, Gregor (1892–1934): Leading Nazi politician. Strasser joined the party after serving in World War I and participated in the Munich putsch of 1923. Leader of the North German wing of the NSDAP during the 1920s, his attempt to propagate a populist 'anti-capitalism' (appropriate, he considered, to the mobilisation of the industrial workers of the north) earned him a reputation as the leader of a supposedly 'left-wing' faction within the party. He came into conflict with Hitler (q.v.) when he negotiated with Schleicher (q.v.) for the post of Vice-Chancellor in 1932, and was forced to withdraw from active politics. He was arrested and murdered during the 1934 purge of the SA.

Strasser, Otto (1897–1974): Brother of Gregor Strasser (see above), and head of propaganda of the North German wing of the NSDAP. Expelled from the party in 1930 following ideological differences with Hitler, he went into exile during the Nazi dictatorship but returned to fascist politics in post-war West Germany.

Strauss, Richard (1864–1949): German composer and conductor. His works include *Till Eulenspiegels Lustige Streiche* (1895), *Also sprach Zarathustra* (1896), *Salome* (1905), *Elektra* (1908), *Der Rosenkavalier* (1910) and *Ariadne auf Naxos* (1912). Arguably the leading figure in German music, Strauss remained in Germany in 1933 and accepted the post of President of the Reich Chamber of Music, which he held until 1935. He was cleared by a de-Nazification trial after the war.

Streicher, Julius (1885–1946): Nazi politician. A Bavarian schoolmaster, Streicher served in World War I and founded his own *Deutsch-Soziale Partei* in 1919, before joining the NSDAP in 1921. In 1923 he founded *Der Stürmer*, a virulently anti-semitic journal, and became *Gauleiter* of Franconia in 1925. He was dismissed from his job for anti-republican activity in 1928 and was elected to the Bavarian *Landtag* in 1929. *Der Stürmer* led the campaign for anti-semitic legislation which culminated in the Nuremberg laws. His unpopularity among other leading Nazis led to his dismissal from party posts in 1940. He was tried and hanged at Nuremberg in 1946.

Stresemann, Gustav (1878–1929): Weimar politician. Before and during World War I Stresemann was a member of the National Liberal Party which he represented in the Reichstag (1907–12 and 1914–18), and was a co-founder of the DVP in 1918, which he represented in the National Assembly (1919) and the Reichstag (1920–33). He was Chancellor at the height of the inflation crisis of 1923, and subsequently Foreign Minister until his death in 1929.

Stroop, Jürgen (1895–1951): SS officer. Stroop served in World War I and was promoted through the ranks of the SS after 1933. He served with the SS in eastern Europe and the USSR after the outbreak of war, and commanded the suppression of the revolt in the Warsaw ghetto in 1943. He was tried and executed in Poland in 1951.

Stuelpnagel, Karl-Heinrich von (1886–1944): German officer, and cousin of Otto von Stuelpnagel. Born in Darmstadt, Stuelpnagel was a career soldier. He was Military Governor of France from 1942 to 1944, during which he time he ordered violently repressive measures against the resistance. He was a leading member of the 1944 conspiracy to overthrow the Nazi regime. After the failure of the plot he unsuccessfully tried to commit suicide and was arrested and hanged in Berlin.

Stuelpnagel, Otto von (1878–1948): German officer. Stuelpnagel earned a reputation for brutality during World War I, which he consolidated as Military Governor of France (1940–42) with reprisal executions and the mass murder of Jews and Communists. He was extradited to Paris after the war and committed suicide while awaiting execution.

Terboven, Josef (1898–1945): Nazi politician. Born in Essen, Terboven served in World War I and studied at Freiburg and Munich. An SA member, he was elected to the Reichstag for Düsseldorf West in the Nazi electoral breakthrough of 1930. *Gauleiter* of Essen from 1933, *Oberpräsident* of the Rhineland from 1935, and Reich Defence Commissioner for District VI (Münster) from 1939, he became Reich Commissioner in Norway in 1940, where he committed suicide in 1945.

Thälmann, Ernst (1886–1944): Leader of the German Communist Party (KPD). Thälmann joined the SPD as a Hamburg dock worker in 1903, the USPD in 1917, and the KPD in 1920. He was a Communist member of the Reichstag from 1924 to 1933 and President of the KPD from 1925. He ran (unsuccessfully) for President in 1925 and 1932. He was arrested in 1933 and died in Buchenwald.

Thierack, Otto (1889–1946): Nazi politician. Born in Saxony into a middle class family, Thierack studied law at Marburg and Leipzig, served in World War I and then practised as a lawyer. An early Nazi, he was appointed Saxon Justice Minister in 1933, and was President of the *Volksgericht* (1936–42). Thierack was instrumental in the murderous exploitation of slave labour. He committed suicide after the war.

Thyssen, Fritz (1873–1951): German Nationalist businessman. Thyssen organised passive resistance during the 1923 occupation of the Ruhr and was an early financial backer of the NSDAP. He joined the party in 1931, mediated between the Nazis and the Rhineland business community, and was rewarded in 1933 by election to the Reichstag in the plebiscite of November of that year. He was also appointed Prussian State Councillor by Goering. He subsequently fled Germany and repudiated the regime. He was arrested by the Vichy French and turned over to the Germans. He died in Argentina.

Todt, Fritz (1891–1942): Nazi Minister for Armaments and Munitions, 1940–42. Born in Baden into an upper middle class family, Todt served in World War I and studied civil engineering at Karlsruhe. He joined the Nazis in 1922 and became an SS Colonel in 1931. In 1933 he was appointed Inspector General of German Roads, a post which gave him responsibility for the construction of the motorways and military fortifications. He was appointed Armaments Minister in 1940, and Inspector General of Roads, Water and Power in 1941. He died in an air crash and was succeeded by Speer (q.v.).

Toller, Ernst (1893–1939): German playwright. Toller volunteered to serve in World War I, but was discharged from the army in 1916 following a breakdown. He became involved in Communist politics in Bavaria after the war, and was imprisoned there for five years for his involvement with the revolutionary government. Most of his important work was written in prison. Toller was Jewish, and fled Germany for the USA in 1933. He committed suicide in New York in 1939.

Tucholsky, Kurt (1890–1935): German writer and journalist. Born in Berlin, Tucholsky studied law and served in World War I before pursuing a career in journalism on the *Weltbühne* (of which he was briefly editor) during the 1920s. He also published satirical essays and poetry. He committed suicide in exile in Sweden in 1935.

Ulbricht, Walter (1893–1973): German Communist politician. Ulbricht joined the Spartacus League in 1918 and was a co-founder of the Communist Party (KPD). He spent several years in the USSR before his election as a Reichstag deputy in 1927. He fled to the Soviet Union in 1933, and commanded a republican army unit in Spain between 1936 and 1938. He returned to Germany after the war to become General Secretary of the Socialist Unity Party and effective leader of East Germany, in which capacity he was responsible for the building of the Berlin Wall.

Veesenmayr, Edmund (b.1904): SS officer. An early Nazi, Veesenmayr pursued a career in the SS and the German foreign service. He had business interests and diplomatic postings in the Balkans, where he became involved in the deportation of local Jewish populations. He was appointed Reich Plenipotentiary in Hungary in 1944, where he organised the deportation of Hungarian Jews. He was sentenced to twenty years at Nuremberg in 1949, but released after two years following US intervention on his behalf.

Wagner, Adolf (1890–1944): Nazi politician. Born in Lorraine, Wagner was a German officer in World War I and joined the NSDAP in 1923. He was elected to the Bavarian *Landtag* in 1929 and appointed *Gauleiter* of Munich-Upper Bavaria in the same year. Bavarian Interior Minister from 1933, and Bavarian Education Minister from 1936, he was appointed Defence Commissioner of Districts VII and XIII (Munich and Nuremberg) in 1939. He lost influence after the outbreak of war.

Wagner, Gerhardt (1888–1938): Nazi functionary. A former *Freikorps* member, Wagner was head of the Nazi Doctors' League from 1932, and was elected to the Reichstag in the 1933 plebiscite. Wagner was an early supporter of euthanasia for the disabled.

Wagner, Robert (1895–1946): Nazi politician. Wagner served in World War I and participated in the Munich putsch while still a *Reichswehr* officer. *Gauleiter* of Baden from 1925, and a member of the Baden *Landtag* from 1929 to 1933, he acquired responsibility for Alsace after the fall of France, initially as Chief of the Civil Administration. He was tried by the French and executed in Strasbourg in 1946.

Weber, Max (1864–1920): German social philosopher. Weber was appointed to Chairs at Freiburg (1894) and Heidelberg (1897) before publishing his best-known work, *The Protestant Ethic and the Spirit of Capitalism*. He established a distinctive method of inquiry in the social sciences and participated in the drafting of the Weimar constitution.

Weill, Kurt (1900–50): German Jewish composer who collaborated with Bertolt Brecht (q.v.). Weill studied at the Berlin High School of Music and began to compose operas in the 1920s. His reputation was established by his work with Brecht on *Der Aufstieg und Fall der Stadt Mahagonny* (1927: *The Rise and Fall of the City of Mahagonny*), and particularly on *Die Dreigroschenoper* (1928: *The Threepenny Opera*). When the Nazis came to power he fled abroad, initially to Paris (1933) and then to London and finally New York (1935) where he re-established himself as a composer of Broadway musicals. He was married to the singer Lotte Lenya (q.v.).

Weiss, Wilhelm (1892–1950): Nazi journalist. A former student at Munich University, *Freikorps* member and participant in the Munich putsch, Weiss joined the *Völkischer Beobachter* in 1927 and became editor in 1938. He was elected to the Reichstag in March 1933 and appointed head of the Reich Association of the German Press by Goebbels in 1934.

Weizsäcker, Ernst Freiherr von (1882–1951): German diplomat. A naval officer in World War I, Weizsäcker joined the German Foreign Office in 1920 and received a number of diplomatic postings before his promotion by Ribbentrop to Chief State Secretary. He was ambassador to the Vatican from 1943 until the end of the war. He was sentenced to five years at Nuremberg, but released after eighteen months, and published apologetic memoirs shortly before his death.

Wels, Otto (1873–1939): German Socialist. Born in Berlin, Wels was a Social Democratic Reichstag deputy from 1912 to 1933 and Chairman of the SPD (1931–33). He fled to Prague in 1933 and led the exiled SPD (SOPADE) from there, and after 1938 from Paris, until his death.

Wessel, Horst (1907–30): Young Nazi stormtrooper killed in a brawl in 1930. Subsequently presented as a martyr, the marching song he composed became the most important anthem of the Nazi movement.

Wiener, Alfred (1885–1964): Leader of the German Jewish community. Born in Potsdam, Wiener studied at Berlin and Heidelberg and wrote a doctorate on Arabic literature. After World War I he became head of the *Centralverein*, Germany's most important Jewish organisation. He fled to the Netherlands in 1933 and documented the Nazi persecution of the Jews at the Jewish Central Information Office, whose collection formed the basis of the Wiener Library in London. The collection is now in Tel Aviv.

Wirth, Christian (1885–1944): SS officer. Wirth served in World War I before pursuing a career in the Württemberg police and subsequently the *Kripo*. He was appointed head of a euthanasia institute in 1939 and transferred to Poland in 1941, where he was head of the death camps' organisation. He was transferred to Trieste in 1943.

Wirth, Josef (1879–1956): Weimar Chancellor. A member of the Baden *Landtag* for the Centre Party from 1913, and of the Reichstag from 1914 to 1933, he was appointed Finance Minister in 1920 and Chancellor in 1922. He emigrated to Switzerland in 1933 but returned after the war and died in his native Freiburg.

Wolff, Karl (b.1900): SS officer. Born in Darmstadt into an upper middle class family, Wolff served in World War I and joined the Nazi Party in 1931. He was promoted through the SS ranks and became a lieutenant-general in the Waffen-SS in 1940. He became Military Governor of occupied nothern Italy in 1943. Wolff went over to the Allies at the end of the war, thereby avoiding prosecution as a war criminal, and although he was later sentenced to four years by a German court, he was released after a week. He was tried again in 1964 for war crimes and sentenced to fifteen years, but was released early (in 1971) a second time.

SECTION VIII
Bibliography

Abbreviations

AHR   *American Historical Review*

CEH   *Central European History*

EHQ   *European History Quarterly*

EHR   *Economic History Review*

ESR   *European Studies Review*

GH   *German History*

HWJ   *History Workshop Journal*

JCH   *Journal of Contemporary History*

JMH   *Journal of Modern History*

JSH   *Journal of Social History*

PP   *Past and Present*

SH   *Social History*

Printed Primary Sources

J Noakes and G Pridham, *Nazism 1919–1945: A Documentary Reader* (3 vols) is as useful for the commentary as for the documents themselves. There are three volumes: 1 *The Rise to Power* (Exeter, 1983), 2 *State, Economy and Society 1933–1939* (Exeter, 1984) and 3 *Foreign Policy, War and Extermination* (Exeter, 1988). This collection is a revised version of an earlier collection in a single volume: J Noakes and G Pridham, *Documents on Nazism* (London, 1974). See also the recently published one-volume collection by Benjamin Sax and Dieter Kuntz, *Inside Hitler's Germany* (Lexington, Mass., 1992).

E L Woodward and Rohan Butler (eds) *Documents on British Foreign Policy 1919–1939*, 2nd series (London, 1947). Vols II–IV cover the depression and the Nazi takeover of power.

There are several sources for Hitler: D C Watt (ed.), *Mein Kampf*, translated by Ralph Mannheim (London, 1992); *Hitler's Secret Book*, introduced by Telford Taylor (New York, 1961); *Hitler's Secret Conversations* (New York, 1972); H R Trevor-Roper (ed.), *Hitler's Table Talk 1941–1944* (London, 1953); W Maser, *Hitler's Letters and Notes* (New York, 1976); W Domarus (ed.), *Hitler's Speeches* (London, 1991); A Kubizek, *The Young Hitler I Knew* (New York, no date); and O Strasser, *Hitler and I* (Oxford, 1940).

Diaries, Memoirs and Autobiographies

On Weimar politics see: Hartmut Pogge von Strandmann (ed.), *Walter Rathenau. Industrialist, Banker, Intellectual and Politician. Notes and Diaries 1907–1922* (Oxford, 1985).

On the Nazis and Nazi Germany see: H Heiber (ed.), *The Early Goebbels Diaries* (London, 1962); F Taylor (ed.), *J Goebbels, Diaries 1939–1941* (London, 1982); Albert Speer, *Inside the Third Reich* (London, 1970); idem, *Spandau. The Secret Diaries* (London, 1977).

See also: Konrad Heiden, *Hitler's Rise to Power* (London, 1944); A Krebs, *The Infancy of Nazism: The Memoirs of ex-Gauleiter Albert Krebs*, ed. by W S Allen (London, 1978).

Secondary Sources

Biographies

On Weimar politics see: K Epstein, *Matthias Erzberger and the Dilemma of German Democracy* (Princeton, 1959); K R Calkins, *Hugo Haase. Democrat and Revolutionary* (Durham, North Carolina, 1979); A Dorpalen, *Hindenburg and the Weimar Republic* (Princeton, 1964); J Wheeler-Bennett, *Hindenburg. The Wooden Titan* (London and New York, 1967); J A Leopold, *Alfred Hugenberg. The Radical Nationalist Campaign against the Weimar Republic* (New Haven and London, 1977); H A Turner, *Stresemann and the Politics of the Weimar Republic* (Princeton, 1963).

The classic biography of Hitler is Alan Bullock, *Hitler. A Study in Tyranny* (London, 1952). See also: Joachim Fest, *Hitler*, (London, 1974); Ian Kershaw, *Hitler* (London, 1991); and Alan Bullock, *Hitler and Stalin. Parallel Lives* (London, 1991). There are biographies of several other leading Nazis, but see especially: R Overy, *Goering. The Iron Man* (London, 1984) and Peter R Black, *Ernst Kaltenbrunner. Ideological Soldier of the Third Reich* (Princeton, 1984). Both combine biography with the broader political context of the subject. See also: J V Lang, *Bormann* (London, 1979); Bradley F Smith, *Heinrich Himmler. A Nazi in the Making 1900–1926*; R Manvell and H Fraenkl, *Heinrich Himmler* (New York, 1965); Richard Breitman, *The Architect of Genocide. Himmler and the Final Solution* (London, 1991); Werner T Angress and Bradley F Smith, 'Diaries of Heinrich Himmler's Early Years', *JMH*, xxxi (1959), pp. 206–24; and Peter Loewenberg, 'The Unsuccessful Adolescence of Heinrich Himmler', *AHR*, lxxvi (1971), pp. 612–41.

German History

There are several standard histories of modern Germany. Perhaps the most accessible is William Carr, *A History of Germany 1815–1945* (London, 1979); G A Craig, *Germany 1866–1945* (Oxford, 1981) and H A Holborn, *A History of Modern Germany*, 2 vols (London, 1969) are also useful introductions. The best history of Germany from the 1890s is V R Berghahn, *Modern Germany. Society, Economy and Politics in the Twentieth Century*, (2nd edn, Cambridge, 1987).

Mary Fulbrook, *Germany 1918–1990: The Divided Nation* (Princeton, 1960) takes a somewhat later starting point. See also R Dahrendorf, *Society and Democracy in Germany* (London, 1967). On the economy G Stolper, *The German Economy, 1870 to the Present* (London, 1967) and G Bry, *Wages in Germany 1871–1945*. On the constitution see H W Koch, *A Constitutional History of Germany in the Nineteenth and Twentieth Centuries* (London, 1984).

The Weimar Republic

There are several useful general texts on the Weimar Republic as a whole. Still among the best is Erich Eyck, *A History of the Weimar Republic* (English edn, Oxford, 1964), while A J Nicholls, *Weimar and the Rise of Hitler* (London, 1968) is among the clearest and most accessible. More recent German work on the Weimar Republic is now available in English, including E Kolb, *The Weimar Republic* (London, 1988) and Detlev Peukert, *The Weimar Republic* (London, 1991).

On the German revolution the best general introduction in English is still F L Carsten, *Revolution in Central Europe* (London, 1972) which deals with both Germany and Austria. A J Ryder, *The German Revolution* (Cambridge, 1967) and Richard M Watt, *The Kings Depart: The German Revolution and the Treaty of Versailles 1918–19* (London, 1968) are also useful; A Mitchell, *Revolution in Bavaria 1918–1919: The Eisner Regime and the Soviet Republic* (Princeton, 1965) and J Tampke, *The Ruhr and Revolution. The Revolutionary Movement in the Rhenish-Westphalian Industrial Region* (London, 1979) are good regional studies of events in particularly turbulent parts of Germany. See also: C B Burdick and R H Lutz, *The Political Institutions of the German Revolution* (Stanford, 1968); J W Mishark, *The Road to Revolution* (Detroit, 1967); D W Morgan, *The Socialist Left and the German Revolution* (Ithaca, 1975) and E Waldmann, *The Spartacist Uprising* (Marquette, 1958). Students should also look at journal literature, particularly R. Rürup, 'Problems of the German Revolution', JCH, 3 (1968), pp. 109–126.

A useful starting point on the economic problems of the inter-war period is still J M Keynes, *The Economic Consequences of the Peace Treaty* (New York, 1920). On Germany's problems during the post-war crisis see: D Felix, *Walter Rathenau and the Weimar Republic: The Politics of Reparations* (Baltimore, 1971); C L Holtferich, *The German Inflation* (Berlin, 1985); F K Ringer (ed.), *The German Inflation of 1923* (New York, 1969); G D Feldman, *Iron and Steel in the German Inflation, 1916–1923* (Princeton, 1977) and G D Feldman et al. (eds), *The German Inflation Reconsidered. A Preliminary Balance* (Berlin and New York, 1982). See also R J Schmidt, *Versailles and the Ruhr* (London, 1968). Although there is no general work on counter-revolutionary politics and the activities of the radical right during the crisis, a number of books on the politics of the period shift the focus away from the revolutionaries to their opponents both within the social and political establishment and beyond. C S Maier, *Recasting Bourgeois Europe* (Princeton, 1975) provides a more general European perspective. On Germany itself see F L Carsten, *The Reichswehr and Politics* (Oxford, 1966). On counter-revolution and the radical right see: G D Feldman, 'Big Business and the Kapp Putsch', *CEH*, iv (1971).

Weimar Politics

General books on Weimar Germany deal extensively with its political problems. See: J M Diehl, *Paramilitary Politics in Weimar Germany* (Bloomington, Ind., 1977); R Heberle, *From Democracy to Nazism. A Regional Case Study on Political Parties in Germany* (New York, 1970). On the left see H Grebing, *A History of the German Labour Movement* (Leamington Spa, 1985), and R N Hunt, *German Social Democracy 1918–1933* (New Haven, 1964) and W L Guttsman, *The German Social Democratic Party 1875–1933* (London, 1981). Specifically on the USPD: D W Morgan, *The Socialist Left and the German Revolution: A History of the German Independent Social Democratic Party*. On the Communist Party see B Fowkes, *Communism in Germany under the Weimar Republic* (London, 1984). See also R Breitman, *German Socialism and Weimar Democracy* (Chapel Hill, 1981) and, on the depression years, R A Gates, 'German Socialism and the Crisis of 1929–33', *CEH*, vii (1974), pp.332–59. Less attention has been paid to the politics of liberal democracy: see B B Frye, *Liberal Democrats in the Weimar Republic. The History of the German Democratic Party and the German State Party* (Carbondale and Edwardsville, Ill., 1985). Similarly, there is little on Christian Democracy and the Centre Party: see K Epstein, *Matthias Erzberger and the Dilemma of German Democracy*, 2 vols (Cambridge, Mass. 1962).

On the right see: A Dorpalen, *Hindenburg and the Weimar Republic* (Princeton, 1964); L Hertzmann, *DNVP: Right-Wing Opposition in the Weimar Republic 1918–1924* (Lincoln, Neb., 1963); J A Leopold, *Alfred Hugenberg. The Radical Nationalist Campaign against the Weimar Republic* (New Haven and London, 1977); H A Turner, *Stresemann and the Politics of the Weimar Republic* (1963); D P Walker, 'The German National People's Party: the Conservative Dilemma in the Weimar Republic', *JCH*, xv (1980), pp.513–32. On the difficulties of German conservatism during the depression see: A Chanady, 'The Disintegration of the German National People's Party 1924–1930', *JMH*, xlix (1967), pp.65–91, and by the same author, 'The Dissolution of the German Democratic Party in 1930', *AHR*, lxxiii (1968) pp.1433–53. See also R R G Moeller,

German Peasants and Agrarian Politics 1914–1924. The Rhineland and Westphalia (Chapel Hill and London, 1986) and J R C Wright, *'Above Parties'. The Political Attitudes of the German Protestant Church Leadership 1918–1933* (Oxford, 1974).

German Society in the Weimar Republic

There have been few attempts to provide a comprehensive social history of Weimar Germany. On society and politics see R Bessel and E J Feuchtwanger (eds), *Social Change and Political Development in Weimar Germany* (London, 1981). On the working class see E Fromm, *The Working Class in Weimar Germany* (Leamington Spa, 1984); J Wickham, 'Working Class Movement and Working Class Life: Frankfurt am Main during the Weimar Republic', *SH*, viii (1983), pp.315–43.

On the middle classes see: H Lebovics, *Social Conservatism and the Middle Classes in Germany 1914–1933* (Princeton, 1969); S J Coyner, 'Class Consciousness and Consumption: The New Middle Class in the Weimar Republic', *JSH*, 11 (1977), pp.310–37; L E Jones, 'The Dying Middle. Weimar Germany and the Fragment-ation of Bourgeois Politics', *CEH* (1972).

On women see R Bridenthal, 'Beyond Kinder, Kirche, Küche: Weimar Women at Work', *CEH*, vi (1973), pp.148–66; B Peterson, 'The Politics of Working Class Women in the Weimar Republic', *CEH*, x (1977), pp.87–111.

Weimar Foreign Policy

See Lee Marshall and W Michalka, *German Foreign Policy 1917–1933: Continuity or Break?* (Leamington Spa, 1987); J Jacobson, *Locarno Diplomacy* (Princeton, 1971). The most important individual figure to determine Weimar foreign policy was Stresemann: see W L Bretton, *Stresemann and the Revision of Versailles* (Stanford, 1953); R Grathwohl, *Stresemann and the DNVP: Reconciliation or Revenge in German Foreign Policy 1924–1928?* (Lawrence, Kan., 1980); H Gatzke, *Stresemann and the Rearmament of Germany* (Baltimore, 1954). See also H L Dyck, *Weimar Germany and Soviet Russia* (London, 1966); S A Stehlin, *Weimar and the Vatican* (Princeton, 1983).

Weimar Culture

The cultural and intellectual life of Weimar Germany is one of the most fascinating aspects of the period. See W Laqueur, *Weimar. A Cultural History* (New York, 1975); P Gay, *Weimar Culture* (New York, 1968) and F Stern, *The Politics of Cultural Despair* (New York, 1961). See also Jeffrey Herf, *Reactionary Modernism: Technology, Culture and Politics in Weimar and the Third Reich* (Cambridge, 1985). More specifically on intellectuals, see: A Phelan (ed.), *The*

Weimar Dilemma. Intellectuals in the Weimar Republic (Manchester, 1985).

The Collapse of the Weimar Republic

The depression and the political crisis of the early 1930s has attracted a great deal of attention from historians. See D Abraham, *The Collapse of the Weimar Republic. Political Economy and Crisis* (2nd, revised edn, New York, 1986); M Broszat, *Hitler and the Collapse of Weimar Democracy* (Leamington Spa, 1987); I Kershaw (ed.), *Weimar: Why did German Democracy Fail?* (London, 1990).

More specifically on the economy, see: H James, *The German Slump. Politics and Economics 1924–1936* (Oxford, 1986); W C McNeil, *American Money and the Weimar Republic. Economics and Politics on the Eve of the Great Depression* (New York, 1986). On the depression and its effects see: R J Evans and D Geary (eds), *The German Unemployed 1918–1936* (London, 1986); P D Stachura (ed.), *Unemployment and the Great Depression in Weimar Germany* (London, 1986); and D Petzina, 'Germany and the Great Depression', *JCH*, iv (1969), pp.59–74.

On the political violence of the last years of the Weimar Republic see: R Bessel, *Political Violence and the Rise of Nazism* (New Haven, 1984); P Merkl, *Political Violence under the Swastika. 581 Early Nazis* (Princeton, 1975); E Rosenhaft, *Beating the Fascists? The German Communists and Political Violence 1929–1933* (Cambridge, 1983); and J Ward, ' "Smash the Fascists . . ." German Communist Attempts to Counter the Nazis', *CEH*, xiv (1981), pp.30–61.

Fascism and Totalitarianism

Nazism was characterised as German fascism by many contemporaries and fascism has been seen as a generic phenomenon (as opposed to one restricted to Italy) since the 1920s. Totalitarian interpretations on the other hand have emphasised the similarities between Nazi Germany and Soviet Russia. Such theories were particularly popular at the height of the cold war and waned when the death of Stalin was followed by limited reform in the USSR and East–West tension was relaxed by *Ostpolitik* and detente. Research in the late 1960s and 1970s concentrated on comparative studies of fascism. The concept of totalitarianism has undergone something of a revival since the early 1980s.

W Laqueur, *Fascism. A Reader's Guide* (London, 1979) is still an invaluable introduction to the comparative study of fascism, which contains important essays on Nazism, above all Hans Mommsen, 'National Socialism. Continuity and Change'. F L Carsten, *The Rise of Fascism* (London, 1982) is an accessible survey of the origins of fascism. S J Woolf (ed.), *Fascism in Europe* (London, 1981) is a useful collection of essays on fascism in a number of European countries. See S J Woolf (ed.), *The Nature of Fascism* (Oslo, 1979) on interpretations of the phenomenon. Stein Ugelvik Larsen et al. (eds), *Who were the Fascists?* (Oslo, 1980) and Detlef Mühlberger, *The Social Basis of European Fascist Movements* (London, 1987) are useful comparative collections on the social bases of European fascist movements. See also Martin Blinkhorn (ed.), *Fascists and Conservatives. The Radical Right and the Establishment in Twentieth-Century Europe* (London, 1990).

A comparative essay on the ideology of Nazism, Italian fascism and the *Action Française*, Ernst Nolte, *The Three Faces of Fascism* (London, 1965) did much to encourage renewed interest in fascism as a generic phenomenon in the 1960s and 1970s. Roger Griffin, *The Nature of Fascism* (London, 1990) also approaches the subject from the perspective of the historian of political ideas. Hannah Arendt, *The Origins of Totalitarianism* (New York, 1951) is the classic introduction to the concept of totalitarianism. See also W Sauer, 'National Socialism: Totalitarianism or Fascism', *AHR*, 73 (1967) pp.404–24; and A L Unger, *The Totalitarian Party: Party and People in Nazi Germany and Soviet Russia* (Washington DC, 1970). See Ian Kershaw, *The Nazi Dictatorship. Problems and Perspectives of Interpretation* (3rd edn, London, 1993), chapter 2 ('The Essence of Nazism: Form of Fascism, Brand of Totalitarianism or Unique Phenomenon?') for a discussion of the different interpretations of Nazism; and Thomas Childers and Jane Caplan (eds), *Re-evaluating the Third Reich* (New York, 1993), especially the appendix by Tim Mason, 'Whatever Happened to "Fascism?" '.

Historiographical Surveys

See: I Kershaw, *The Nazi Dictatorship. Problems and Perspectives of Interpretation* (3rd edn, London, 1993); P Ayçoberry, *The Nazi Question* (London, 1981); J Hiden and J Farquharson, *Explaining Hitler's Germany. Historians and the Third Reich* (London, 1983); K Hildebrand, *The Third Reich* (London, 1984). The second edition of Kershaw's book (London, 1989) contains a chapter on the *Historikerstreit* of the mid-1980s, and the third edition has a new chapter on 'Shifting Perspectives: Historiographical Trends in the Aftermath of Unification'. A collection of important contributions to that debate has now (rather belatedly) been published in English, translated by James Knowlton and Truett Cates, *Forever in the Shadow of Hitler* (Atlantic Highlands, New Jersey, 1993). See also R Evans, *In Hitler's Shadow* (London, 1989) and his earlier article, 'The New Nationalism and the Old History: Perspectives on the West German "*Historikerstreit*" ', *JMH*, 59 (1987), pp.761–97; C Maier, *The Unmasterable Past* (Cambridge, Mass., 1988).

The Nazi Party
The standard introduction is still D Orlow, *The History of the Nazi Party*, 2 vols (Pittsburgh, 1969–70). See also M H Kater, *The Nazi Party* (Cambridge, Mass., 1983); Jeremy Noakes, *The Nazi Party in Lower Saxony* (Oxford, 1971); J Nyomarky, *Charisma and Factionalism in the Nazi Party* (Minneapolis, 1967). See also G Pridham, *Hitler's Rise to Power: The Nazi Movement in Bavaria, 1923–1933* (London, 1973); and H J Gordon, *Hitler and the Beer Hall Putsch* (Princeton, 1972).

The distribution of support for the Nazi Party before 1933 has attracted a great deal of scholarly attention. See T Childers, *The Nazi Voter. The Social Foundations of Fascism in Germany 1919–1933* (Chapel Hill, 1933), and by the same author, 'The Social Bases of the National Socialist Vote', *JCH*, xi (1976), pp.17–42 and 'Who, indeed, did vote for Hitler?', *CEH* xvii/1 (1983), pp.45–53. Childers has also edited a collection of essays on the subject: T Childers (ed.), *The Formation of the Nazi Constituency 1918–1933* (London, 1986). Heated debate has been generated about the extent of working class support for Nazism. See: C Fischer, *Stormtroopers: A Social, Economic and Ideological Analysis 1929–1935* (London, 1983) and 'Class Enemies or Class Brothers? Communist-Nazi Relations in Germany 1929–1933', *EHQ*, xv/3 (1985), pp.259–80 along with the response to this article by Dick Geary, 'Nazis and Workers', *EHQ*, xv/4 pp.453–64. See also R F Hamilton, *Who Voted for Hitler?* (Princeton, 1982), and 'Braunschweig 1932: Further Evidence on the Support for National Socialism', *CEH*, xvii/1 (1984), pp.3–36. Also on the question of the relationship between industrial labour and Nazism, see: T Mason, 'National Socialism and the Working Class, 1925–May 1933', *NGC*, xi (1977), pp.49–93, and Detlef Mühlberger, 'The Sociology of the NSDAP: the Question of Working Class Membership', *JCH*, xv (1980), pp.493–512.

The relationship between the Nazis and social groups from the middle classes is covered by a number of specialised studies, including: Hans Speier, *German White Collar Workers and the Rise of Hitler* (New Haven and London, 1986); M S Steinberg, *Sabers and Brown Shirts: The German Student's Path to National Socialism* (Chicago, 1977).

On the contentious issue of the relationship between big business (or 'capital') and Nazism see H A Turner, *German Big Business and the Rise of Hitler* (New York, 1985) and the following articles by the same author: 'Big Business and the Rise of Hitler', *AHR*, 75 (1969), pp.56–70; 'The Ruhrlade. The Secret Cabinet of German Heavy Industry in the Weimar Republic', *CEH*, iii (1970). See also D Abraham, *The Collapse of the Weimar Republic*, and above all his article 'Big Business, Nazism and German Politics at the

End of Weimar', *EHQ* xvii (1987), pp.235–45, which is very critical of Turner.

See also P Stachura, *Nazi Youth in the Weimar Republic* (Santa Barbara, 1975); P Merkl, *The Making of a Stormtrooper* (Princeton, 1980); and R Waite, *Vanguard of Nazism. The Freecorps Movement in Postwar Germany 1919–1933* (Cambridge, Mass., 1952).

On the transition from democracy to dictatorship (often misleadingly characterised as a 'seizure of power' by the Nazis) see M Broszat, *Hitler and the Collapse of Weimar Germany* (Leamington Spa, 1987); Ian Kershaw (ed.) *Weimar. Why did German Democracy Fail?* (London, 1990); P D Stachura (ed.), *The Nazi Machtergreifung* (London, 1983); D Abraham, 'Constituting Hegemony. The Bourgeois Crisis of Weimar Germany', *JMH*, 51 (1979) pp.417–33. See also W S Allen, *The Nazi Seizure of Power: The Experience of a Single German Town 1930–1935* (2nd, revised edn. London, 1984); N E Hayward and D S Morris, *The First Nazi Town* (Aldershot, 1988).

The Third Reich

Ernst Fraenkel, *The Dual State* (New York, 1940) and Franz L Neumann, *Behemoth: The Structure and Practice of National Socialism 1933–1944* (New York, 1944) are still useful. There are remarkably few good comprehensive surveys of the Third Reich in English. Among the most useful is the collection of documents in three volumes by J Noakes and G Pridham, *Nazism 1919–1945. A Documentary Reader* (Exeter, 1983–88). Karl Dietrich Bracher, *The German Dictatorship: The Origins, Structure and Consequences of National Socialism* (London, 1971) is now somewhat dated. Martin Broszat, *The Hitler State: The Foundation and Development of the Internal Structure of the Third Reich* (London, 1981) provides a 'structuralist' interpretation of the 'polycratic' nature of the Third Reich, while Klaus Hildebrand, *The Third Reich* (London, 1984) offers an 'intentionalist' interpretation, neglecting a number of broader domestic political issues to concentrate on Hitler and his 'programme'. See also Norbert Frei, *The Führer State* (Oxford, 1993); J Noakes (ed.), *Government, Party and People in Nazi Germany* (Exeter, 1980); G Hirschfeld and L Kettenacker (eds), *The Führer State'* (Stuttgart, 1980); P Stachura (ed.), *The Shaping of the Nazi State* (London, 1978); H A Turner (ed.), *Nazism and the Third Reich* (New York, 1972); J Fest, *The Face of the Third Reich* (London, 1975).

The central debate on the nature of the Nazi political system concerns the role of Hitler. Studies which depart from the strictly biographical and place Hitler in his historical and political context are: W Carr, *Hitler. A Study in Personality and Politics* (London,

1978); I Kershaw, *The Hitler Myth. Image and Reality in the Third Reich* (Oxford, 1987); idem, *Hitler* (London, 1991). See also Eberhard Jäckel, *Hitler in History* (Hanover and London, 1984); E N Peterson, *The Limits of Hitler's Power* (Princeton, 1969). K D Bracher 'The Role of Hitler: Perspectives of Interpretation' and H Mommsen, 'National Socialism: Continuity and Change', both in W Laqueur (ed.), *Fascism. A Reader's Guide* (London, 1979) constitute two of the earliest contributions to the debate between intentionalists and structuralists. Mommsen's article is reprinted in Hans Mommsen, *From Weimar to Hitler* (Cambridge, 1991) along with a number of other essays hitherto available only in German.

Nazism and the Economy

There is no useful comprehensive work on the nature of the Nazi economy. One of the most important issues has been the relationship between economic interests (especially big business and industry) and politics. See: T Mason, 'The Primacy of Politics – Politics and economics in National Socialist Germany' in H A Turner (ed.), *Nazism and the Third Reich* (New York, 1972); Alan Milward, 'Fascism and the Economy' in W Laqueur (ed.), *Fascism. A Reader's Guide* (Harmondsworth, 1979). Of particular interest on this issue is a recent study of the company most closely associated with the Nazi regime: P Hayes, *Industry and Ideology. IG Farben in the Nazi Era* (Cambridge, 1987).

On the Nazi economy see: Avraham Barkai, *Nazi Economics* (London, 1990); B Carroll, *Design for Total War. Arms and Economics in the Third Reich* (The Hague, 1968); Alfred Sohn-Rethel, *The Economy and Class Structure of German Fascism* (London, 1987); A Milward, *The German Economy at War* (London, 1965); R J Overy, *The Nazi Economic Recovery 1932–1938* (London, 1982); B H Klein, *Germany's Economic Preparations for War* (Cambridge, Mass., 1959); W Carr, *Arms, Autarky and Aggression. A Study in German Foreign Policy 1933–1939* (2nd edn, London, 1979); R J Overy, *Goering. The Iron Man* (London, 1984); T Mason, 'Some Origins of the Second World War', *PP*, 29 (1964), pp.67–87; 'Hitler's War and the German Economy. A Re-interpretation', *EHR*, xxxv (1982), pp.272–91. See also A Schweitzer, *Big Business in the Third Reich* (New York, 1972), and on agriculture: J E Farquharson, *The Plough and the Swastika* (London, 1976); Gustavo Corni, *Hitler and the Peasants. Agrarian Policy in the Third Reich* (New York, Oxford and Munich, 1990).

German Society under the Nazis

There is no good general social history of Nazi Germany. For a review of the literature to 1984 see R Bessel, 'Living with the Nazis: Some Recent Writing on the Social History of the Third

Reich', *EHQ*, xiv (1984), pp.211–20. R Grunberger, *A Social History of the Third Reich* (London, 1971) deals with a number of aspects of German society during the period, but given the ground it attempts to cover is inevitably rather superficial. R Bessel (ed.), *Life in the Third Reich* (Oxford, 1986) contains a number of essays reprinted from *History Today* and D Peukert, *Inside Nazi Germany. Conformity and Opposition in Everyday Life* (London, 1989) is a useful contribution to the social history of the Nazi dictatorship. D Schoenbaum, *Hitler's Social Revolution* (London, 1966) has stimulated discussion about the relationship between 'modernisation' and fascism. See also J Stephenson, 'War and Society: Germany in World War II', *GH* (1983).

Much has been written in German on the working class under Nazism, but little has appeared in English. See: T Mason, *Social Policy in the Third Reich* (Oxford, 1993); idem, 'Labour in the Third Reich 1933–1939', *PP*, xxxiii (1966) and 'The Workers' Opposition in Nazi Germany', *HWJ*, xi (1981); S Salter, 'Structures of Consensus and Coercion: Workers' Morale and the Maintenance of Work Discipline 1939–1945' in David Welch (ed.), *Nazi Propaganda. The Power and the Limitations* (London, 1983); I Kershaw, *Popular Opinion and Political Dissent: Bavaria 1933–1945* (Oxford, 1984).

On women in Nazi Germany see J Stephenson, *Women in Nazi Society* (London, 1975), and *The Nazi Organisation of Women* (London, 1981); C Koonz, *Mothers in the Fatherland* (New York, 1986); R Bridenthal et al. (eds), *When Biology Became Destiny* (New York, 1984); R J Evans, 'German Women and the Triumph of Hitler', *JMH* (1976); T Mason, 'Women in Nazi Germany 1925–1940: Family, Welfare and Work', *HWJ*, i (1976) pp.74–113 and ii pp.5–32. On young people see Detlev Peukert, 'Youth in the Third Reich' in R Bessel, *Life in the Third Reich* (Oxford, 1987) and Detlev Peukert, *Inside Nazi Germany* (London, 1987). See also P L D Walker, *Hitler Youth and Catholic Youth* (Washington DC, 1970). The relationship between the Nazi regime and German society has been discussed in terms of consensus and coercion, opposition and compliance. Important issues in this field are raised by I Kershaw, *Popular Opinion and Political Dissent: Bavaria 1933–1945* (Oxford, 1984).

Histories of the resistance to Hitler in Germany tend to concentrate on the military and the churches. The best collection of essays is F R Nicosia and L D Stokes (eds) *Germans against Nazism: Nonconformity, Opposition and Resistance in the Third Reich* (New York, 1990). See also G Ritter, *The German Resistance* (London, 1958); T Prittie, *Germans against Hitler* (London, 1964); H Graml et al., *The German Resistance to Hitler* (London, 1970) and David Clay Large (ed.), *Contending with Hitler. Varieties of German*

Resistance in the Third Reich (Cambridge, 1991). On the relationship between the Nazi regime and the churches see J S Conway, *The Nazi Persecution of the Churches* (London, 1968); and E C Helmreich, *The German Churches under Hitler* (Detroit, 1979).

The SS State
See: H Krausnick and M Broszat, *Anatomy of the SS-State* (London, 1968); G C Browder, *Foundations of the Nazi Police State. The Formation of Sipo and SD* (Lexington, Kentucky, 1990); H Höhne, *The Order of the Death's Head* (London, 1969); R L Koehl, *RKFDV: German Resettlement and Population Policy 1939–1945* (Cambridge, Mass., 1957) and *The Black Order. The Structure and Power Struggles of the Nazi SS* (Wisconsin, 1983); B Wegner, *The Waffen–SS: Organisation, Ideology and Function* (Oxford, 1990); Herbert G Ziegler, *Nazi Germany's New Aristocracy. The SS Leadership 1925–1939* (Princeton, 1989). On the development and activities of the Gestapo see R Gellately, *The Gestapo and German Society. Enforcing Racial Policy 1933–1945* (Oxford, 1990).

Racial Policy
More recent research has sought to place the Holocaust in the wider context of institutionalised racism and the formulation of a racial policy by the Nazi regime. See: Michael Burleigh, *Germany turns Eastwards: A Study of 'Ostforschung' in the Third Reich* (Cambridge, 1988); R J Lifton, *The Nazi Doctors. A Study in the Psychology of Evil* (London, 1986); Berno Müller-Hill, *Murderous Science: Elimination by Scientific Selection of Jews, Gypsies and Others. Germany 1933–1945* (Oxford, 1988); Robert N Proctor, *Racial Hygiene: Medicine under the Nazis* (Cambridge, Mass., 1988); and Paul J Weindling, *Health, Race and German Politics between National Unification and Nazism 1870–1945* (Cambridge, 1989).

Anti-Semitism and the Holocaust
On the ideological underpinnings of the racist radical right and the development of anti-semitism see G L Mosse, *Towards the Final Solution: A History of European Racism* (New York, 1978) and *The Crisis of German Ideology: Intellectual Origins of the Third Reich* (New York, 1971); H Graml, *Antisemitism in the Third Reich* (Oxford, 1992). The debate between 'intentionalists' and 'structuralists' has also influenced writing on the Holocaust. More or less intentionalist approaches are taken by L S Dawidowicz, *The War against the Jews 1933–1945* (London, 1977) and Gerald Fleming, *Hitler and the Final Solution* (Oxford, 1986). More or less structuralist interpretations include those of K A Schleunes, *The Twisted Road to Auschwitz: Nazi Policy towards German Jews 1933–1939* (London, 1972), and Hans Mommsen, 'The Realization of the Unthink-

able: The "Final Solution of the Jewish Question" in the Third Reich', in Gerhard Hirschfeld (ed.), *The Policies of Genocide: Jews and Soviet Prisoners of War in Nazi Germany* (London, 1986), pp. 97–145. See also Avram Barkai, *From Boycott to Annihilation: The Economic Struggle of German Jews 1933–1954* (New England, 1989); Y Bauer, *A History of the Holocaust* (New York, 1982); C R Browning, *The Final Solution and the German Foreign Office* (New York, 1978); *Fateful Months. Essays on the Emergence of the Final Solution 1941–42* (New York, 1985), *Ordinary Men*, and *Path to Genocide* (idem); H Friedlander and S Milton (eds), *The Holocaust. Ideology, Bureaucracy and Genocide* (Milwood, NY, 1980); L Kochan, *Pogrom. 10 November 1938* (London, 1957); M Marrus, *The Holocaust in History*; M Gilbert, *Auschwitz and the Allies* (London, 1981), *Atlas of the Holocaust* (London, 1982) and *The Holocaust. The Jewish Tragedy* (London, 1986); S Gordon, *Hitler, Germans and the Jewish Question* (Princeton, 1984); L Gross, T*he Last Jews in Berlin* (London, 1983); R Hilberg, *The Destruction of the European Jews* (New York, 1983); G Hirschfeld (ed.), *The Policies of Genocide. Jews and Soviet Prisoners of War in Nazi Germany* (London, 1986); R Hoess, *Commandant of Auschwitz* (London, 1959); S Milton (ed.), *The Stroop Report* (London, 1979); G Sereny, *Into that Darkness. From Mercy Killing to Mass Murder* (London, 1974); I Trunk, *Judenrat. The Jewish Councils in Eastern Europe under Nazi Occupation* (London, 1977).

On popular responses to Nazi anti-semitism and the Holocaust, see: David Bankier, *The Germans and the Final Solution: Public Opinion under Nazism* (Oxford, 1992); Ian Kershaw, 'The Persecution of the Jews and German Popular Opinion in the Third Reich', *Leo Baeck Institute Year Book*, xxv (1980); Otto Dov Kulka and Aron Rodrigue, 'The German Population and the Jews in the Third Reich: Recent Publications and Trends in Research on German Society and the "Jewish Question"', *Yad Vashem Studies*, xvi (1984).

Discussion of Nazi racial policies has understandably been dominated by the mass murder of the Jews. Other consequences of the Nazis' preoccupation with the creation of a racially pure state have been relatively neglected. M Burleigh and W Wipperman, *The Racial State 1933–1945* (Cambridge, 1991) deals extensively with the persecution and murder of the gypsies (Sinti and Roma); see also M Berenbaum (ed.), *A Mosaic of Victims: Non-Jews Persecuted and Murdered by the Nazis* (London, 1990). Burleigh and Wippermann also deal with the case of the so-called Rhineland 'bastards' (children of German women and occupation soldiers from the French colonies), and with the Lusatian Sorbs. On the Rhineland 'bastards' see also S Marks, 'Black Watch on the Rhine: A Study in Propaganda, Prejudice and Prurience', *ESR*, xiii (1983), pp.297–334; on the Sorbs see T Huebner 'Ethnicity

Denied: Nazi Policy towards the Lusatian Sorbs 1933–1945', *GH*, vi (1988), pp.250–77. More generally on the Sorbs: G Stone, *The Smallest Slavonic Nation: The Sorbs of Lusatia* (London, 1972). M Burleigh, *Germany turns Eastwards* (Cambridge, 1988) discusses the complicity of German academics in the development and application of racial ideology. The neglect of some aspects of Nazi racial policy seems to have arisen from the persistence of ambivalent attitudes towards the victims. West Germany officially views the persecution of 'Gypsies' by the Nazis until 1943 as 'legitimate'. Nazi legislation on homosexuality was retained by successive conservative governments in the 1950s and 1960s, and was only repealed in 1969. On the persecution of homosexuals by the Nazis see R Plant, *The Pink Triangle: The Nazi War against Homosexuals* (New York, 1986). For an autobiographical account see H Heger, *The Men with the Pink Triangle* (London, 1980). See also R Lautmann, 'Gay Prisoners in Concentration Camps' in M Berenbaum (ed.), *A Mosaic of Victims: Non-Jews Persecuted and Murdered by the Nazis* (London, 1990).

Diplomacy, Rearmament and War
On the armed forces see F L Carsten, *The Reichswehr and Politics* (London, 1973); M Cooper, *The German Army 1933–45* (London, 1978); R J O'Neill, *The German Army and the Nazi Party 1933–39* (London, 1966); W Deist, T*he Wehrmacht and German Re-armament* (London, 1981); K-J Müller, *The Army, Politics and Society in Germany 1933–45. Studies in the Army's Relation to Nazism* (Manchester, 1987).

On the early years of Nazi foreign policy see G Stoakes, *Hitler and the Quest for World Dominion: Nazi Ideology and Foreign Policy in the 1920s* (Leamington, Spa, 1986); Gerhard Weinberg, *The Foreign Policy of Hitler's Germany. Diplomatic Revolution in Europe* (London/ Chicago, 1970). See also, W Carr, *Arms, Autarky and Aggression* (London, 1972).

On the origins of World War II see also P M H Bell, *The Origins of the Second World War in Europe* (London, 1986); W Carr, *Poland to Pearl Harbour: The Making of the Second World War* (London, 1985); G Weinberg, *The Foreign Policy of Hitler's Germany. Starting World War II* (Chicago/London, 1980).

There are several overlapping debates in this area. The issue of Hitler's role in German foreign policy has implications for the debate between 'intentionalist' and 'structuralist' historians of the Third Reich. It also has a bearing on debates about continuity and change in German foreign policy, and the question of the importance of domestic considerations in the formulation and implementation of foreign policy. Beyond these questions there is a further debate, primarily among 'intentionalists' on the extent of Hitler's ambitions.

An early exponent of the 'intentionalist' or 'programmatist' school was Hugh Trevor-Roper. His response to A J P Taylor, *The Origins of the Second World War* (London, 1963) is reprinted, along with a further exchange between the two, in E M Robertson (ed.), *The Origins of the Second World War* (London, 1971). The chief exponents of the 'intentionalist' school in West Germany (whose work is readily available in English) have been Klaus Hildebrand and Andreas Hillgruber. See K Hildebrand, *The Foreign Policy of the Third Reich* (London, 1973) and A Hillgruber, *Germany and the Two World Wars* (London, 1981). Hillgruber and Hildebrand also belong to the sub-school of 'globalists', who argue that Hitler's ultimate objective was world mastery. See also M Hauner, 'Did Hitler want a World Dominion?' *JCH*, 13 (1978), pp.15–32 and M Michaelis, 'World Power Status or World Dominion', *HJ*, 15 (1972), pp.331–60. See also N Rich, *Hitler's War Aims* 2 vols (New York, 1973, 1974; reissued 1992).

Different interpretations are offered by T Mason, 'Some Origins of the Second World War', *PP*, 29 (1964), which argues that Hitler's decision-making was influenced by domestic constraints. See also R Overy, 'Germany, "Domestic Crisis" and War in 1939', *PP*, 116 (1987) pp.138–68, and Mason and Overy in *PP*, 172 (1989) pp.205–40. See also K H Jarausch 'From Second Reich to Third Reich: The Problem of Continuity in German Foreign Policy', *JCH*, 13 (1978), pp.15–32.

On World War II see O Bartov, *The Eastern Front 1941–45* (London, 1985); J Erickson, *The Road to Stalingrad* (London, 1975); and idem, *The Road to Berlin* (London, 1984). See also W Deakin, *The Brutal Friendship: Mussolini, Hitler and the Fall of Italian Fascism* (London, 1962).

On the occupation of Europe and the 'New Order' see: A Dallin, *German Rule in Russia 1941–45. A Study in Occupation Politics* (London, 1981); J T Gross, *Polish Society under German Occupation. The Generalgouvernement 1919–1944* (Princeton, 1979); E L Homze, *Foreign Labor in Nazi Germany* (Princeton, 1967); U Herbert, 'Labour and Extermination: Economic Interest and the Primacy of *Weltanschauung* in National Socialism', *PP* (1993); R C Lucas, *Forgotten Holocaust. The Poles under German Occupation 1939–1944* (Kentucky, 1986); A Milward, *The German Economy at War* (London, 1965); idem, *The New Order and the French Economy* (London, 1970); idem, *The Fascist Economy in Norway* (London, 1972); idem, *War, Economy and Society* (London, 1987).

SECTION IX
Sources

The following texts and reference works have been used in compiling the material in the text and tables.

Statistisches Jahrbuch für das deutsche Reich (Berlin, 1942), p. 278

W Abelshauser et al. (eds), *Sozialgeschichtliches Arbeitsbuch 1914–1945* (Munich, 1978)

V Berghahn, *Modern Germany, Society, Economy and Politics in the Twentieth Century* (2nd edn, Cambridge, 1987)

Martin Broszat and Norbert Frei (eds), *Das Dritte Reich im Überblick* (Munich, 1989)

Gerhard Bry, *Wages in Germany 1871–1954* (Princeton, 1960)

Herschel B Chipp, *Theories of Modern Art* (Berkeley, 1968)

K D Erdmann, *Das Ende Des Reiches und die Neubildung deutscher Staaten* (Stuttgart, 1976)

J Falter, Th Lindenberger and S Schuchmann, *Wahlen und Abstimmungen in der Weimarer Republik* (Munich, 1986)

Michael Freeman, *Atlas of Nazi Germany* (London, 1987)

Gerhard Granier, Josef Henke and Klaus Oldenhage, *Das Bundesarchiv und seine Bestände* (3rd edn, Boppard am Rhein, 1977)

Ulrich Herbert, *Fremdarbeiter, Politik und Praxis des "Ausländer-Einsatzes" in der Kriegswirtschaft des Dritten Reiches* (Berlin, 1985)

W Hoffmann, *Das Wachstum der deutschen Wirtschaft seit der Mitte des 19 Jahrhunderts* (Berlin, 1965)

Edward L Homze, *Foreign Labor in Nazi Germany* (Princeton, 1967)

Burton H Klein, *Germany's Economic Preparations for War* (Cambridge, Mass., 1959)

M C Kaser and E A Radice (eds), *The Economic History of Eastern Europe 1919–1975*, 3 vols (Oxford, 1986)

Helmut Krausnick and Martin Broszat, *Anatomy of the SS State* (London, 1973)

Longman Dictionary of 20th Century Biography (London, 1985)

Jeremy Noakes and Geoffrey Pridham, *Nazism. A Docu\` Reader.* Vol. 1 *The Rise to Power 1919–1934* (Exeter. ` State, Economy and Society 1933–39* (Exeter, 19° Policy, War and Racial Extermination* (Exeter, 1988`

Richard Plant, *The Pink Triangle, The Nazi War ag\` (New York, 1986)

Gerhard Schulz (ed.), *Weimarer Republik. Eine Nation im Umbruch* (Freiberg/Würzberg, 1987)

Hans-Gerd Schuhmann, *Nationalsozialismus und Gewerkschaftsbewegung. Die Vernichtung der deutschen Gewerkschaften und der Aufbau der "Deutschen Arbeitsfront"* (Hanover, 1958)

John Stevenson (ed.), *Macmillan Dictionary of British and European History since 1914* (London, 1991)

John Willet, *The Weimar Years. A Culture Cut Short* (London, 1984)

Dörte Winkler, *Frauenarbeit im Dritten Reich* (Hamburg, 1977)

Robert Wistrich, *Who's Who in Nazi Germany* (London, 1982)

The following are more specific references to material which has been used or adapted to construct tables and summaries.

I Politics and the State: The Weimar Republic and the Rise of Nazism
4.3   Falter et al., p.46
4.4   Ibid.
5   Schulz, pp.209–18
      Erdmann, pp. 408–19
6.2   Noakes and Pridham, pp.86–7
6.3   Abelshauser, p.131
6.4   Noakes and Pridham, p.83

II Politics, State and Party: The Third Reich
3   Erdmann, pp.420–21
4.1   Broszat and Frei, pp.242–3
4.2   Ibid.
4.3   *Statistisches Jahrbuch* (1942), p.9
5.1   Krausnick et al., *Anatomy of the SS State*, pp.576–7
5.2   Broszat and Frei, pp.248–9

III Economy, Society, Culture
1.1   *Statistisches Jahrbuch* (1936), pp.7, 35; (1942), pp.9, 66
1.2   Abelshauser, p.22
1.3   *Statistisches Jahrbuch* (1942), p.7
1.4   Ibid.
1.5   Ibid.
1.6   *Statistisches Jahrbuch* (1942), p.22
1.7   Ibid.
1.8   *Statistisches Jahrbuch* (1936), p.11; (1942), p.25
2.1   *Statistisches Jahrbuch* (1936), p.17; (1942), p.33
2.2   Ibid.
2.3   *Statistisches Jahrbuch* (1936), p.17
2.4   *Statistisches Jahrbuch* (1936), p.18
2.5.1 *Statistisches Jahrbuch* (1936), p.19; (1942), p.34
2.5.2 *Statistisches Jahrbuch* (1936), p.19
2.5.3 *Statistisches Jahrbuch* (1936), p.20
2.5.4 Winkler, p.201
3.1   *Statistisches Jahrbuch* (1936), p.27
3.2   *Statistisches Jahrbuch* (1942), p.63
3.3   *Statistisches Jahrbuch* (1942), p.664
4.1   Abelshauser, p.61
4.2   Hoffmann, p.342
4.3   Hoffmann, pp.354, 362
5.1   Abelshauser, p.68
5.2   Abelshauser, p.73
6.1   Abelshauser, p.68

6.2   *Statistisches Jahrbuch* (1942), p.278
7.1.1   Hoffmann, p.19
7.1.2   Abelshauser, p.98
7.2.1   *Statistisches Jahrbuch* (1942), p.384
7.2.2   *Statistisches Jahrbuch* 1942), p.383
7.3   Berghahn, p.304
7.4.1   Berghahn, p.284
7.4.2   Falter et al., p.38
7.5   Herbert, pp.49, 56; Homze, p.232
7.6.1   Berghahn, p.307
7.7.1   Schuhmann, p.177
7.7.2   Schuhmann, p.178
7.7.3   Schuhmann, p.168
7.8.1   *Statistisches Jahrbuch* (1942), p.362
7.8.2   Hoffmann, p.586f
7.8.3   *Statistisches Jahrbuch* (1936), p.294; (1942), p.376
7.8.4   *Statistisches Jahrbuch* (1942), p.448
7.8.5   Freeman, p.18
8.1   *Statistisches Jahrbuch* (1942), p.362
8.2   Hoffmann, p.586f
8.3   *Statistisches Jahrbuch* (1942), p.376
8.4   *Statistisches Jahrbuch* (1942), p.448
8.5   Freeman, p.18
9   *Statistisches Jahrbuch* (1936), p.14
10.1   *Statistisches Jahrbuch* (1942), p.79
10.2   Abelshauser, p.153
10.3   *Statistisches Jahrbuch* (1942), p.90
11.2   Abelshauser, pp.165–7
11.3   Freeman, p.86; Abelshauser, p.132
11.4   Abelshauser, p.169
11.4   *Statistisches Jahrbuch* (1936), pp.544–5
11.4.3 *Meldungen aus dem Reich*, p.835
11.4.4 *Meldungen aus dem Reich*, pp.5, 782–3
11.4.5 Ibid.
11.5   Noakes and Pridham, p.420
12.1   *Sopade*, 1936, p.786
12.2   Ibid., pp.805–6
12.3   Ibid., pp.787
12.4   Oron J Hale, *The Captive Press in the Third Reich*,
        Princeton, 1964, p.324
12.5   *Sopade*, 1936, p.820

IV Diplomacy
2.1   Sources include Cook and Stevenson, *Longman Handbook
        of World History*, p.255f; Schulz, pp.176–9
2.2   Sources include Erdmann, *Das Ende Des Reichs*, p.381

The figures used within the table are taken from the publication: Ferdinand Friedensburg, *Die Weimarer Republik* (1946), pages 103–5.
The table is based on table 24, 'Deutsche Reparations-leistunger nach dem Ersten Weltkrieg' in Gebhardt, *Handsbuch der deutscher Geschichte*, 9th, new revised edition, edited by Herbert Grundmann. Vol. 4: *Die Zeit der Weltkriege*, edited by Karl Dietrich Erdmann, page 826.

3.1	Berghahn, p.296
3.2	Willi A Boelcke, 'Kriegsfinanzierung im internationalem Vergleich' in Friedrich Vorstmeier and Hans-Erich Volkmann (eds), *Kriegswirtschaft und Rüstung 1939–1945* (Düsseldorf, 1977), p.34, 40f.
3.3	Paul Kennedy, *The Rise and Fall of the Great Powers: Economic Change and Military Conflict from 1500 to 2000* (London, 1988), p.418; Burton H Klein, *Germany's Economic Preparations for War* (Cambridge, Mass., 1968) p.99
4.2	Kaser and Radice, vol. ii, p.309.
4.2.1	Kaser and Radice, vol. ii, p.456
4.2.2	Ibid., p.463
4.3	Noakes and Pridham, vol. iii, pp.923–5; Kaser and Radice, vol ii, p.310
4.5	Kaser and Radice, vol. ii, pp.310–11
6	Broszat and Frei, p.286; Noakes and Pridham, voi. iii, p.874
7.1	Freeman, p.9
7.2	Noakes and Pridham, vol. iii, pp.1220–1
7.3	Noakes and Pridham, vol. iii, p.1222

V Antisemitism

2	*Statistisches Jahrbuch* (1936), p.14
3	*Statistisches Jahrbuch* (1936), p.15
4	Ibid.
5	*Statistisches Jahrbuch* (1942), p.96
6	Ibid.
7.1	Noakes and Pridham, vol. iii p.1208

VII Biographies

Broszat and Frei (eds), *Das Dritte Reich im Überblick*
Chipp, *Theories of Modern Art*
Granier, et al., *Das Bundesarchiv und seine Bestände*
Longman Dictionary of 20th Century Biography
Schulz (ed.), *Weimarer Republik*
Stevenson (ed.), *Macmillan Dictionary of British and European History since 1914*
Willet, *The Weimar Years*
Wistrich, *Who's Who in Nazi Germany*

Index

Aachen, 44, 55, 124, 135, 220, 222
abortion, 51
Abyssinia, 127
Agrarian League, see *Landbund*
Albania, 130, 150
Alsace, 76, 150, 241;
 Alsace-Lorraine, 74, 137, 163,
 194
alte Kämpfer, 59, 175
Amann, Max, 61, 112, 183, 193
Amsterdam, 117–18, 193
Anglo-German Naval Agreement,
 127–8, 130, 139
Anhalt, 47, 75, 83, 90, 101, 112,
 167, 234
Anschluss, 129, 146, 175, 208,
 227, 231, 234, 236
Anti-Comintern Pact, 128,
 139–40, 175
Ardennes offensive, 135
Arnhem, 135
'asocials', 66, 161, 176, 177
Athens, 135
Atlantic Charter, 132, 141
Atomic bomb, 136, 205, 207, 214
Augsburg, 77, 90, 199
Auschwitz, 55, 67, 69, 163–6, 218,
 222, 226, 231
Auslandsorganisation, 63
Austria, 40, 41, 53–5, 74, 76, 84,
 97, 119, 123–4, 127–9, 137–8,
 142, 146–8, 151, 161–2, 172,
 175–6, 178, 196, 200, 203–4,
 211, 217, 220–1, 234–7
Austro-German customs union,
 14, 126
Autarky, 176, 232

Babi Yar, 176
Backe, Herbert, 58
Baden, 27, 44, 49, 63–4, 75, 89,
 97, 101, 112, 150–1, 163, 167,
 170, 233, 239, 242
Baku, 133
Baltic States, 131–2, 140, 224
Balkans, 142
Bamberg meeting, 41
'Barbarossa', operation, 132, 185
Bauer, Gustav, 10, 25–8
Bauhaus, 114–17, 212, 219–21,
 226, 233
Bavaria, 4, 9, 10, 12, 17, 19, 44,
 49, 50, 55, 63–5, 75, 83, 89, 97,
 101, 112, 151, 167, 170, 205,
 210, 215–16, 240
Bavarian Peasants' League, 18, 28
Bayreuth, 64
Beauty of Labour, 51, 187
Beck, Ludwig, 129, 194–5, 213,
 223
Beckmann, Max, 114, 117
Belgium, 11, 54, 74, 123, 125,
 131, 137, 139, 150, 172, 206
Belgrade, 135, 206
Belorussia, 194, 224
Belzec, 67, 69, 164–5, 210
Berg, Alban, 115, 118, 195, 233
Bergen-Belsen, 69, 222
Berlin, 5, 9, 13, 18, 44, 52, 55,
 63–5, 76–7, 83, 90, 97, 101,
 108, 109, 112–16, 118, 120, 125,
 135, 139, 151, 164, 167, 170,
 193, 195, 196, 198–9, 201,
 206–10, 212, 214–16, 219, 221,
 224, 226–38, 240–2
Bialystok, 54, 66, 221
'Blitz', 131, 176
Blitzkrieg, 176, 212
Blomberg, Werner von, 38, 53,
 56–7, 196, 208, 220
'Blood and Soil', 118, 177
Bochum, 77, 90

Bohemia, 40–1, 90, 130, 147, 162, 188, 201, 204, 208, 214, 226
Bonhoeffer, Dietrich, 196
Bonn, 108, 194, 232, 233
Bormann, Martin, 54, 57, 61, 196–7, 214, 222
Bouhler, Philipp,· 61, 197–8
Brandenburg, 63–4, 83, 97, 112
Braun, Eva, 198
Braun, Otto, 23, 198
Brauchitsch, Walther von, 133, 196, 198
Brecht, Bertolt, 115, 117, 120, 199, 223, 241
Bremen, 9, 49, 75, 77, 83, 89, 90, 101, 112, 151, 167, 169, 204
Breslau, 44, 77, 90, 109, 194, 197, 222, 233
Brest-Litovsk, Treaty of, 3, 123
Bretton Woods Conference, 135
Britain, 124–5, 127–35, 137, 139, 141–3, 145, 151–2, 184, 188, 199, 201, 212, 219; battle of, 131, 176, 211, 213, 221, 230
Brüning, Heinrich, 14, 35–6, 42, 126, 177, 199, 211, 216
Brunswick, 44, 47, 63–4, 75, 83, 89, 101, 112, 167, 231
Buch, Walter, 61, 200
Bucharest, 135, 206
Buchenwald, 69, 199, 239
Budapest, 135
Bulgaria, 138, 142, 150, 172, 202
burning of books, 50, 117
BVP, 13, 17, 19, 21, 177: in cabinet, 25–6, 30, 32–6; election results, 21

Carinthia, 63–4, 75, 90, 146, 147, 210; South Carinthia, 76–150
Casablanca, (conference), 133, 142
Centre Party, 5, 7, 11, 13–14, 17, 19, 37, 48, 50, 199, 205, 207, 227, 235, 242: in cabinet, 24–36; election results, 21
Chamberlain, Neville, 129, 130, 175, 184
Chelmno, 67, 69, 164, 165–6, 210
Chemnitz, 77, 90; Chemnitz-Zwickau, 44

Chetnik movement, 132
China, 138, 142
Christian Democratic Union, 17, 235
Christian Social Party, 177, 203, 234
Churchill, Winston, 131, 142
'Citadel', operation, 134, 185
Cologne, 77, 90, 138, 199, 233; Cologne-Aachen, 44, 63–4, 125
Comintern, 18, 177, 202
Communist Party, German: see KPD
concentration camps, 49, 65–7, 69, 177, 183, 207, 222–4
Concordat, 50, 127
Condor Legion, 128
'Co-ordination': see *Gleichschaltung*
Council of People's Deputies, 5, 9, 24, 168, 178, 204, 232
Councils, Workers' and Soldiers', 5, 9, 24
Coventry, 132
Cracow, 149, 163, 181; Cracow-Plaszow, 69
Creditanstalt, 14, 126, 178
Crete, 132
Croatia, 132, 150
Cuno, Wilhelm, 11, 28–9, 124, 225
Curtius, Julius, 33–5
Czechoslovakia, 41, 53, 74, 123–5, 129–30, 138–9, 147–8, 172, 183–4, 188, 195–6, 211, 217, 225, 232

Dachau, 52, 69, 166, 205–6, 218, 222, 227
Dada, 203, 205, 212–13, 228
DAF, 50–1, 59, 62, 178, 182, 223–4, 233
Daluege, Kurt, 52, 66, 201
Danzig, 69, 74, 84, 90, 97, 130, 137, 148, 178, 207, 208, 211
Danzig-West Prussia, 54, 63–4, 75–6, 148–9
DAP (Bohemia), 40
DAP (Germany), 9, 10, 16, 40–1, 204, 206, 216
Darmstadt, 10, 44, 112, 123, 195, 238, 242

Darré, Richard Walter, 56–8, 61, 194, 201
Dawes Plan, 7, 12, 13, 31, 124–6, 140, 141, 178, 232
'D-Day', 134, 178
DDP, 5, 7, 10–11, 13, 17, 34, 209, 228, 232: in cabinet, 24–35; election results, 21
death camps, 67, 69, 177, 198, 218, 226, 242
de Gaulle, Charles, 135, 180, 201
'degenerate art', 119, 177, 222, 224, 227, 234
Denmark, 10, 54, 74, 117, 123, 131, 135, 137, 172, 195, 199
Dessau, 116–17, 212
DEST, 67
Deutsche Arbeiterpartei, see DAP
Deutsches Frauenwerk, 233
Deutsche Staatspartei, 17, 35, 36
Deutsch-Völkische Freiheitsbewegung, 19
Dietrich, Otto, 61, 113, 202
Dix, Otto, 114–16, 202–3
DNVP, 6–8, 13, 16, 19, 31, 33, 126, 178, 183, 208–9, 218: in cabinet, 32, 34, 35–8; election results, 21, 31
Döblin, Alfred, 116, 203
Doenitz, Karl, 55, 58, 136, 203, 229, 235
Dorpmüller, Julius, 57–8, 203
Dortmund, 77, 90, 113, 195
Dresden, 77, 90, 109, 193, 202, 203, 212, 221; Dresden-Bautzen, 44
Drexler, Anton, 16, 204, 206
Duisburg, 11, 77, 90, 124, 125, 200
Dumbarton Oaks Conference, 142
Dunkirk, 131
Düsseldorf, 11, 44, 63–4, 77, 90, 113, 119, 124–5, 195, 221, 239
DVP, 6,7, 12, 13, 16, 200, 225, 235, 238: election results, 21, 27; in cabinet, 27, 30–5

East Prussia, 11, 44, 54, 63–4, 83, 112, 123, 148, 196, 210, 221
Ebert, Friedrich, 4–5, 9–10, 13, 24, 204, 228
Edelweiss Pirates, 179
EDES, 132

Egypt, 138, 214
Eichmann, Adolf, 162–3, 204–5, 219
Einsatzgruppen, 53, 162–3
Einstein, Albert, 115, 117, 205, 228
Eisenhower, 133, 136, 151
Eisner, Kurt, 9–10
El Alamein, 133
ELAS, 179
Eltz von Rübenach, Paul Freiherr, 37–8, 57
Enabling Act, 17, 47–8, 50, 52, 217, 233
Epp, Ritter Franz von, 49, 61, 205
Erzberger, Matthias, 10–11, 25–6, 205
Essen, 63–4, 77, 90, 113, 200–1, 239
Estonia, 126, 194, 231
Ethiopia, 127
Eupen and Malmédy, 11, 54, 84, 137, 149
Euthanasia Programme, 162–4, 175, 197, 198, 209, 234, 236, 240, 242
Ewige Jude, Der, 119

Faith and Beauty, 53, 109, 181
Fasci di combattimento, 179
Feder, Gottfried, 207
Fehrenbach, Konstantin, 11, 27
final solution, 179, 204, 226
Finland, 131, 135
Fischer, Fritz (controversy), 179
'flag decree', 33
Flick, Friedrich, 207
Four-Year Plan, 52, 128, 161, 179–80, 182, 194, 210, 221, 232
France, 4, 7, 117–18, 123, 124–5, 127, 129–31, 137, 139, 151, 163, 172, 183, 188–9, 203, 205–6, 215, 225, 230–1, 238, 241
Franco, Francisco, 128
Franconia, 44, 63–4, 97, 207, 238
Frank, Anne, 207
Frank, Hans, 56–7, 59, 61, 149, 208
Frankfurt am Main, 10, 77, 90, 109, 123, 193, 207, 216
Frankfurt an der Oder, 44
Free French, 180

freemasons, 52
Freiburg, 109, 207, 214, 219, 226, 239, 241, 242
Freikorps, 10, 18, 52, 180, 187, 194, 197, 201, 205–6, 208, 211, 215, 218, 224, 240, 241
Freisler, Roland, 55, 208
Freud, Sigmund, 119, 208
Frick, Wilhelm, 14, 38, 49, 55–8, 61, 65–6, 76, 147, 208
Fritsch, 53, 128, 196, 208
Führer Chancellery, 197
'fulfilment' (policy), 7, 27, 32, 180
functionalists, 59, 180
Funk, Walter, 57–8, 209

Galen, Clemens Graf von, 209
gas chambers, 165–6
Gelsenkirchen, 77, 90
Gereke, Günther, 38, 39
German Labour Front: see DAF
German People's Freedom Party (DVFP), 31, 41, 44
German-Polish non aggression pact, 139
German Revolution, 181
German Workers' Party: see DAP
Gessler, Otto, 26–34, 125, 209
Gestapo, 48, 51–3, 55, 65–6, 181, 183, 186–7, 195–6, 201, 207, 211, 215, 226, 232
Glaube und Schönheit: see Faith and Beauty
Gleichschaltung, 48–50, 76, 181
Globocnik, Odilo, 163, 210
Goebbels, Joseph, 13, 49, 55–8, 61, 135, 165, 206, 210, 218, 236, 241
Goering, Hermann, 39, 49, 52, 56–8, 65–6, 161, 163, 179, 181, 196, 197, 202, 210–11, 215, 221–2, 232, 239
'Gomhorra', operation, 134
Government General, 49, 162
Graz, 147, 219, 236
Greece, 59, 76, 130–1, 134
'Green', operation, 129
Groener, Wilhelm, 5, 9, 27–9, 34–6, 123, 125–6, 209, 211–12
Gropius, Walther, 114, 117–19, 212, 226

Grosz, George, 114, 212
Grynszpan, Herschel, 161, 212
Guernica, 128
Gürtner, Franz, 37, 38, 54, 56–8, 212–13
Gypsies: see Sinti; Roma

Haase, Hugo, 3, 10, 24
Halder, 129, 133, 195, 213
Halle, 77, 90, 97, 108, 109, 215, 219, 236; Halle-Merseburg, 63–4
Hamburg, 9, 11, 12, 44, 49, 63–4, 75, 77, 83, 89, 90, 97, 101, 109, 112, 119, 134, 138, 167, 170, 193, 195, 207, 220, 233, 239
Hanover, 44, 63–4, 77, 83, 90, 97, 112, 194, 218, 231, 234
Harzburg Front, 14, 204, 218, 232
Heartfield, John, 119, 213–14
Heidegger, Martin, 116, 214, 219
Heidelberg, 108–9, 196, 200, 207, 210, 219, 222, 241
Henlein, Konrad, 129, 214
Hess, Rudolf, 51, 54, 56–7, 59, 61, 132, 197, 214
Hesse, 44, 49, 63–4, 75, 83, 89, 97, 101, 112, 151, 167, 170, 195, 227
Hesse, Hermann, 215
Heydrich, Reinhard, 52–3, 65–6, 133, 147, 160, 162–4, 186, 195, 201, 215, 220
Hilferding, Rudolf, 29, 34, 215
Himmler, Heinrich, 13, 49, 50–2, 55, 58, 62, 65–6, 147, 149, 163, 165–6, 181, 186, 187, 194, 196–7, 202, 205, 208, 210–11, 215–16
Hindemith, Paul, 116, 216
Hindenburg, Paul von, 3, 13–14, 23, 32, 36, 38, 48, 51, 127, 180, 216–17, 224
Hiroshima, 136
Hirschfeld, Magnus, 50, 117
Hitler, Adolf, 216–18: and DAP, NSDAP, 11, 16, 41, 61; rise to power, 6, 8, 10, 11, 13–16, 23, 36, 37, 41, 115, 116, 193, 214, 216, 218, 230, 232, 235, 237; appointment as Chancellor,

15, 38–9, 42, 47, 126, 159, 233;
and Nazi Regime, 47–51,
56–60, 196–7, 204, 211–13,
219–20, 226–7, 230; and police
state, 65–7; and holocaust, 67,
160, 163; and armed forces,
53, 127–30, 195, 196, 198; and
foreign policy, war, 127–30,
150, 175; opposition and
resistance, 54, 135, 196, 214,
223, 230, 237; suicide, 55, 136
Hitler Youth, 53, 59, 109–10, 135,
176, 182, 200
holocaust, 69, 182, 210, 215, 217,
237
homosexuals, 49, 51, 66, 177, 185
Hossbach memorandum, 128,
182, 218
Hugenberg, Alfred, 38, 56, 126,
218
Hungary, 127, 134, 138, 142, 147,
150, 172, 240
Husserl, Edmund, 116, 119, 214,
218–19

IG-Farben, 67, 182, 195, 197, 204,
223
intentionalists, 59, 182
Italy, 124–5, 127–31, 133–4, 136,
139, 142, 145, 166, 172, 178,
185, 188, 213, 223, 242

Japan, 125–6, 128, 132–3, 136,
137, 139, 145, 188
Jehovah's Witnesses, 50, 51, 52, 66
Jena, 108, 109, 223
Jews, 50, 55, 66, 67, 106, 130, 134,
149, 159–72, 177–8, 182, 185,
194, 197, 204, 206–7, 209–10,
212, 214–15, 217, 228, 231,
237–8, 240, 242
Jodl, Alfred, 136, 219
Joyce, William, 219
Jud Süss, 120, 210, 213
July plot, 135, 195, 200, 201, 206,
208–10, 213, 218, 223, 237
Jünger, Ernst, 119, 219
Jungmädelbund, 182
Junker, 16, 182

Kaiser, Georg, 120, 219

Kaltenbrunner, Ernst, 219–20
Kandinsky, Wassily, 115, 117, 220
Kapp putsch, 6, 10, 26, 182, 200
Karajan, Herbert von, 220
Kassel, 77, 90
Kästner, Erich, 116, 120
Katyn, 134
Kautsky, Karl, 220
Keitel, Wilhelm, 136, 196, 220
Kellog-Briand Pact, 125, 127
Kerrl, Hans, 52, 56, 57
Kiel, 4, 9, 77, 90, 108, 123, 196,
209, 234
Kiev, 132, 134
Klee, Paul, 119, 221
Koblenz, 138; Koblenz-Trier, 44,
150
Koch, Erich, 26–7, 34, 221
Kokoschka, Oskar, 119, 221
Kolberg, 120, 213
Kollwitz, Käthe, 117–18, 222
Königsberg, 77, 90, 109, 182, 210,
222
KPD, 9–13, 15, 18, 30, 50, 182,
187–8, 239, 240: election
results, 21, 36; resistance, 18,
51, 55
Kraft durch Freude: see Strength
through Joy
Kreisau circle, 55, 201, 223
Krupp, Alfried, 222
Kurhessen, 63–4
Kursk, 133–4

Labour Education Camp, 176
Lammers, Hans-Heinrich, 57, 58,
222
Landbund, 19, 175, 183
Landsberg, Otto, 24, 25
Landsberg prison, 13, 41, 198,
214
Landtage, 21, 76, 198–9, 207, 223,
227, 234, 238, 240–2
Lang, Fritz, 114, 117, 223
Latvia, 126, 172
Lausanne conference, 126, 141
League of German Girls, 109–10,
176
League of Nations, 5, 11, 13,
125–7, 137, 178, 199
Lebensborn, 52, 183

Leipzig, 44, 77, 90, 109, 193, 209, 210, 214, 239
Leningrad, 134
Lenya, Lotte, 117, 223, 241
Ley, Robert, 50, 61, 223–4
Lidice, 133
Liebknecht, Karl, 10, 18, 187, 224, 225
Linz, 90, 204, 216, 219
Lippe, 75, 83, 90, 101, 112, 167
Lithuania, 137, 172, 229, 230
Litvinov Protocol, 126
Locarno Pact, 7, 13, 32, 125, 127–8, 139
London, 18, 119, 196, 208, 241; London Conferences, 11, 124–6, 140
Lord Haw Haw: see Joyce, William
Lorraine, 76, 150
Lower Austria, 76, 146
Lower Danube, 63–4, 75, 76, 90, 146, 147
Lower Silesia, 63–4, 83, 112
Lübeck, 9, 83, 101, 112, 133, 167
Lublin, 69, 149, 163, 210; Lublin Committee, 135, 143
Ludendorff, Erich, 3, 5, 9, 12, 23, 41, 123, 184, 216–17, 224–5
Lueger, Dr Karl, 177
Luther, Hans, 13, 29–33, 225
Luxembourg, 76, 150, 172
Luxemburg, Rosa, 10, 18, 187, 224, 225

Madagascar, 163, 183
Magdeburg, 44, 63–4, 77, 97, 113, 235
Majdanek, 69, 135, 164
Manchuria, 126, 136
Mann, Heinrich, 114, 117–18, 225
Mann, Klaus, 117–18
Mann, Thomas, 115–19, 225
Mannheim, 77, 90
Marburg, 108, 109, 195, 201, 213, 239
Marienwerder, 11, 123, 148
Marx, Wilhelm, 12, 13, 23, 30, 31, 33, 34, 225
Mauthausen, 69, 166, 221
Mecklenburg, 44, 47, 63–4, 75, 83, 89, 101, 112, 167

Meinecke, Friedrich, 225–6
Mein Kampf, 12, 13, 115, 183, 193, 217
Meissner, Otto, 58–9
Memel, 74, 84, 124, 130, 137, 138
Mengele, Josef, 226
Mihailović, Draža, 132
Minsk, 164, 216, 226
Modernisation theory, 183–4
Moeller van den Bruck, Arthur, 115, 188
Montenegro, 150
Moravia, 90, 130, 147, 162, 201, 208, 226
Moscow, 18, 123, 132, 142, 202; Moscow Declaration, 134
Moselland, 63–4, 150
MSPD, 18, 24–8, 188; in cabinet, 24–6, 28
Müller, Hermann, 10, 13, 14, 25–6, 34, 226
Müller, Heinrich, 226
Munich, 9, 11–13, 16, 40, 49, 59, 63–4, 77, 90, 109, 113–14, 118, 161, 193, 195, 197–9, 201, 205–6, 208–10, 213, 215–16, 220, 227–8, 232, 236, 239, 240–1
Munich Agreement, 129, 147, 184, 188
Munich putsch, 6, 8, 16, 41, 184, 202, 204, 211, 213, 215, 217, 230–1, 234, 237, 241
Münster, 108, 194, 209, 239
Musil, Robert, 120
Mussolini, 124, 127, 128, 130, 134, 136, 223

National Assembly, 5, 10, 21, 24, 185, 198, 204, 235, 238
National Socialist Factory Cell Organisation: see NSBO
National Socialist Motor Corps: see NSKK
Nazi Party: see NSDAP
Nazi-Soviet Pact, 130, 140, 148, 230
Nazi Women's League, 233
Nedić, Milan, 132
Netherlands, 9, 196, 207, 220, 231–2, 242

Neue Sachlichkeit, 115, 184, 193, 203, 212
Neurath, Konstantin Freiherr von, 37–8, 56, 57–9, 147, 196, 226, 230
New Order, 184
Niemöller, Martin, 53, 226
Night of the Long Knives, 48, 51, 186, 194, 200, 202, 204, 215, 227, 230, 233
North Schleswig, 10, 137
Norway, 118, 131, 165, 172, 206, 228, 234, 239
Noske, Gustav, 25–6
NSBO, 62, 97, 184
NSDAP, 16, 19, 30, 61–4, 184, 187, 213, 230: origins, 40–1, 204, 206, 207, 216–17, 220; during Weimar Republic, 10–15, 208, 237, 239; electoral support, 21, 36–7, 39, 41–2, 44, 47; financial support, 50, 207, 213, 233, 239; membership, 16, 42–3, 50, 53, 193–4, 196, 200–2, 207, 209–11, 214–15, 219–20, 223, 231–4, 236, 238, 240, 242; in government, 38, 42, 47, 50, 56–60, 159
NS Frauenschaft, 62, 184
NSKK, 62, 147, 184
NSV, 184
Nuremberg, 77, 90, 160, 161, 182, 209, 236, 240
Nuremberg laws, 52, 160, 217, 233, 238
Nuremberg Trials, 193, 194, 196–7, 203, 208–9, 211, 214, 218–20, 222, 229–32, 235–6, 238, 240–1

Ohnesorge, Wilhelm, 57–8
Oldenburg, 47, 75, 83, 89, 101, 112, 167
Olympic Games, 52, 118
Oradour, 134
Orff, Carl, 119, 227
Ossietzky, Carl von, 118, 119, 227

Pact of Steel, 130, 185
Palatinate, 44, 83, 97, 151
Palestine, 130

Pan-German movement, 40, 218
Papen, Franz von, 14, 15, 37–8, 42, 47, 50, 213, 216, 227, 233–4
Paris, 11, 18, 26, 117, 123–4, 126, 131, 135, 140, 165, 193, 212, 219–20, 223–4, 227–8, 238, 241
Partisans, 132, 134, 183
Pavelic, Ante, 132, 150
Pétain, 131, 201, 228
Piscator, Erwin, 114–15, 117, 199, 228
Poland, 53–4, 67, 74, 76, 84, 124–7, 129–32, 135, 137, 139–40, 142, 147, 148–50, 155, 159, 162–3, 165, 172, 178, 181, 185, 196, 205, 208, 211–12, 217, 220–1, 225, 231, 238, 242
police state, 65–9
Pomerania, 44, 63–4, 83, 112, 196
Posen, 54, 74, 83, 109, 137, 148
Potsdam, 44, 50, 114, 143, 242
Prague, 18, 136, 162, 206, 241
presidential elections, 23, 225
Preuss, Hugo, 25, 228
Preussenstreich, 14, 48, 198
prisoners of war, 67
Prussia, 14, 47, 48–50, 65, 75, 83, 89, 101, 112, 167, 170, 183, 198, 211, 215

Quebec Conference, 184
Quisling, 133, 228

Rapallo, Treaty of, 11, 124, 138–9, 229
Rathenau, Walter, 11, 28, 229, 231
rationing, 53–4
Rauschining, 211, 229
Ravensbrück, 69, 166, 209
Red army, 177, 217
Reich Chamber of Culture, 51
Reich Chancellery, 51–2, 222
Reich Entailed Farm Law, 51, 159
Reich Food Estate, 19, 50, 147, 186
Reich Press Chamber, 54, 193
Reichsbank, 49, 52–3, 225, 231–2
Reichskristallnacht, 53, 66, 161, 186
Reichsrat, 21, 186
Reichssicherheitshauptamt, 53, 66, 186, 195, 215, 219, 220, 232

Reichstag, 3–4, 9–10, 18, 21, 25, 31–2, 35, 37, 42, 47, 49, 52, 125–6, 186, 189, 198, 215, 218, 223–6, 238: elections, 6, 11, 13, 14, 19, 20–2, 26, 31–2, 36–7, 39, 41, 44, 49, 51, 199, 200, 202, 204–8, 210–11, 220, 223–4, 231–2, 235, 239, 240–2; fire, 47, 49, 189, 202, 224
Reichsstatthalter, 76
Reichswehr, 12, 127, 194, 196, 213, 219, 235, 241
Reich Trustees of Labour, 50
'Reinhard' operation, 163–4, 166, 210
Reinhardt, Max, 114, 118, 202, 214
Remarque, Erich Maria, 116, 229
reparations, 11–14, 27, 18, 123, 124–6, 140–1, 143, 199
resistance, 18, 51, 52, 55, 67, 132–6, 215, 223
Rhineland, 7, 14, 19, 52, 83, 97, 112, 125, 128, 138, 209, 210, 217, 220, 233, 239
Ribbentrop, Joachim von, 53, 57, 58, 128, 193, 230, 241
Riefenstahl, Leni, 118, 230
Riga, 164
Röhm, Ernst, 51, 56, 202, 204, 205, 230
Roma, 52, 53, 66, 160–1, 163, 165, 187
Romania, 126, 129–31, 134, 142, 172, 183
Rome, 134, 226
Rome-Berlin Axis, 128, 140
Rommel, Erwin, 132, 230
Roosevelt, F D, 132, 142
Rosenberg, Alfred, 54, 58, 61, 115, 117, 132, 209, 231
Rostock, 108, 230
Rostov, 133–4
Ruhr, 10–13, 27, 29, 97, 124–5, 134, 140–1, 151, 205, 207, 220, 237, 239
Russia, 4, 123, 159, 194, 220, 229
Ruthenia, 130, 147
Rust, Bernhard, 56, 57, 58, 231

SA, 11, 14, 41, 48–9, 51, 61, 65–6, 127, 147, 159, 181, 186, 197, 211, 215, 224, 230, 237, 239
Saarland, 75, 90, 101, 137, 163, 200; plebiscite, 51, 127
Sachsenhausen, 69, 209, 218, 222, 227
Salzburg, 63–4, 75, 90, 146, 147
Sauckel, Fritz, 231
Saxony, 12, 49, 63–4, 75, 83, 89, 97, 101, 112, 167, 170
Schacht, Hjalmar, 49, 51, 53, 56, 58–9, 209, 231–2
Schaumburg-Lippe, 49, 75, 83, 90, 101, 167
Scheidemann, Philipp, 9, 24, 25, 232
Schirach, Baldur von, 61
Schlegelberger, Franz, 54, 58, 193, 232
Schleicher, Kurt von, 15, 37, 38, 42, 211, 216, 233, 237
Schleswig-Holstein, 44, 63–4, 83, 112, 123, 199, 203, 224, 227, 235
Schmidt, Robert, 25, 26, 29, 30
Schmitt, Carl, 233
Scholtz-Klink, G, 62, 233
Schoenberg, Arnold, 118, 195, 233
Schönheit der Arbeit: see Beauty of Labour
Schwarz, Franz, 61, 234
Schwerin von Krosigk, Johann Ludwig, 37–8, 56–8, 234–5
Schwitters, Kurt, 118, 234
SD, 65–6, 163, 179, 183, 195, 199, 215
'Sealion', operation, 131
Seeckt, Hans von, 30, 125, 235
Seldte, Franz, 39, 57, 58, 204, 235
Serbia, 132, 150
Severing, Carl, 34, 235
Seyss-Inquart, Arthur, 58, 59, 129, 146, 149, 235
Silesia, 11, 54, 124, 149
Sinti, 52–3, 66, 160, 161, 163, 165, 177, 186–7
slave labour, 67, 207, 222, 231, 239
Slavs, 40, 67
Slovakia, 130, 135, 147
Slovenia, 150
Smolensk, 132, 134

Sobibor, 67, 69, 164, 166, 210
'social Darwinism', 40
SOPADE, 18, 187, 241
Spain, 131, 240
Spanish Civil War, 128
Spartacist League, 10, 18, 180,
    187, 224, 225, 240
SPD, 3–4, 7–8, 10–14, 17–18,
    27–8, 31–3, 36, 48, 50, 187–8,
    203–4, 220, 223–6, 232, 235,
    239, 241: in cabinet, 29–30,
    34–5, see also MSPD; election
    results, 21; resistance, 52, 55,
    see also Sopade
special courts, 50
Speer, Albert, 54, 58, 119, 133,
    236, 239
Spengler, Oswald, 115, 236
SS, 14, 49, 51–2, 62, 65–9, 147,
    175–8, 181, 183, 184, 186–7,
    189, 200–2, 205, 207, 209–10,
    215–16, 220–2, 232, 238–9, 242
'stab-in-the-back-myth', 4, 178
Stahlhelm, 49, 126, 187, 204, 221,
    235
Stalin, Joseph, 132
Stalingrad, 133, 187, 217, 228
Stangl, Franz, 236–7
Stauffenberg, Claus Schenk Graf
    von, 55, 223, 230, 237
Stettin, 77, 90, 138, 163, 187
Stockholm, 119, 196
Stormtroopers: see SA
Strauss, Richard, 118, 237
Strength through Joy, 51, 182
Stresa Front, 127, 188
Stresemann, Gustav, 7, 12, 14, 17,
    27, 29–35, 124–6, 139, 225, 238
Strasser, Gregor, 37, 41, 206, 237
Strasser, Otto, 237
Stuttgart, 26, 77, 90, 234
Styria, 63–4, 75, 76, 90, 146;
    Lower Styria, 76, 150
Sudetenland, 41, 53, 63–4, 74, 75,
    76, 90, 128–9, 184, 188, 214
Swabia, 63–4, 97
Sweden, 166, 240
Switzerland, 118, 198–9, 215–16,
    219, 221, 225, 229, 242

Tehran (conference), 134, 142

Terboven, Josef, 206, 239
Thälmann, Ernst, 23, 49, 239
Thierack, Otto Georg, 55, 58
Thule Society, 41
Thuringia, 12, 14, 41, 47, 63–4,
    75, 83, 89, 97, 101, 112, 167,
    204, 208, 231
Thyssen, Fritz, 239
Tiso, Josef, 147
Tito, Josip Broz, 132, 134, 203
Tobruk, 133
Todt, Fritz, 54, 58, 62, 236, 239
Toller, Ernst, 114, 118, 119,
    239–40
trades unions, 50, 95–6
Treblinka, 67, 69, 164–5, 210, 236
Tsolakoglu, Georgios, 132
Tübingen, 109, 196, 209
Turkey, 138, 166, 216, 227
Tyrol, 76, 90, 146, 147, 236;
    Tyrol-Vorarlberg, 63–4, 75

Ukraine, 133
United States, 4, 9, 117–18, 124,
    132–6, 141–3, 145, 151–2, 184,
    198–9, 203, 205, 212–13, 216,
    223, 225–6, 231, 233–4, 240
Upper Austria, 76, 147, 216
Upper Danube, 63–4, 75, 76, 90,
    146, 147
Upper Silesia, 11, 63–4, 83, 112,
    124, 137, 149, 201
USPD, 3–4, 9–11, 18, 28, 187–8,
    199, 203, 215, 220, 239: in
    cabinet, 24; election results,
    21, 26
USSR, 11, 54, 76, 117, 124–7,
    130–6, 138–40, 142–3, 145,
    151–2, 163, 172, 185, 194, 199,
    202, 209, 220–1, 228–9, 238, 240

Vatican, 50, 127, 237, 241
Versailles, Treaty of, 5–6, 10,
    16–17, 22, 123, 127, 137–8, 153,
    180, 186, 217, 229, 235
Vichy, 133, 165, 180, 189, 193,
    199, 201, 212, 223, 228, 239
Vienna, 40, 63–4, 75–6, 90, 108–9,
    118–19, 127, 136, 146–7, 163,
    195, 200, 208, 210, 216, 220,
    223, 227, 229, 232–6

Völkischer Beobachter, 197, 204–5, 213, 241
völkisch movement, 40, 231
Völkisch-Nationaler Block, 19, 44
Vorarlberg, 146–7
V-weapons, 135–6, 189, 198

Wagner, Adolf, 206, 240
Wannsee Conference, 54, 164, 204
War Economy Decrees, 53
Warsaw, 131, 134–5, 148–9, 165, 194, 196, 238
war losses, 152
Wartheland, 54, 63–4, 75–6, 148–9, 162, 211
Washington (conference), 124, 142; (Pact), 133, 142
Wehrmacht, 189, 196, 198, 208
Weill, Kurt, 116–18, 199, 223, 241
Weimar, 5, 10, 114, 185, 193
Wels, Otto, 18, 241
Wessel, Horst, 242
Westmark, 63–4, 150
Westphalia, 44, 63–4, 83, 97, 209, 233

West Prussia, 11, 83, 112, 123, 137, 229
Wilhelm II, Emperor of Germany, 4, 9, 17, 138
Wirth, Josef, 11, 12, 19, 26–8, 35, 242
Wirtschaftspartei, 19, 20, 35
Works councils, 10, 95
Wuppertal, 77, 90
Württemberg, 44, 49, 63–4, 75, 83, 89, 97, 101, 112, 151, 167, 170, 242

Yalta Conference, 135, 143, 151
Young Plan, 13, 126, 141, 218, 232
Yugoslavia, 54, 76, 123, 132, 135, 142, 150, 172, 183, 185

Zagreb, 132, 175
Zentralarbeitsgemeinschaft (ZAG), 9, 190
Zentrum: see Centre Party
Zhukov, 133, 151
Zyklon B, 164, 182